A
LASTING
IMPRESSION

A
LASTING
IMPRESSION

Coastal, Lithic, and Ceramic Research in New England Archaeology

Edited by Jordan E. Kerber
Foreword by Brona G. Simon

Native Peoples of the Americas
Laurie Weinstein, General Editor

Westport, Connecticut
London

Library of Congress Cataloging-in-Publication Data

A lasting impression / coastal, lithic, and ceramic research in New England archaeology /
    edited by Jordan E. Kerber ; foreword by Brona G. Simon.
        p.   cm.—(Native peoples of the Americas, ISSN 1521–5091)
    Includes bibliographical references and index.
    ISBN 0–89789–849–4 (alk.   paper)—ISBN 0–89789–850–8 (pbk. : alk.   paper)
    1. Indians of North America—New England—Antiquities.   2. Indian pottery—New
England.   3. Stone implements—New England.   4. Coastal archaeology—New England.   5.
New England—Antiquities.   I. Kerber, Jordan E., 1957–   II. Series.
    E78.N5L37   2002
    974'.01—dc21   2002070877

British Library Cataloguing in Publication Data is available.

Library of Congress Catalog Card Number: 2002070877
ISBN: 0–89789–849–4
        0–89789–850–8 (pbk.)
ISSN: 1521–5091

First published in 2002

Praeger, 88 Post Road West, Westport, CT 06881
An imprint of Greenwood Publishing Group, Inc.
www.praeger.com

Printed in the United States of America

The paper used in this book complies with the
Permanent Paper Standard issued by the National
Information Standards Organization (Z39.48–1984).

10 9 8 7 6 5 4 3 2 1

In memory of Barbara E. Luedtke
1948–2000

Barbara E. Luedtke. Photo by Michael Davis,
Michael Davis Photography, November 1993.

Contents

Illustrations

FIGURES

TABLES

Series Foreword

As General Editor of the *Native Peoples of the Americas*, I am truly
honored to include *A Lasting Impression: Coastal, Lithic, and Ceramic
Research in New England Archaeology* as the latest book in the series.
Dr. Jordan E. Kerber pulled together an outstanding group of scholars
to pay tribute to the late Barbara E. Luedtke. The three sections of the
book each demark the areas of research to which Barbara had dedicated
her life: coastal archaeology (the islands off Boston Harbor) and lithic
and ceramic analyses. What makes the book particularly impressive is
that the contributors worked with each other so that each section is internally consistent and each chapter leads to the next.

While I did not know Dr. Luedtke well, I did know that she was a
genuinely compassionate person as well as a scholar. Whenever I spoke
to her, she was always patient and kind and she was willing to work
with me, whether it was about an article I was submitting for the *Bulletin
for the Massachusetts Archaeological Society* or a research question regarding the Wampanoag Indians. She touched everyone's lives in myriad
ways and in myriad ways she inspired us all to take up the challenge of
New England archaeology and ethnohistory.

Readers will appreciate the numerous chapters in *A Lasting Impression*
that refer to the Woodland and Contact cultural time periods. Much of
the archaeology in New England is biased toward the Late Archaic, not
by design, but by necessity, since so many sites are dated to the Late

Archaic. What is also unique about this volume is that it looks at the new identities that natives were creating for themselves during the Woodland and Contact cultural time periods, whether those identities were fashioned in stone or clay.

I predict that this book, like another series title, *The Archaeological Northeast*, edited by Levine, Sassaman, and Nassaney (1999), will become a classic in New England archaeology for years to come.

The series, *Native Peoples of the Americas*, covers indigenous peoples in North, Middle, and South America. Each volume explores the history and cultural survival of native peoples by telling their unique stories. Some volumes focus on competing ethnicities and the struggle for resources; other volumes illuminate the archaeology and ethnohistory of particular regions; and still others explore gender relations, warfare, and native cosmologies and ethnobotanies. Yet, despite the particular foci or theoretical frameworks of the editor and his or her contributors, all volumes reveal the rich cultural tapestry of the American continents. Together they chronicle a common historical theme: despite the invasion of foreign explorers, traders, militia, missionaries, and colonists beginning in the sixteenth century, despite rapid native depopulation because of disease and overt Anglo policies of ethnocide, and despite the penetration of a capitalistic market system into tribal economies, the native peoples have survived.

Laurie Weinstein
General Editor
Native Peoples of the Americas

Foreword

"A Lasting Impression" is an appropriate way to describe the contributions Barbara E. Luedtke has made to New England archaeology. Through her many publications and teaching career, she has left an everlasting imprint of her enthusiasm, love, and support for archaeology and archaeologists, both professional and avocational. Always helpful in offering advice, encouragement, and support, Barbara was a breath of fresh air and positivism in a field that is inherently rife with super-criticism, petty jealousies, and territoriality. Her untimely death in 2000 has left a void in New England archaeology and in our lives. The contributors to this book are joined by common threads of research interests that they shared with Barbara—coastal archaeology, lithic analysis, and ceramic analysis. To some of the authors, Barbara was a mentor; to others, a friend; but to all, a colleague. The authors have recognized the contributions Barbara made, and are striving to make further advances to the foundations she laid. In publishing this book, the editor and I hope that it will encourage researchers to delve even more deeply into New England archaeology, and further our understanding of the past.

When Barbara first came to teach at the Department of Anthropology at the University of Massachusetts at Boston in 1974, she immediately dove into New England archaeology, by undertaking the first-ever systematic survey of 12 of the islands in Boston Harbor (Luedtke 1975, 1978a). In her survey of the islands, Luedtke remarked, "To our surprise, we found it virtually impossible to dig a 1-meter test pit anywhere on the islands without finding at least some cultural material" (Luedtke 1978a:100). The Boston Harbor Islands, a short boat ride from the UMass/Boston campus, turned out to be a rich laboratory for Luedtke's lifelong study of human adaptations to coastal ecosystems (see Luedtke, this volume). The good preservation of faunal and floral remains, and artifacts made of bone in the shell middens that litter the harbor islands, resulted in great discoveries to which Luedtke devoted hours of painstaking research and about which she published prolifically (Luedtke 1980a, 1980b, 1988, 1996a, 1998a, 1998b, 2000, n.d.). Kerber's and Bernstein's chapters on shell middens offer significant new perspectives on Native American subsistence, settlement, and ceremonialism in southern New England and New York. Dincauze and Décima's chapter provides fresh insights into the technological, social, and ecological implications of the results of the most recent archaeological investigation of the Boylston Street Fishweir complex in Boston. Barbara's interest in island archaeology led her to Nantucket (Luedtke 1980c), but unfortunately, not to Martha's Vineyard. Chilton and Doucette's chapter is a welcome new addition to the study of coastal archaeology through their archaeological investigations of an important site on Martha's Vineyard.

Barbara's area of expertise in lithics fit in perfectly with the archaeological record of Native American New England, where severe soil acidity results in poor preservation of classes of organic artifacts. Lithics are frequently the only type of cultural material found on New England sites. "Archaeologists working in all areas and time periods have often recognized 'exotic' materials that could not have originated in the vicinity of the site where they were found, and which must have been brought or traded from a distance. If the original source of such materials can be determined, hypotheses about trade and social interaction can be tested, forming the basis for higher-level studies of adaptation, cultural change, and the development of complex economies" (Luedtke 1978b:414). This lofty goal was the subject of Barbara's doctoral dissertation (Luedtke 1976) at the University of Michigan, and led her to use trace-element analysis as a means of identifying different sources of lithics throughout her career (Hermes et al. 2001; Luedtke 1978b, 1979, 1987a; Luedtke and Meyers 1984; Luedtke et al. 1998). Her comprehensive publication, *An Archaeologist's Guide to Chert and Flint* (Luedtke 1992), is recognized globally as the sourcebook and reference guide for all archaeologists engaged in studies of chert and flint.

Having spent her graduate and post-graduate studies in analyzing cherts from the Midwest, Barbara devoted the same level of scrutiny and interest in the "grotty" lithics common to New England. New England has few sources of chert or jasper; the dominant lithics include rhyolite, quartz, quartzite, fine-grained volcanics, hornfels, and some metamorphic stones (see Calogero, Ritchie, and Volmar and Blancke [this volume]). Barbara's use of trace-element analysis identified Pennsylvania as the source of jasper found on Middle Woodland sites in eastern Massachusetts, as opposed to the more local jasper sources in New England and New York (Luedtke 1987a). Petrographic and geochemical analyses helped Luedtke identify "Melrose green" as a fine-grained rhyolite commonly misidentified by archaeologists as a New York chert (Hermes et al. 2001; Luedtke et al. 1998). Through archival research and field inspection, she was able to "rediscover" the quarry site of "Melrose green" in a modern suburb of Boston.

Combining her research interest in sourcing lithics and understanding settlement systems, Luedtke's recent study of the distribution of lithics on the harbor islands revealed what she believed is a pre-Contact territorial boundary across the middle of Thompson Island and across the middle of the harbor along what is now called the Nantasket Road (see Luedtke, this volume). Luedtke suggested that this boundary existed during the Middle and Late Woodland periods (ca. 2000–500 years before present [B.P.]) and the Contact period (after 500 B.P.), between the Native groups on the mainland to the north and to the south of the Boston area. Ritchie's chapter delves further into this research topic on the mainland.

Luedtke always felt that "there are enough research topics to go around" (personal communication). She had four key recommendations for lithic studies: (1) more articles need to be published on lithic sources in the region; (2) locations and spatial extent of secondary deposits of lithics need to be identified (e.g., glacial, river, and stream deposits); (3) additional petrographic and geochemical studies should be done on additional types of lithics; and (4) communication among lithic experts in the region should increase (Luedtke 1993:58–59). She advocated for regional lithic databases and working groups. Through time, she amassed an enormous type collection of lithic materials at UMass/Boston, the largest in the greater Boston area. Her specific recommendation for lithic sourcing publications was to provide "a careful description of a [lithic] material's dimensions (color, luster, texture, etc.), along with suggestions as to its possible provenance" (Luedtke 1986a:92). She encouraged her colleagues to use petrographic and geochemical analysis rather than simply "eyeball identification" (Luedtke 1993). Lithic artifact classifications and styles could be greatly confused with the actual functional use of the tool, Luedtke noted (Luedtke 1986a:90–91). She recommended use-wear studies and accurate descriptions of tools.

I have always found the monograph on the archaeology of the Shattuck Farm Site as an exemplary site report (Luedtke 1985). Of particular interest to the readers of Section III in this book are the pages that Barbara devoted to the description and analysis of ceramics (Luedtke 1985:210–256). She presents an introduction to the region's ceramics, providing an overview of the technological aspects of pottery-making. She gives a chronology of the changes in sherd thickness, temper, shape, and decoration through the Early (ca. 3000–2000 B.P.), Middle, and Late Woodland periods. In addition, decorative motifs are described and tools used to make certain motifs are illustrated. Furthering her interest in ceramic studies, Luedtke later described her analysis of regional differences in ceramics from sites in northeastern Massachusetts, Boston Harbor Islands, and Nantucket, all located within the coastal lowlands (Luedtke 1986b). She observed changes through time in such attributes as sherd thickness, temper, temper particle size, and major decorative elements, and she offered explanations for these differences (Luedtke 1986b).

For ceramic studies, Luedtke emphasized that "ceramics are very sensitive indicators of a variety of cultural dynamics, including both macro-trends relevant to areas as large as the Northeast, and micro-traditions relevant only to individual river valleys" (Luedtke 1986b:132). Ceramic analysis offers great potential for addressing questions concerning settlement systems, economics, trade networks, social relationships, kinship/clan membership, individuality, rules of domestic residency, and possibly ideology and ritual. Luedtke once remarked, ". . . it should be encouraging to Massachusetts archaeologists to learn that our prehistoric ceramics hold great potential for the elucidation of prehistoric cultures, and are not the hopeless confusion of styles that many may have feared" (Luedtke 1986b:132). The chapters by Goodby, Lavin, Pretola, and Bunker certainly attest to this optimistic prognosis.

Early in her career, Luedtke viewed ceramics and lithics as technologies. She even used technological analysis to publish articles on historic period gunflints (Luedtke 1998c, 1999a, 1999b). But Luedtke's research interests expanded beyond the purely technological aspects of Native American lithics and ceramics. She was interested in exploring questions of cultural identity (Luedtke 1996b), social territories and boundaries (Luedtke n.d.), and ideological implications of the preference for certain lithic materials like Pennsylvania jasper or Braintree hornfels (Luedtke 1987a:44–45; 1998a:28).

Luedtke's research over a quarter of a century has helped to sort out cultural chronologies in southern New England. She has established research frameworks for coastal sites and settlement studies. She has contributed to the establishment of a regional lithic source database. She has used archaeological sciences in her research—geochemical and petrographic analysis, palynology, AMS radiocarbon dating—and urges us to fill the "archaeometry gap" in our research of new sites and existing collections (see Luedtke, this volume). Twenty-five years have given us a lasting impression and even more exciting work to do.

Brona G. Simon

Preface

Jordan E. Kerber

This volume brings together a wide range of studies on coastal, lithic, and ceramic research in New England archaeology. At first glance, these topics may appear to be unrelated. The principal reason for making them the focal point here, indeed the intellectual rationale for this book, is that these three areas represent the major research interests of the late distinguished archaeologist Barbara E. Luedtke. All the papers in this volume raise issues that are directly relevant, if not central, to Barbara's work. As discussed in the Foreword, during her 25-year career in New England archaeology, Barbara not only actively pursued research on coastal archaeology, lithic analysis, and ceramic analysis, but by so doing she paved the way for many other investigations of these topics and inspired numerous archaeologists in the region. Her scholarship has made an enormous impact, a lasting impression, both on the development of New England archaeology and on her many colleagues.

This book consists of 12 chapters, written by 15 authors and organized in three parts. All but two of the chapters were composed specifically for the volume. All the contributors discuss various topics pertaining primarily to Native American settlement, subsistence, and technology in New England (and occasionally New York) during the prehistoric (pre-Contact) and Contact periods, from as early as ca. 12,000 B.P. until about 300 B.P. They also present methodologies, results, analyses, interpretations, and syntheses of important regional studies, undertaken recently and several years ago, which both complement and challenge existing models and knowledge. *A Lasting Impression* is unique insofar as no other publication focuses on coastal, lithic, and ceramic research in New England archaeology. Further, because some of the papers present current methodological approaches, the volume is relevant to other geographic areas, since it provides a comparative framework for evaluating archaeological research elsewhere.

Part One, Coastal Archaeology, consists of five chapters that are written by seven authors. The first two chapters, by Barbara E. Luedtke and Jordan E. Kerber, are reprinted. In this, one of her last publications, Luedtke offers a retrospective view of her 25 years of doing archaeology on the Boston Harbor Islands. She reflects on some of the especially interesting or significant issues, reviews much information gathered over the years, comments on what is still unknown, and suggests directions for future research in the coastal zone in general and on the Boston Harbor Islands in particular. Kerber, in his chapter, attempts to expand existing subsistence-dominated notions of marine shell deposits by exploring the possibility that symbolism and ceremonialism were associated with some of these features during the Woodland period (ca. 3000–500 B.P.) in New England and New York. In addition to discussing the Lambert Farm site in Rhode Island, he raises numerous questions and generates speculation concerning so-called shell middens and the use of shellfish, in the hope that further consideration will be pursued by others. In Chapter 3, David J. Bernstein addresses evidence of coastal resource utilization from the van der Kolk site at Mount Sinai Harbor on Long Island, New York, during the Late Woodland period (ca. 1000–500 B.P.). He reconstructs a pattern of generalized resource use and argues that the late prehistoric Native Long Islanders rarely utilized products that could not be readily found within a few hundred meters of their coastal settlements. Focusing on their recent excavations at the multicomponent Lucy Vincent Beach site on Martha's Vineyard, Elizabeth S. Chilton and Dianna L. Doucette, in the next piece, discuss preliminary results, analysis, and interpretations. They maintain that not only will diverse archaeological information recovered from this site contribute to understanding the complex relationship between environmental change and the lifeways of the region's Native coastal inhabitants, but it will also elucidate the history of the Wampanoag Aquinnah tribe on the island. The last chapter in Part One, co-authored by Dena F. Dincauze and Elena Décima, focuses on the renowned "Boylston Street fishweir" in Boston. Drawing on data from excavations immediately south of the original site, the authors challenge the long-held interpretation of this weir as a single huge structure with its thousands of stakes over many acres, implying a large organized workforce to build, operate, and maintain. Instead, they argue that the facility consisted of a series of successive small tidal weirs along an inundating shore, over a time span of about 1500 years during the Late Archaic period (ca. 5000–3000 B.P.).

The three chapters in Part Two, written by four contributors, focus on analysis of lithics utilized by Native Americans in New England. Barbara L.A. Calogero addresses the benefits of microscopic examination of thin sections of stone tools and chipping debris to identify more accurately lithic types and source areas. Referring largely to collections from Connecticut, she offers petrographic evidence of the variety and qualities of stone materials used by prehistoric toolknappers. In Chapter 7, Duncan Ritchie discusses the shift in lithic resource use in eastern Massachusetts to local sources during the Late Woodland period. Using petrography and geochemistry to trace rock types to their source areas, he hypothesizes that certain lithic materials served as markers of identity or territory for Native Americans after about 1100 B.P. In a similar vein as Luedtke's piece (this volume) on the Boston Harbor Islands, Ritchie notes that Late Woodland lithic resource use patterns appear to conform to drainage basins that may also mark group territories. In their co-authored chapter, Michael A. Volmar and Shirley Blancke stress the value of examining the microscopic scale at archaeological deposits in general and at two sites in Massachusetts and Rhode Island in particular. The authors demonstrate how microstructural analysis of lithics, soils, and sediments enables them to refine interpretations of depositional history, to locate minute evidence of human activities, and to augment and challenge field observations of site and feature formation processes.

In the final section of the book, the authors of the four chapters analyze and interpret Native American ceramics in New England (and New York). The chapter by Robert G. Goodby critiques the common assumption that the Shantok ceramic tradition is associated with the historic Pequot-Mohegan people of Connecticut. He draws on studies of seventeenth-century Native American ceramics from adjacent areas of southeastern New England to argue that these artifacts did not function as ethnic or tribal markers during this period, that the ethnicity or tribal affiliation of particular potters cannot be inferred from either the stylistic or technological attributes of these vessels, and that the Shantok construct should be abandoned. In the next chapter, Lucianne Lavin attempts to explain why collared pottery styles dating near the end of the Late Woodland period (ca. A.D. 1350–1500) in New England, eastern New York, and northern New Jersey are nearly identical to contemporaneous "Iroquoian" ceramics in central New York. Her hypothesis involves the dynamics of inter-group relations, associated language groups or dialects, and stable settlement patterns. Similar to Lavin, John P. Pretola in Chapter 11 examines the puzzling existence of "Iroquoian" ceramic traits in eastern New York and southern New England. He utilizes ceramic petrography and optical mineralogy to study vessel paste composition, construction, and design execution, based on 91 sherds from Mohawk, Hudson, Housatonic, and Connecticut River valley sites, dating to the end of the Late Woodland period. The author concludes that Algonquian and Iroquoian groups interacted in an open and fluid system that allowed association and mixture of people and ideas, and that the use of the term "Iroquoian" to describe any eastern New York and southern New England ceramic trait should be abandoned. In the last chapter, Victoria Bunker presents descriptions of two early Vinette I-type ceramic vessels, dating to nearly 3500 B.P., excavated at the Beaver Meadow Brook and Eddy sites along the Merrimack River in New Hampshire. She asserts that both discoveries are significant as they possess the oldest radiocarbon-dated associations of Native pottery in New England, and they provide much-needed information on early ceramic manufacture technology through attribute analysis.

The 15 contributors to this volume, along with Brona G. Simon who wrote the Foreword, are fortunate to have counted Barbara E. Luedtke as a colleague, friend, and/or mentor. This book clearly demonstrates the far-reaching and profound effect she has had on archaeological research in New England, and is proudly dedicated to her memory, in tribute to her lasting impression.

I wish to acknowledge the vital contribution of numerous individuals for assisting me in the preparation and completion of this book. I extend my heartfelt thanks to all the contributors to the volume for their commitment to this publication and for their diligence in completing and revising their manuscripts. Judith Zeitlin, Barbara Davis, and Dennis Howe provided important assistance, as well. I am grateful for permission obtained from Margaret and Charles Luedtke, Barbara's parents, to reprint her article; from Charles Cobb, editor of *Northeast Anthropology*, to reprint my article; and from Michael Davis to use his photograph of Barbara. Also worthy of recognition are Jane Garry of Greenwood Publishing Group, Inc. and Laurie Weinstein, *Native Peoples of the Americas* General Editor, for their support and valuable advice. I acknowledge Colgate University for providing me with a supportive environment in which to produce this book. Lastly, I am deeply grateful to my wife, Mary Moran, and to my children, Pearl and John, for having given me the time needed to complete this project, and along with my parents, Sidney Kerber and the late Pauline Kerber, for being eternal sources of inspiration and encouragement.

PART I

COASTAL ARCHAEOLOGY

Archaeology on the Boston Harbor Islands after 25 Years

Barbara E. Luedtke

The year 1999 marked my 25th year doing archaeology on the Boston Harbor Islands. Milestones are always a good time for retrospection, so this paper will reflect on some of the things we've learned over these years, comment on what we still don't know, and suggest directions for future research in the coastal zone in general, and on the Boston Harbor Islands in particular. This chapter is not meant to be a comprehensive summary of our knowledge of the Islands, which would require a book, but simply presents some of the issues that I consider especially interesting or significant. I will first discuss several topics regarding coastal sites that are primarily meaningful to New England archaeologists, and then discuss what the coast and islands might have meant to the pre-Contact native peoples who left these sites.

ISSUES OF SIGNIFICANCE TO ARCHAEOLOGISTS

First, as is true everywhere in Massachusetts, the total number of known sites has grown enormously. In 1974 there was no official state site file, and the Massachusetts Archaeological Society had by far the most complete list of archaeological sites in the Commonwealth. The only Boston Harbor Islands sites known officially were those recorded by Dena Dincauze in the course of her survey of the Greater Boston Area. According to my count, 19 sites were known then, and 60 ± are

Table 1.1
Types of Sites on Boston Harbor Islands

Surveys	N	Shell Middens	Scattered Shell	No Shell
Long Island[1]	6	33%	17%	50%
World's End[2]	10	50%	10%	40%
Thompson I.[3]	20	50%	10%	40%

References: 1, Luedtke 1984a; 2, Luedtke 1990; 3, Luedtke 1996a.

known now (depending on how one counts areas that are now connected to the mainland but that used to be islands). This increase is the result of a great deal of fieldwork by many institutions, including the University of Massachusetts at Boston, Harvard University, Public Archaeology Laboratory, Inc., the Boston City Archaeologist, Boston University's Office of Public Archaeology, Timelines, Inc., and others.

However, I am quite certain that more than 60 sites still exist on the Islands. Some of the Harbor Islands have never been surveyed, some have only been partially surveyed, and many others need to be re-surveyed because the survey methods used in the early days would now be considered woefully inadequate (Luedtke 1975, 1978a). We probably found most of the big shell middens on the 12 islands we studied in 1974, but I know we missed most of the non-midden sites, which we now realize make up a substantial proportion of the total. For example, for the three islands that have been most intensively surveyed by more modern methods (Table 1.1), 40 to 50% of the sites we found had no shell, and another 10% had very little shell. Some of these shell-less sites are early, dating to the Middle and Late Archaic, before the shellfish beds developed (Luedtke 1990:39–47). Others date to periods when shellfish were available, but were simply not deposited at these particular sites. For example, several shell-less sites may be Late Woodland farming hamlets, located away from the shellfish beds but adjacent to the best soils for farming (Luedtke 1987b). There could even be a Paleoindian site among the as-yet undiscovered sites on the Islands; with the Neponset/Wamsutta site just 25 km away (Carty and Spiess 1992), it is hard to believe that Paleoindians never came to this area. Therefore, my first recommendation for future work on the Islands is that we do more survey, to fill in the remaining gaps in our knowledge of site locations.

Coastal sites are especially significant to New England archaeologists because a wider range of materials are preserved than at most inland sites. But this just heightens the frustration of the "archaeometry gap," that is, the ever-widening gap between the analyses we *could* do on our sites and artifacts, and those we can actually *afford* to do. For just a few examples, we now could obtain AMS radiocarbon dates from very tiny samples of charcoal or shell, and find out the age of many of our "sites of unknown age"; we could determine the season during which clams were harvested through study of their growth rings (Lightfoot and Cerrato 1989); we could reconstruct the paleocoastlines (Aubrey 1994); we could study erosion patterns and shoreline change (Kellogg 1995); we could perform the microstratigraphic studies of soils that might help elucidate complex stratigraphy and features (Currie 1994); we could core all the saltmarshes on the islands and study changes in pollen and plant macrofossils (Simon 1991); we could use petrographic and geochemical methods to securely determine the sources of lithic materials (Strauss and Hermes 1996); we could do stable isotope studies of domestic dog bones, to obtain insight into the diets of the people who kept those dogs (Cannon, Schwarcz, and Knyf 1999). Any issue of the *Journal of Archaeological Science* or *Archaeometry* will suggest numerous other procedures, all potentially capable of producing fascinating data. Thus, my second recommendation is that in the future, any Cultural Resource Management projects on the islands should try to include at least some of these kinds of analysis in their scope of work. Also, graduate students working on MA theses and Ph.D. dissertations should be aware that there is tremendous potential for exciting and significant projects, based on existing collections from the Islands or with a little additional fieldwork.

Site formation processes may not actually *be* more complex on the coast, but coastal shell midden sites often appear especially complex stratigraphically because of the ways shell is transformed by natural and cultural processes (Ceci 1984). Unlike the massive shell piles at sites such as Damariscotta (Sanger and Sanger 1986), Boston Harbor Islands' shell middens are usually less than 50 cm thick and take the form of numerous overlapping lenses and features, just what you'd expect if shellfish were being gathered as part of a diverse diet and discarded in small dumps or pits, during the course of multiple visits spanning hundreds and sometimes thousands of years. Some of these middens are a fairly uniform mixture of soil and shell, in which it can be difficult to see intrusions; I remember our surprise at uncovering a 1930s hammer head near the base of what had appeared to be undisturbed midden (Luedtke 1990:25). In some cases microstratigraphy is present, but Dena Dincauze has voiced the suspicion that some of it may be the result of bioturbation, and may even be ephemeral (Dincauze, personal communication). In other cases there are no visible strata, but as one trowels down, one can *feel* trample surfaces where the shells are lying flat. Modified Harris matrices may help us to deal with this complexity (Shaw 1994), but this will only work in conjunction with rather broad-scale excavations, not the scattered test pits we have generally used. Thus, my third recommendation: we need more broad-scale excavations of large contiguous areas (Mrozowski 1994:60).

This is also one solution to the final archaeological concern I want to mention here, which is site destruction resulting from storms and sea level rise. We have laws requiring mitigation when development threatens a site, but none to deal with attacks from Mother Nature. As others have also pointed out (Kerber 1999), coastal sites are among our most endangered, primarily due to erosion (but also because of increasing pressure from people who wish to build and play in the coastal zone). Sea level rise has been a long-term trend throughout the Holocene, it is still occurring, and it will accelerate if global warming is a reality. Although much of my research has been focused on finding sites and then leaving them undisturbed as much as possible, we now face the possibility that most of those carefully documented sites will erode away during the next generation while we all sit back and watch. My fourth recommendation is that we begin to develop a priority list of endangered coastal sites and start excavating them while we still can.

ISSUES OF SIGNIFICANCE TO SITE INHABITANTS

I would like to shift gears now and try to consider what the Boston Harbor Islands might have meant to the people who lived on them in the past. Of course, the significance of the Islands to native peoples must have varied over time, both because cultures change and because the environment changes. For an obvious example, the first people living in the area that is now Boston Harbor were really living on the shores of river estuaries, not islands. We have recovered artifacts dating from the Early Archaic on (Luedtke 1984a:7–8), but the islands only began to separate from the mainland during the Late Archaic (Aubrey 1994). The Middle and Late Woodland periods are most heavily represented on the islands, but we have to assume that many sites from earlier periods could have been lost to erosion.

First, the Islands must have had considerable economic significance to people in the past. For all coastal periods, the Boston Harbor Islands would have been a *dependable* source of food in any season (certainly for shellfish, probably for certain waterbirds, and possibly for certain fish and crustaceans). This is not of minor significance to people who can't drive to the Stop and Shop when they run low on food. In certain seasons, such as when large numbers of migratory fish or birds visit the harbor, the coastal zone was also a source of *abundant* resources. What one would expect, given these characteristics, and what I see in the archaeological record, is a pattern of repeated visits to the coast, especially during the seasons of abundance but sometimes at other times of the year as well. Fall seems to have been an especially popular time to visit the Islands (Luedtke 1980a), but some sites appear to represent spring or summer camps (Luedtke 1996a:47–53). I see no evidence for sedentism at any period; these islands were simply too small to support a group of people for a whole year, and the raw and frigid winds make them thoroughly unpleasant in the winter.

Very few of the Boston Harbor Islands sites have food remains representing only coastal resources; more often floral and faunal remains indicate use of a wide range of both marine and terrestrial resources (Table 1.2). Though 64 species of plants and animals have been identified from Harbor Islands sites, three species (deer, cod, and soft-shell clam) predominate in their categories not only in terms of how frequently they are found, but also in terms of the minimum number of individuals represented. In the case of soft-shell clam, this is simply a reflection of availability, as this is the most common clam found in the harbor today as it has been for the last two thousand years (Braun 1974). Deer also must have been the most abundant and easily available large herbivore in the area, as they were throughout most of the Eastern Woodlands. Deer did live on some of the islands (Wood 1977:61), and may have visited others by swimming, by crossing at low tide, or by crossing on the ice when the harbor was frozen in winter. Some of the deer bone found at sites may also have been brought to the islands as scrap for making bone tools, which appear to have been manufactured at many of the sites (Luedtke 1990:22–24). Cod has been an important fish in the New England economy for many centuries (Ross 1991:145–149), but it may be impossible to determine whether it was actually the most abundant fish in Boston Harbor, or whether it was simply especially favored by the native peoples who fished there.

The Harbor Islands also provided a number of non-food resources that may have been valued, including flakable stone cobbles on the beaches, clay deposits, shell for beads, and even sun and wind. The juxtaposition of land, which heats and cools quickly, and the sea, which warms and cools slowly, creates a thermal gradient along the coast, resulting in a nearly permanent breeze. On Thompson Island we have found a number of features on the tops of hills that appear to be locations where foods were sun and/or smoke dried (Luedtke 1996a:43–44). Thus, my fifth rec-

Table 1.2
Species Found at Boston Harbor Islands Sites

Scientific name	Common name	# of BHI sites where species was identified ($N=31$)
MAMMALS		
Odocoileus virginianus	deer	12
Canis familiaris	dog	11
Procyon lotor	raccoon	5
Castor canadensis	beaver	5
Phoca vitulina	harbor seal	2
Sylvilagus sp.	rabbit	2
Erethizon dorsatum	porcupine	1
Sciurus carlinensis	grey squirrel	1
Urocyon or *Vulpes*	fox	1
Mustela sp.	weasel, mink	1
BIRDS		
Phalacrocorax auritus	double crested cormorant	5
Maleagris gallopavo	turkey	4
Branta bernicla	brant	2
Branta canadensis	Canada goose	2
Gavia immer	common loon	2
Anas rubripes	black duck	2
Aythini sp.	bay duck	2
Pinguinnis impennis	great auk	1
Alca torda	razorbill auk	1
Phalacrocorax carbo	common cormorant	1
Corvus sp.	crow	1
Cygnus sp.	swan	1
Melanitta sp.	scoter (duck)	1
Bucephala sp.	goldeneye (duck)	1
Gavia sp.	loon	1
Family *Accipitrine*	hawk	1
Family *Tetraoninae*	grouse	1
Family *Laridae*	gull	1
Family *Ardeidae*	heron	1
FISH		
Gadus morhua	cod	10
Acipenser sp.	sturgeon	5
Squalus acanthias	spiny dogfish	3
Lophius americanus	goosefish	3
Melanogrammus aeglefinus	haddock	2
Alosa pseudoharengus	alewife	1
Pomatomus saltatrix	bluefish	1
Tautogolabus adspersus	cunner	1
Brosme brosme	cusk	1
Pollachius virens	pollock	1

Table 1.2 Continued

Scientific name	Common name	# of BHI sites where species was identified (*N*=31)
Tautoga onitis	tautog	1
Microgadus tomcod	tomcod	1
Family *Serranidae*	bass	1
Family *Bothidae*	flounder	1
Family *Labridae*	wrasse	1
MOLLUSCS		
Mya arenaria	soft-shell clam	29
Mytilus edulis	mussel	16
Crassostrea virginica	oyster	10
Mercenaria mercenaria	quahog	10
Argopecten irradians	scallop	5
Ensis directus	razor clam	5
Lunatia heros	moon snail	4
Family *Buccinidae*	small whelk	3
Spisula solidissima	surf clam	2
Crepidula fornicata	slipper shell	2
Geukensia demissa	ribbed mussel	1
PLANTS		
Chenopodium sp.	lambsquarters	13
Carya sp.	hickory	10
Rubus sp.	blackberry, raspberry	10
Rhus sp.	sumac	6
Zea mays	corn	3
Quercus sp.	oak (acorn)	1
Polygonum sp.	smartweed	1
Portulaca sp.	purslane	1
Mollugo sp.	carpetweed	1

ommendation: we need more sophisticated modeling of resource use for the coastal zone, based in part on more thorough identifications of faunal and floral remains in existing collections and also on consideration of non-food resources.

It is worth noting that there are no resources available on the Islands that are not also available on the mainland, with the possible exception of access to deep water close to land. There are shallow and extensive tidal flats along much of the mainland, requiring anglers to either drag their canoes a long way over the tide flats at low tide, or to fish a dangerously long way from shore at higher tides. But this is a minor consideration, and my major point is that people probably did not visit the Boston Harbor Islands solely for economic reasons. Social, ideological, and even aesthetic factors may also have been important motivations for island visits.

The Boston Harbor Islands would also have been significant to people as part of a social landscape, with potential for shared or restricted access. I suggested early on in my career that the use and social significance of the Islands might have changed during the Late Woodland, after the introduction of farming (Luedtke 1980a). Before this economic innovation, the islands might have functioned as a "commons," with access fairly unrestricted as long as one belonged to the appropriate regional group. People visiting the islands therefore generally chose to use the closer and bigger islands, and they generally camped at the "best" locations on those islands, that is, on flat well-drained land near a spring, shellfish beds, and good coves for landing canoes. Later in the Late Woodland, some of the bigger and closer islands appear to have been suitable for small farming hamlets, and thus became incorporated into family territories. People who were not closely related to the families farming on a particular island probably felt uncomfortable visiting there. The resulting archaeological pattern, which has held up well over 25 years of research, is for large multicomponent sites to be occupied up until about A.D. 1200, and then apparently abandoned. Most sites dating after A.D. 1200 are located adjacent to good farming soil, or on the smaller outer islands, which may have still been considered "commons."

There are also new data relevant to the social landscape of the Boston Harbor Islands, based on proportions of Saugus jasper, Melrose green rhyolite, and Braintree hornfels flakes in assemblages. During our survey on Thompson Island, I noted that sites at the northern end of the island often had large proportions of raw materials from the north shore of Boston Harbor, while at sites on the southern part of the island, southern materials predominated. I then plotted proportions of these key materials for other Harbor Islands sites, and found that the same pattern distinguished sites on islands in the northern part of the Harbor from those in the southern part. Some time ago, Dincauze suggested that during the Late Woodland period the Charles River functioned as a boundary between two different, although closely related, groups (Dincauze 1974: 56), and my data suggest that this boundary also extended right across Boston Harbor, following approximately the shipping route known as Nantasket Road (Luedtke 1997). As mentioned previously, the boundary cuts right through Thompson Island, and it may not be coincidental that the two sites located adjacent to that boundary produced most of the exotic lithic materials we found during our survey, including jasper, Onondaga chert, and chert from the Champlain Valley (Luedtke 1996a). My sixth recommendation is that we investigate this possible boundary further, in order to determine whether the pattern I found is also evident on other islands, and whether it is apparent in any other aspect of material culture, such as ceramic decoration motifs or minor lithic style differences. Were people more likely to trade with each other at sites along such boundaries? Is this in any way related to the development of social complexity, which Bragdon has suggested occurred along the coast in late pre-Contact times (Bragdon 1996)?

Finally, the Islands surely had symbolic significance to the native peoples who visited them. The coastal zone in general would have been the portion of the pre-Contact landscape most susceptible to rapid and dramatic changes, as chunks of land were eroded into the sea, barrier beaches formed or were breached, and sand spits migrated up and down coastlines (Luedtke and Rosen 1993). The coastal zone is also fundamentally liminal, a threshold between the very different domains of land and sea. For the native peoples of the East Coast, it was also the "end of the known world," the edge of the turtle's shell (Bragdon 1996:214). Like other liminal states and places, the coastal zone is both benevolent to those who know how to use it properly, and harmful to those who do not. Food is always available in Boston Harbor, but the rocks, sand bars, and nine-foot tidal range have drowned many a careless fisherman or shellfish gatherer. There is always a cool breeze along the coast, providing welcome relief from summer's heat, but during a nor'easter the coast is also a place of great danger and destruction.

Would the dynamic, ambivalent, and liminal character of the coastal zone have made it an especially important location for ceremonial activities? Was it indeed favored for burials, as has been suggested (Kerber 1999:3; see also Kerber, this volume)? Two pre-Contact burials have been excavated on the Harbor Islands (Dincauze 1974), and others are said to have eroded out in the past (Luedtke 1996a:20). My final recommendation for future research is that we attempt to investigate the symbolic or ideological aspect of the islands and coast, both through oral traditions and through some innovative hypothesis testing using archaeological data. We might also start using remote sensing methods to locate graves on the islands, not so that they can be excavated, but so that they can be protected from accidental exposure and from erosion. There are probably more pre-Contact graves, and on some of the islands there are definitely a large number of unmarked graves dating to the last few centuries. The Islands have recently been designated the Boston Harbor Islands National Recreation Area, and they are certain to face increased development over the next few years. The various owners of the islands could spare themselves a great deal of trouble and bad publicity if they determine ahead of time which areas should not be developed, because of the presence of unmarked graves.

SUMMARY

After 25 years, I know some of the Boston Harbor Islands themselves in intimate detail, but I feel that I still have a lot to learn about how people have used them. In part, this is because my research has focused on survey and minimal testing. Beyond this, though, I believe there is simply a great deal to learn about. The increased range of materials preserved at coastal sites provides opportunities to study traditional archaeological issues such as typology, culture history, and adaptation. In addition, though, the archaeological richness of the coastal zone may also allow us to deal with so-called "post processual" concerns such as ideology, detecting the activities of the sub-groups that make up any human population, such as men, women, children, and the elderly, accounting for the origin of social inequality, and determining the relations within and between social groups. I want to end this retrospective by encouraging the next generation of New England archaeologists to focus on the coastal zone in this new century. Come on in; the archaeology is just beginning to warm up!

ACKNOWLEDGMENTS

This chapter was first prepared for the 1999 meeting of the Conference on New England Archaeology, held in Portsmouth, NH. I thank the organizers of that conference for their invitation to reflect upon coastal matters.

2

Interpreting Diverse Marine Shell Deposits of the Woodland Period in New England and New York: Interrelationships among Subsistence, Symbolism, and Ceremonialism

Jordan E. Kerber

INTRODUCTION

In this chapter I intend to expand our notions of marine shell deposits and the ways in which diversity is expressed in these features at sites from New England and New York. However, the topic of shell midden diversity, which has been discussed in the literature by Barber (1983), Boissevain (1943), Ceci (1984), and Lightfoot (1985), among others, is not the focus of this chapter. Instead I explore the larger issue of diversity within the context of prehistoric human use of marine shellfish, specifically molluscs.[1] In this conceptual framework, I offer an alternative, less conventional interpretation. I argue that prehistoric shell deposits and the use of shellfish may have reflected more than just subsistence economies. It is conceivable that in some instances, perhaps more than we might assume, the shells themselves possessed symbolic meaning and ceremonial significance. I should state at the outset, of course, that subsistence, symbolism, and ceremonialism are not necessarily unrelated, nor are they mutually exclusive. The same shellfish could have been collected for both consumption of the meat and ideology of the shell. Further, the shellfish meat may have been eaten for ceremonial purposes. I conclude by presenting data from the Lambert Farm site in Rhode Island. While this information does not necessarily prove my speculation, it provides the inspiration for much of the theoretical discussion in this chapter.

SHELLFISH USE AND SHELL DEPOSITS

Prehistoric human use of marine shellfish in New England and New York has been seen almost exclusively within the context of subsistence. It is no secret that past populations in the region and elsewhere usually collected molluscs to consume the extracted meat and discarded the shells because they could not be eaten. But were shellfish meat and shells utilized in ways other than human consumption and food refuse? For the Contact period in the Northeast, wampum comes immediately to mind, though shellfish meat in the quahog and whelk shells, from which the shell beads were fashioned, may have been eaten. Other artifacts were made of shell, including hoes to cultivate Woodland period [ca. 3000–500 B.P.] gardens, and crushed shell was used as temper for prehistoric ceramics. Shellfish meat may have been used as bait on hooks or in nets to attract fish (Claassen 1991a:253). We may be hard pressed to think of other examples. As Rollins et al. (1990:474) maintain, molluscs throughout the New World, Oceania, and elsewhere have a "passive use," in addition to their subsistence use. They state that marine shells functioned as important ritual symbols, as items of ascribed value, or both (Rollins et al. 1990:474). Is this true for New England and New York during the Woodland period? I suspect so and will elaborate shortly.

Evidence for use of shellfish is abundant along the shores of the Northeast, as well as many other coastlines around the world. The most conspicuous evidence, of course, are the shellfish remains, which are often discovered in dense deposits, so-called shell middens, that may contain other types of cultural materials. In addition to their high visibility, dense deposits of molluscan remains are often a treasure trove of data and objects as the calcium carbonate in the shells tends to contribute to the preservation of bone, charcoal, nut and seed remains, and other organics that may have been left in these features. Dense shell deposits are notorious, however, for often containing complex microstratigraphy and evidence of multiple episodes of use, thereby posing difficulties in excavation and interpretation (Dincauze 1996; Shaw 1994; Stein 1992).

Northeastern sites containing shell-rich deposits have had a relatively long history of investigation, spanning over 150 years, initiated by geologists and naturalists and later continued by archaeologists (Christenson 1985). In 1867, Wyman introduced the term "shell heap" into the literature on northeastern archaeology when he wrote about the dense shellfish remains of Salisbury, Massachusetts. Soon, use of the synonymous terms "shell heap," "shell midden," and "kitchen midden" became commonplace. The word "midden," according to Stein (1992:6), has its roots in the Scandanavian languages, meaning an accumulation of refuse about a dwelling.

While all shell middens are, by definition, dense shell deposits, it does not follow that all dense shell deposits are necessarily shell middens, even if they contain discarded food remains. Clearly, the vast majority of shell-rich features contain the remains of consumed meals of molluscs and other food. But calling all such deposits shell middens simply because they consist of dense shellfish remains is misleading and makes it difficult to interpret them in ways other than just subsistence. For this reason, some archaeologists (Claassen 1991a; Stein 1992) prefer the term "shell-bearing site," instead of "shell midden," to refer to a site containing shell deposits. I do not propose at this time that the term "shell midden" be replaced, but rather that we expand our notions of so-called shell middens in more complex ways. In this paper I consciously attempt to use the more inclusive terms "shell deposit," "shell feature," and "shellfish remains" to downplay the primarily subsistence-related connotations associated with the term "shell midden."

Since we usually see shell deposits in economic terms, particularly as food refuse, we have for many years analyzed the archaeological remains of molluscs in order to reconstruct subsistence and related topics, including diet and nutrition, seasonality, settlement, population size, and environmental change. Shellfish and shell middens have been at the center of several debates among northeastern coastal archaeologists, for instance: Were molluscs a supplement versus a staple (or seasonal staple [Claassen 1991a:269]) to prehistoric diets? Were changes in the distribution of shellfish species in features a result of changes in technology, cultural preferences, environmental conditions, taboos, and/ or other factors? How is it possible to obtain representative samples from shell middens? And how accurate are shell-growth studies for identifying season(s) of death? Despite the disagreements in these debates, the "message in the midden" is still heard loud and clear: subsistence.

DIVERSITY

Although shell deposits tend to be interpreted primarily as food refuse, and the dense ones are treated as a single type of site or feature (i.e., shell midden), archaeologists still recognize the considerable diversity among and often within these remains (Barber 1983; Ceci 1984; Lightfoot 1985). The fact that no two shell features are the same comes as no surprise. Why would we expect them to be? Variability among these deposits is found in their measurable attributes, a few of which are size, shape, and depth, as with any feature, and density of shells and frequency of shellfish species. They range from thin scatters of fragmented shells of one species to deep deposits (exceeding one meter) containing thousands of shells and the remains of numerous shellfish species, in addition to artifacts and other non-molluscan materials. Some were used only once, some only one season, and others multiple seasons and even years. Many, if not most, were situated adjacent to paleoshorelines (some of these deposits are now submerged by rising sea levels), while others were located farther from their contemporaneous coasts. Some appear as mounds, situated above or below ground; others are shallow pits. Their functions are often interpreted variously as "kitchen middens"; special-purpose processing camps; bulk procurement locations; "dinnertime" camps; seasonal, short-term, and long-term residential bases; and occasionally shell-bead production loci (Lightfoot and Cerrato 1989:41; Schaper 1989:17). Diversity may be seen in other areas, including Dunford's (1998:8) provocative interpretation of Woodland period shell middens of Cape Cod as "actively constructed markers with both familial and political significance."

It is not my intention in this paper to construct a typology of shell deposits. But there may be yet another way, often overlooked, in which variability exists among these features. Although difficult to prove, it is conceivable that some shell deposits contain the remains of molluscs that were more than just discarded food refuse (excluding the use of shell as artifacts). I want to raise the possibility that in certain contexts, shells, individually or collectively, had important symbolic meaning to the people who used them for reasons other than, or in addition to, their associated meat content. What are these contexts? I have been suspicious, over the years, of human and animal burials that exist within features also containing shellfish remains, and I suspect that ideology and ceremonialism were as much a part of many of these shell deposits as was subsistence. I realize that my separation of ideology and ceremonialism from subsistence, as traditional as it is, was probably far less rigid among Native Americans. Nevertheless, the literature contains references spanning this century to burials of humans and dogs (and rarely non-domesticated animals) situated within deposits that also contain shells at several sites in New England and New York.[2] Archaeologists in the region have known for a long time what Beauchamp (1901:462) stated nearly 100 years ago, "Near the sea the dead were sometimes buried in shell heaps, and in a few cases dogs were carefully interred. For burial purposes the shells were neatly arranged." Lacking in the literature, however, are discussions of the potential ideological aspect of shell-burial associations and their relevance as a measure of diversity for both shell features and shellfish use. There is one notable exception (see Claassen 1991b), which I discuss at the end of this chapter.

It is important to make a distinction here. I am not attempting to understand why burials are preserved in deposits containing shellfish remains. Clearly, the alkaline nature of the shells is the cause of organic preservation bias of these features. Nor am I claiming that shell deposits were the preferred or most common method of mortuary treatment in the region. Similarly, I am not arguing that burials are highly associated with shell deposits or vice versa. Rather, I am attempting to understand why burials occur at all in features that also hold shells, regardless of how many burials were interred, or are still preserved, outside of shell contexts. In other words, I am particularly curious of the myriad reasons why burials were put within deposits also containing shellfish remains, and conversely, why shells individually or collectively were placed in burials. I should also state clearly that shell-burial associations to which I refer consist of at least three variations: burials occurring within dense accumulations of shells, burials situated "immediately," "directly," or "just below" (rarely reported as "above") such shell concentrations, and "isolated" shells placed next to interred skeletal remains. All three may occur in the same feature, as described below.

Admittedly, some shell-burial associations may have little or nothing to do with ideology and ceremonialism. For instance, it is possible, perhaps even likely, that previously created "refuse pits" containing shellfish and other remains were occasionally emptied by prehistoric Native Americans in order for the pits to be used for interring one or more burials. Once in the ground, the burial(s) in each pit could be backfilled with the shell-rich contents of the "refuse pit." Such a scenario was reconstructed as early as 1909 by Skinner in his discussion of "shell-heaps" in New York City and vicinity:

Under and near most of these deposits ["deep shell-heaps"] may be found scattered "pits" or fire holes, which are bowl-shaped depressions in the ground filled with layers of stained earth, shells, and other refuse, with an occasional layer of ashes. Some pits are as large as ten feet wide by six feet deep, but the average is four feet deep by three feet wide. It is supposed that they were used as ovens or steaming holes and afterwards filled up with refuse. Some contain human skeletons, which may have been interred in them during the winter season when grave digging was impossible. These pits generally contain more of interest than the ordinary shell-heap. (Skinner 1961:15)

It is also conceivable that some burial pits were unwittingly excavated into previously created shell-rich deposits. Thus, the discovery of burials within features containing dense concentrations of shellfish remains does not necessarily imply a deliberate attempt to associate burials with shells, and it is not always possible to determine whether the association was intentional.[3]

Nevertheless, other shell-burial associations may reflect ideology and ceremonialism, and as such raise numerous questions. For instance, was it significant to prehistoric peoples that shells, individually or collectively, covered or were placed near specific burials and similarly that other burials were placed intrusively within deposits of molluscan remains? If so, why? Did the whiteness of the shells represent their value as mortuary items?[4] Were any of these shells the remains of ritual feasting in connection to burying the dead?[5] In short, were any of these features more than just shell middens? We may ask other relevant questions as well. I do not presume, however, that all these questions can be answered definitively at present or in the future. But I am convinced that such questions and others ought to be asked of many shell-burial associations and that their answers attempted, as speculative as they may be. If not, we will continue to interpret diversity of both shellfish use and shellfish remains in limited ways. Indeed, almost a century ago Bolton alluded to speculation surrounding the topic of multifunctional shell deposits in Manhattan when he stated that "[t]he use of shell pits partly for shells only, partly for the debris of feasts, partly for dog or fish burials and partly to cover human remains is a subject open to conjecture" (Bolton 1909:93).

In the remainder of this chapter I present a brief case study in which I raise the possibility that shells from two features at Lambert Farm, a Woodland site in southern New England, possessed symbolic importance as raw materials for animal burials. In this situation and perhaps others, the use of shellfish may have been as centrally related to spirituality and ceremonialism as it was to subsistence.

CASE STUDY

Lambert Farm (RI-269) dates primarily to the Late Woodland period (ca. 1000–500 B.P.) and is located in Warwick, Rhode Island, approximately 1.6 km (one mile) west of Narragansett Bay (Figure 2.1). Intensive archaeological research co-directed by the author and Alan Leveillee of the Public Archaeology Laboratory, Inc. between 1988 and 1990 resulted in the completion of 523 50×50 cm shovel test pits, most of which were placed at 2.5 m intervals, and 122 excavation units (mostly

Figure 2.1
Location of Lambert Farm and Other Archaeological Sites Discussed in the Text

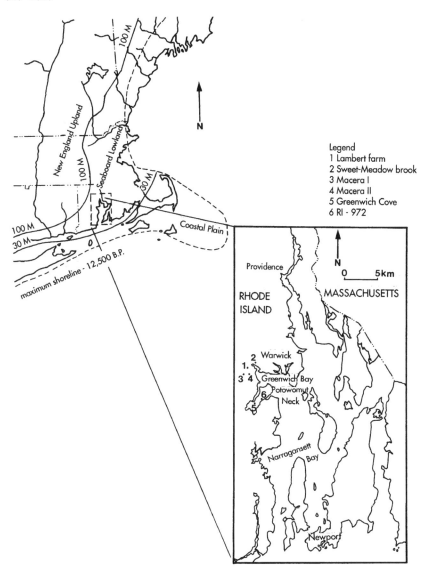

From Kerber, *Lambert Farm, 1st edition*, by © 1997. Reprinted with permission of Wadsworth, an imprint of the Wadsworth Group, a division of Thompson Learning. Fax 800 730-2215.

Figure 2.2
Location of Features 2 and 22 and Completed Sample Units at Lambert Farm

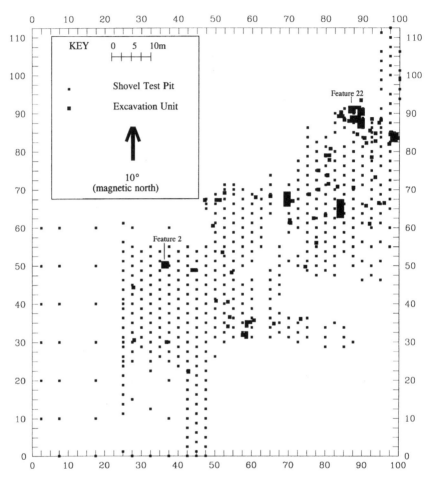

1×1 m) within a .6 ha (1.5 acre) area (Figure 2.2). This distinguishes Lambert Farm as one of the most thoroughly hand-tested sites in New England. Fieldwork revealed 49 features, most containing some number of marine shells, varying greatly in both horizontal and vertical distributions. Several deposits consisted entirely of one or two species of molluscs, while others had six or more. Most of the shell features at Lambert Farm contained discarded food remains in the form of both animals (invertebrates and vertebrates) and non-domesticated plants. Two features (designated numbers 2 and 22), however, were remarkably different from the rest because they were the largest, each holding more than one thousand pounds of shells, and they contained a total of three burials of domesticated dog (*Canis familiaris*). It is these two features that provide insight into an alternative interpretation of shellfish use and shell deposits.[6]

The partially crushed, articulated remains of two immature dogs approximately four months old were discovered in separate burial deposits associated with Feature 2, and the articulated remains of an adult male dog, five or six years old, were unearthed in a burial deposit associated with Feature 22, about 65 m to the northeast of Feature 2 (Figure 2.2). In addition to the dog interment, Feature 22, like Feature 2, held an extremely dense accumulation of shells, as well as charcoal, pottery sherds, chipping debris, fire-cracked rock, non-domesticated plant remains, and disarticulated bones. Feature 2 also contained a steatite platform smoking pipe. The remains of six shellfish species were recovered in Feature 22 and those of seven shellfish species in Feature 2. In both features the shells were situated between about 25 and 85 cm below ground surface and were in the shape of mounds. Many of the shells in the two features were unbroken, and occasionally the bivalves were unopened. The skeletal remains of one immature dog recovered in Feature 2, EU 3, were situated directly beneath a stone slab at the bottom of the shell mound, and a knobbed whelk and a valve of a soft-shell clam were the only other mortuary items in this grave besides the burial (Figure 2.3). The skeletal remains of the second immature dog buried in Feature 2, EU 8, were encountered within the same shell mound, at 73 cm below ground surface. The skeleton of the adult dog in Feature 22 was situated immediately below the other shell mound, and surrounding the skull were several complete soft-shell clamshells (Figure 2.4). None of the three burials appeared to be intrusive in the two shell features. An uncorrected radiocarbon sample of quahog shell at the bottom of the mound in Feature 2 dates to 870 ± 80 B.P. (Beta 27937) (Kerber et al. 1989: 168), while a corrected AMS radiocarbon sample of rib bone from the dog burial in Feature 22 dates to 810 ± 45 B.P. (AA-11784) (Kerber 1997a:32). The latter is the only known radiocarbon date of a prehistoric dog in Rhode Island. Using the calibration computer program CALIB REV 3.0.3 (Stuiver and Reimer 1993a, 1993b), which entails a 95% level of confidence, the two calibrated radiocarbon dates overlap between 790–660 B.P.

Other dense shell deposits containing dog burials also dating to the Woodland period exist at two sites in the vicinity of Lambert Farm. The first is Sweet Meadow Brook near Apponaug Cove, which incidentally also contained the skeletons of an adult man and woman, a child, and a mature dog within a single grave in the same shell feature (Fowler 1956: 5). The second is RI-972 on Potowomut Neck (Kerber 1984). Also on Potowomut Neck is the Greenwich Cove site. Although it lacked dog

Figure 2.3
Plan View of Two Dog Burials and Other Remains Recovered from Feature 2 at Lambert Farm

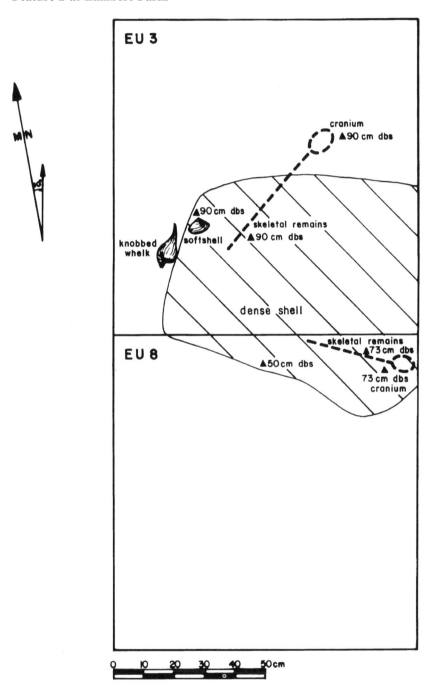

Jordan E. Kerber, Alan D. Leveillee, and Ruth L. Greenspan. "An Unusual Dog Burial Feature at the Lambert Farm Site, Warwick, Rhode Island: Preliminary Observations." *Archaeology of Northeastern North America*, 17 (1989): 165–174, Figure 3, 170. Eastern States Archaeological Federation.

Figure 2.4
**Portion of Single Dog Burial in Feature 22, EU 55 at 90 cm Below
Ground Surface at Lambert Farm**

Shell mound below which dog was interred is visible in the western and northern side
  walls of EU 55 (arrow points north). From Kerber, *Lambert Farm, 1st edition*, by
  © 1997. Reprinted with permission of Wadsworth, an imprint of the Wadsworth
  Group, a division of Thompson Learning. Fax 800 730-2215.

burials, the site's large shell midden contained the intrusive skeletal re-
mains of a child, dating to the Late Woodland or early Contact period
(Bernstein 1993a:160). All three of these sites are situated along the coast
(Figure 2.1). In comparison, what is strikingly different about Lambert
Farm is its location at a greater distance from the shore.

It is interesting that the occupants of Lambert Farm transported the
enormous quantities of shells recovered from Features 2 and 22 some
1.6 km (one mile) uphill to this site. Clearly, it would have been easier
had they carried the substantially lighter preserved meat and left the
shells at the coast. If the extracted meat were not preserved (e.g., by
smoking), however, leaving the meat in the shells and keeping them wet
with seaweed would have delayed spoiling for days at the site. Possible
reasons for not preserving the extracted meat at the shore include planned
consumption within a few days, availability of firewood, amount of effort, taste (including "wetness") preferences, and/or use of the shells at
the site.

Thus, the discovery of the three dog burials within and below both shell mounds may help to explain why such large numbers of shells were brought to Lambert Farm. Indeed, it may be no coincidence that the two densest concentrations of shellfish remains discovered at the site also held dog burials. Of course, shells that were not associated with burials were also transported to this site and others situated away from the coast (e.g., Macera I and Macera II [Morenon 1981], both of which are located nearby, see Figure 2.1). Also, I readily admit that some, if not most, of the shellfish remains in Features 2 and 22 were food refuse, given their contextual association with other non-molluscan subsistence remains. Perhaps these meals were even eaten as part of ritual feasting associated with the burying of dogs. Nevertheless, it is conceivable that many of the shells in both features also possessed symbolic importance as raw materials for the two burial mounds. I speculate that large quantities of shells were brought to the site, not only because of consumption (and temporary preservation) of shellfish meat, but also because they were needed to construct the two mounds for the dog burials. Granted, testing such an hypothesis would be difficult, but the possibility of an ideological function of shells is an intriguing one that few have discussed in the literature. In particular, Claassen (1991b) makes a similar argument for Shell Mound Archaic sites in Kentucky, Tennessee, and Alabama, even though they contain freshwater and not marine shells. She proposes that because the shells in the large mounds served as burial environments for people and, interestingly, dogs, the shells were the objects of collection, rather than their meat (Claassen 1991b:289). According to Claassen, the shells themselves had symbolic importance and ritual significance as they were associated with value, procreation, and death (Claassen 1991b:294–295).

CONCLUSION

What I initially thought to be two typical shell middens that happened to contain three dog burials at Lambert Farm, I now believe to be much more complex than that. Though they contained discarded food refuse in both shell and non-shell forms, Features 2 and 22 suggest, as perhaps other shell-burial associations do, that not all activities represented at shell deposits were limited to subsistence. We may never know the various reasons why prehistoric burials of humans and animals exist within features that also contain shells, but the fact that they occasionally do ought to be considered in our interpretations of diversity of both shellfish use and shell deposits. I hope that my questions and speculation will warrant further consideration of this elusive topic.

ACKNOWLEDGMENTS

The author wishes to thank Susan Bender and Elizabeth Chilton for the opportunity to present a version of this chapter in their co-organized session at the 63rd Annual Meeting of the Society for American Archaeology in Seattle, and Dena Dincauze and Barbara Luedtke, discussants in this session, for their helpful comments. Archaeological research at the Lambert Farm site was performed under the aegis of the Public Archaeology Laboratory, Inc. and co-directed by Alan Leveillee and the author. Ruth Greenspan completed faunal analysis of the three dog burials at Lambert Farm. Funding to support this faunal analysis and the AMS radiocarbon date from one of the dog burials was provided by the Colgate University Research Council. The Rhode Island Historical Preservation Commission provided funding to support the radiocarbon date from the other dog burial. Christine Rossi prepared Figure 2.1, Imogene Lim prepared Figure 2.3, and the author took the photograph in Figure 2.4.

NOTES

1. In this chapter, "shellfish" refers to the edible organism and its surrounding shell.

2. The following is a short list of such references: Bernstein (1993a:160); Bolton (1909: 79,87–88,92); Bullen and Brooks (1948:14); Butler and Hadlock (1949:28); Byers (1979:24,35–36,48,64); Finch (1909:70–71); Fowler (1956:5); Harrington (1909:176); Kerber (1997a:66–78); Little (1986:51); Lopez and Wisniewski (1958:14,17); Nelson (1989:29); Ritchie (1959:29); Rogers (1943: 26,29); Skinner (1909:7, 1919a:56, 1961:57–61); and Solecki (1947:44). (See also Chilton and Doucette, this volume.) Other shell-burial associations undoubtedly exist in the archaeological record but have not yet been discovered. Also, shellfish remains that actually were associated with reported burials may not have been discussed as part of the associations. Of course, sea level rise and recent development, among other disturbances, have obliterated countless sites in the region, some of which may have contained undocumented shell-burial associations.

3. Even if shells were deliberately placed within and above burials, the shells may have played a "practical" role in discouraging animals from disturbing the graves, as argued by Skinner (1961:47).

4. Hamell (1987:66) asserts that for northern Iroquoians and central and eastern Algonquians of the Great Lakes region white was a very important color category, and shells such as wampum that manifest this color had symbolic significance. Based on fundamental concepts synthesized from a panchronic

study of myth among these northeastern Woodland Indians, the color white played a "cognitive role . . . in categorizing and semantically charging biosocial experience" (Hamell 1987:66). Also, white was a primary material manifestation of the "traditional concept of wealth as physical, spiritual, and social well-being" for these people (Hamell 1987:66).

5. Skinner (1961:47) speculates that "feasts of the dead," which occurred at the time of burial interment, included ceremonial meals of shellfish and other food.

6. This section contains a brief summary of pertinent information from Features 2 and 22. For the intricate details of both features, the reader is referred to Kerber (1997a, 1997b, 1994) and Kerber et al. (1989).

3

Late Woodland Use of Coastal Resources at Mount Sinai Harbor, Long Island, New York

David J. Bernstein

This chapter discusses the utilization of coastal resources during late prehistoric times at Mount Sinai Harbor on the north shore of Long Island, New York (Figures 3.1 and 3.2). Research conducted over the last two decades indicates that for thousands of years prior to the European arrival this was one of the most densely populated areas of the Long Island Sound region (Bernstein et al. 1993; Gwynne 1979, 1982; Kalin and Lightfoot 1989). Mount Sinai Harbor has witnessed a variety of excavations since the mid-1970s, including cultural resource management studies (Bernstein 1993b; Bernstein et al. 1993; Kalin and Lightfoot 1989), avocational excavations (described by Gwynne 1982, 1985), and traditional "academic" endeavors (Bernstein et al. 1994; Gramly and Gwynne 1979; Gwynne 1979, 1982, 1984). The results of fieldwork undertaken prior to the early 1980s are synthesized in a doctoral dissertation written by Gwynnc (1982).

After providing a brief introduction to the Mount Sinai Harbor area, I summarize some of the recent work that has taken place at one Late Woodland (ca. 1000–500 B.P.) site on the harbor: van der Kolk (Figure 3.2). Van der Kolk is especially informative about late prehistoric lifeways as it appears that the midden at the site can reasonably be interpreted as having been deposited during the course of a single year.

The region treated in this chapter is shown in Figure 3.1. Long Island and the other islands of Long Island and Block Island Sounds are located in the Atlantic Coastal Plain Physiographic Province (Hunt 1967),

Figure 3.1
Map of Long Island, Showing Locations Discussed in the Text

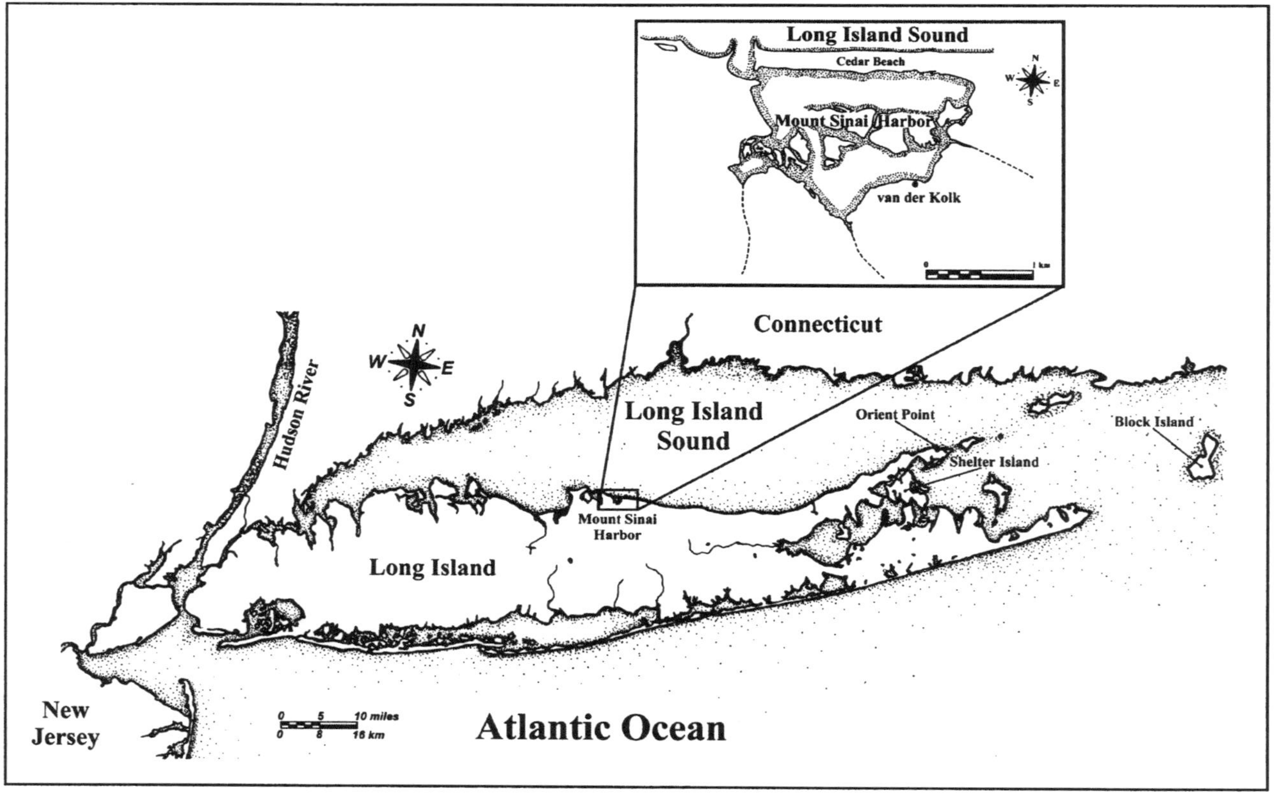

28

Figure 3.2
Map of Mount Sinai Harbor, Showing Locations of Archaeological Sites Discussed in the Text

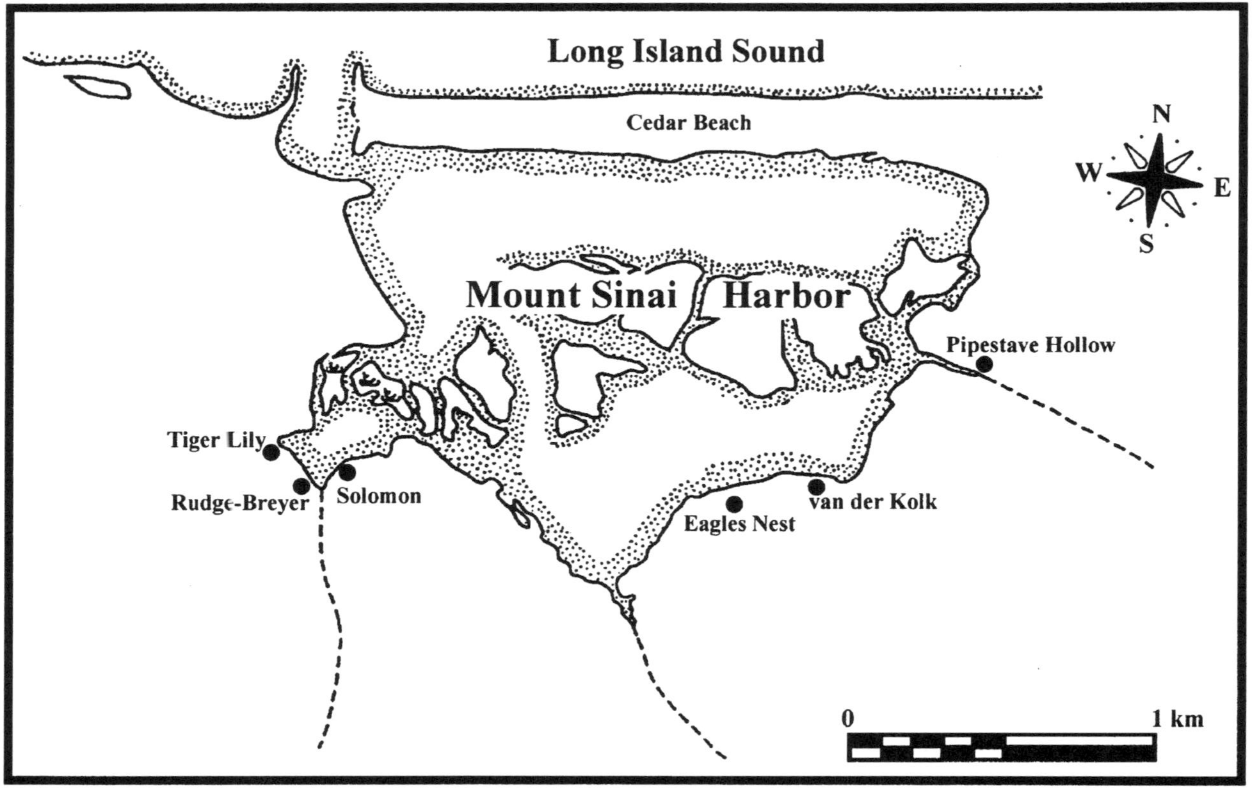

and the oak-chestnut zone of the northern temperate forest (Shelford 1963). General background on the late prehistory of the region is found in Bernstein (1999), Ceci (1990a), Dincauze (1990), Grumet (1995), Lavin (1988a), Lightfoot et al. (1987), Ritchie (1959, 1980), and Silver (1991).

MOUNT SINAI HARBOR

Mount Sinai Harbor is located on the north shore of Long Island, approximately halfway between New York City and Orient Point on the eastern end of the island (Figure 3.1). The small, shallow harbor is very well sheltered and for this reason is today a popular anchorage for pleasure and fishing boats. At its north end, a barrier bar separates the harbor from Long Island Sound. The inlet shown in Figure 3.2 provides access to the Sound. The position of the passage has changed over time, but Mount Sinai Harbor has been open to the Sound for at least the last few thousand years. The harbor is bordered on three sides by steep slopes that are part of the eroded Harbor Hill Moraine (Sirkin 1982). In the past, three freshwater streams emptied into Mount Sinai Harbor (Figure 3.2). Today, none of the three flows regularly, but they often hold fresh water for extended periods (Gwynne 1982:14–15). Freshwater seeps are found at frequent intervals along the south shore of the harbor.

The area surrounding Mount Sinai Harbor has a long record of prehistoric occupation, possibly extending as far back as eight to ten thousand years ago. Fluted and bifurcated-base projectile points have been recovered by amateur excavators, suggesting a great antiquity to the human presence in this region. Due to lower sea level, the harbor did not exist in its present form until well after its shores had been heavily settled for thousands of years. Results to date indicate that the area was densely populated well before marine resources were locally available. Sites dating to before the inundation are often very large and contain dense and diverse quantities of artifactual materials. Further, they frequently contain great numbers of features (i.e., pits, hearths, post molds, etc.) that also indicate a sizable Native American presence (Bernstein et al. 1993, 1997). One very prominent example of the early occupations is the Eagles Nest site, which borders the van der Kolk property to the west (Bernstein et al. 1993; Lenardi 1998). By Long Island standards, Eagles Nest is quite large, encompassing three to four hectares. Over a hundred features (pits, hearths, etc.) were identified in the limited excavations conducted at Eagles Nest. Radiocarbon dates were run on wood charcoal from 10 of the features, the vast majority of which date to the Late

Archaic period (ca. 5000–3000 B.P.). No prehistoric shellfish remains were found at Eagles Nest. Presumably, this results from the fact that the harbor had not yet been inundated during the major occupation at the site, which appears to have been between 6000 and 4000 B.P.

VAN DER KOLK

Van der Kolk was discovered in 1991 during a cultural resource management survey and excavated by SUNY-Stony Brook field schools in 1992 and 1996 (Bernstein 1991, 1993b). The portion of the site relevant to the present discussion is a small shell midden dating to the Late Woodland period that was studied during the first field season (Figure 3.3). The midden is on a steep slope, and the upper levels have been disturbed by downward movement of the deposit. In addition, residential construction just north of the excavations has destroyed a substantial portion of the site. Radiocarbon dates run on shell taken from the top and bottom of the midden (undisturbed strata) yielded identical radiocarbon assays of 1200 ± 60 B.P. (Beta-55877; $\delta^{13}C = -0.7\%o$; calibrated 2σ range=A.D. 1062 to 1306 and Beta-55878, $\delta^{13}C = -1.10\%o$ calibrated 2σ range=A.D. 1062 to 1306). When corrected for the reservoir effect, both samples yield a calibrated age of A.D. 1222.

A total of slightly over 8 m² was excavated in the midden. This constitutes virtually the entire undisturbed portion of the deposit. Vertical control during excavation was maintained through the use of five-centimeter arbitrary levels excavated within natural and cultural stratigraphic horizons. Five sediment fractions were retained. Nested field screens were used to recover materials caught in ¼- and ⅛-inch (6- and 3-mm) mesh. Three flotation fractions were also studied. These include a heavy component caught on two-millimeter mesh, and flotable (light) and near-flotable fractions caught on 0.4-mm screen.

The shell-bearing deposit is small in areal extent, but is nearly a meter thick in places. In terms of its contents, van der Kolk is fairly typical of midden features on the north shore of Long Island. Most particularly, the density and diversity of materials other than shell (i.e., animal bones, lithic tools and debitage, fire-cracked rock, wood charcoal, pottery, bone tools) suggest that deposits such as these are not remnants of specialized sites geared towards the exploitation of the very abundant local shellfish resources. Rather, they are features containing refuse from a whole host of activities including shellfish processing, butchering and processing of vertebrate fauna, stone tool manufacturing, and cooking. The van der Kolk midden is, however, somewhat rare in that it accumulated over

Figure 3.3
Stratigraphic Profile of the Shell Midden at the van der Kolk Site

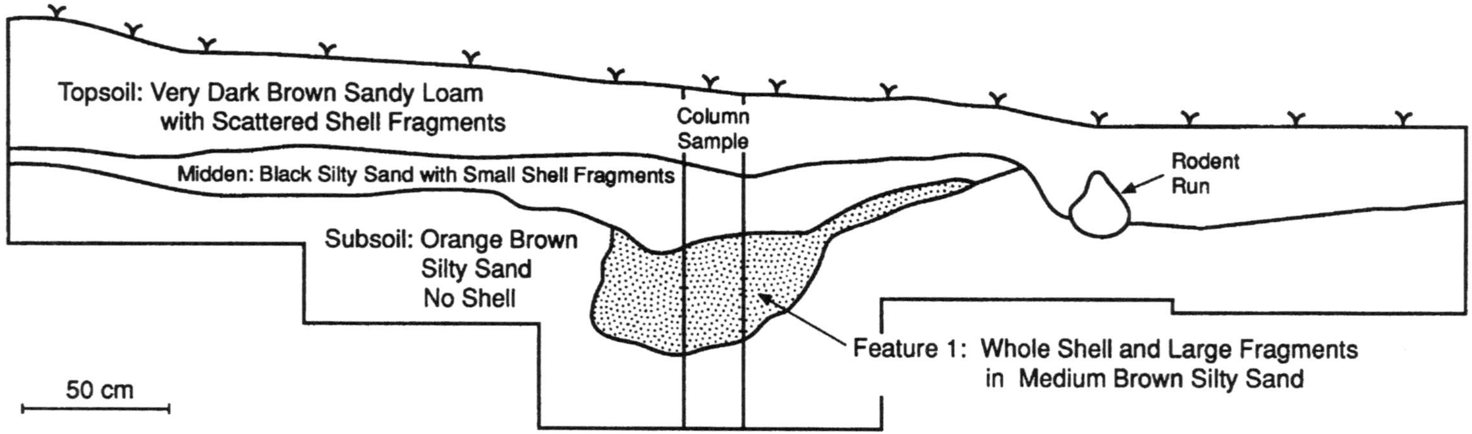

Rodent
Run

Topsoil: Very Dark Brown Sandy Loam
with Scattered Shell Fragments

Midden: Black Silty Sand with Small Shell Fragments

Subsoil: Orange Brown
Silty Sand
No Shell

Column
Sample

Feature 1: Whole Shell and Large Fragments
in Medium Brown Silty Sand

50 cm

what seems to be a very short period of time, quite possibly a single year (see below).

Molluskan Assemblage

The bulk of the shellfish remains at van der Kolk are soft-shell clam (*Mya arenaria*), with oyster (*Crassostrea virginica*), scallop (*Aequipecten irradians*), whelk (*Busycon* sp.), ribbed mussel (*Modiolus demissus*), slipper (*Crepidula fornicata*), and hard clam (*Mercenaria mercenaria*) also represented. Based on minimum number of individual counts (cf., Bernstein 1993a; Mason et al. 1998), soft-shell clam constitutes nearly 93% of the molluskan assemblage (Bernstein 1993b). This dominance of soft-shell clams characterizes Woodland period (ca. 3000–500 B.P.) middens in the Mount Sinai region (Gwynne 1982), and many other areas in the coastal Northeast (Bernstein 1993a; Braun 1974; Snow 1980; Yesner 1983). Oyster typically is more heavily represented in earlier deposits.

Season-of-Death of the Soft-Shell Clam (*Mya Arenaria*)

The study of growth patterns in the soft-shell clams from van der Kolk has produced some very interesting preliminary results. Robert Cerrato and Heather Wallace of the Marine Sciences Research Center at SUNY-Stony Brook, working with archaeologist Kent Lightfoot, have demonstrated, based on a series of modern control samples, that microgrowth increments (tidal and seasonal) are visible in the chondrophore of the soft-shell clam (Figure 3.4), not just the growing edge of the shell (Cerrato et al. 1991). As anyone who has excavated a shell midden in southern New England is aware, these appendages are often found in the thousands at coastal sites. While the valves of this species are thin and easily eroded and damaged, the chondrophore is quite durable and is typically recovered intact in middens.

The study of seasonal patterns in the soft-shell clam focuses primarily on observations of optical density and growth features observable at the edge of the chondrophore (Lightfoot et al. 1993). For example, spring begins with the transition from irregular to regular growth increments and the production of a spawning band. It ends when the opaque, spring layer changes to a translucent, summer pattern. In contrast, winter is marked by a dark, opaque region and irregular growth increments on the edge of the chondrophore.

Figure 3.3 shows the stratigraphic section exposed during the midden

Figure 3.4
Idealized Drawing of the Soft-Shell Clam (*Mya arenaria*), Showing Gross Features Used in Determining Season of Death

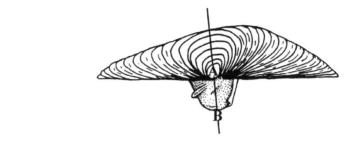

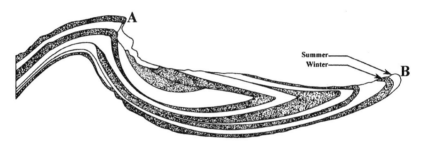

Most recent growth is on the edge of the chondrophore labeled "B." Drawings are after illustrations in Cerrato et al. 1991.

excavations at the van der Kolk site. One hundred and sixty-three clams from 16 excavation levels were analyzed by Cerrato and Wallace for season-of-death information (Figure 3.5). The four lowest shell-bearing levels (18–21)—the bottom of Feature 1 in Figure 3.3—contain shells that all died during the winter (Figure 3.5). A good number of these apparently were taken during the late winter. The shells at the top of the feature (levels 15–17) contain individuals that died during the winter and spring (Figure 3.5). Immediately above the feature, in the layer designated as "midden" on the stratigraphic profile, are shells that were taken primarily during the summer and fall (Figure 3.5). Above this, all seasons are represented in fairly equal numbers (Figure 3.5), a finding that suggests post-depositional mixing and disturbance. This interpretation is consistent with stratigraphic indicators and information on bone breakage patterns from the midden. For example, both the shell and bone remains in the upper levels in the midden are much more fragmented and eroded than is the case for the lower levels.

Figure 3.5
Season of Death Estimates for Soft-Shell Clams Recovered at the van der Kolk Site

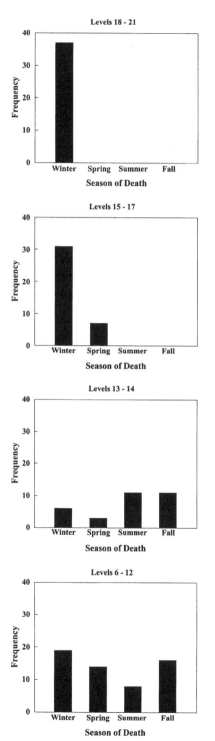

Oldest excavation levels are represented in the top graph and most recent levels are depicted in the one at the bottom.

It is possible that a sequence of no more than a single year is represented in the undisturbed, lower portions of the midden sample. Moving from bottom to top, there is (1) a winter collection; (2) a spring collection; and (3) a summer/fall collecting episode or episodes. As discussed above, the radiocarbon dates from the top and bottom of this section of the deposit are identical. Above this is a mixture of redeposited materials. It is, of course, also plausible that seasons from different years are represented in the van der Kolk midden rather than just one sequence of less than 12 months. While it is impossible to rule out this alternative interpretation, the sequential arrangement of the clusters of season-of-death estimates combined with the radiocarbon dates and taphonomic data are strongly suggestive that the midden feature accumulated over a short period of time.

Exploitation of Vertebrate Fauna

A remarkable diversity of vertebrate fauna is represented at van der Kolk (Table 3.1). As at virtually all Long Island sites, white-tailed deer (*Odocoileus virginianus*) was the most important vertebrate species (Bernstein 1993b). Other mammals represented include dog (*Canis* sp.), raccoon (*Procyon lotor*), Eastern gray squirrel (*Sciurus carolinensis*), Eastern chipmunk (*Tamias striatus*), cottontail rabbit (*Sylvilagus* sp.), seal (most likely the harbor seal *Phoca vitulina*), and possibly elk (*Cervus* sp.). At least four finfish species are present: sturgeon (Acipenseridae), flounder (Bothidae), sea bass (Serranidae), and cod (Gadidae). Birds include ducks or geese (Anatidae), wild turkey (*Meleagris gallapavo*), and shore birds (Laridae). Two species of snakes, including the timber rattlesnake (*Crotalus horridus*), and turtles (Testudinata) are also present.

Few of the vertebrate species are good seasonal indicators. The best is probably the migratory harbor seal, which visits Long Island Sound primarily during the winter and early spring (Connor 1971:54). The seal bone was recovered from the same excavation level (16) that yielded clams determined to have been taken during this time of year.

Members of the sea bass family (Serranidae) are typically found in Long Island Sound during the warmer months of the year. Again there is consistency between the clam season-of-death estimates and the species availability data. In this case, the single sea bass represented in the midden was recovered from an excavation level (13) that yielded clams taken during the summer and/or fall.

Table 3.1
Taxonomic List of Faunal Remains Recovered from the van der Kolk Site

Class: Gastropoda (Single-Valved Mollusks)
  Busycon sp. (Whelk)
  Crepidula fornicata (Common Slipper Shell)
Class: Pelecypoda (Bivalve Mollusks)
  Mercenaria mercenaria (Quahog)
  Mya arenaria (Soft-Shell Clam)
  Aequipecten irradians (Bay Scallop)
  Crassostrea virginica (Common Oyster)
  Modiolus demissus (Ribbed Mussel)
Class: Osteichthyes (Bony Fish)
  Family Acipenseridae (Sturgeons)
  Family Gadidae (Codfish)
  Family Serranidae (Sea Basses)
  Family Bothidae (Flounders)
Class: Reptilia (Reptiles)
  Order Testudinata (Turtles)
  Family Colubridae (Colubrid Snakes)
  Crotalus horridus (Timber Rattlesnake)
Class: Aves (Birds)
  Family Anatidae (Swans, geese, and ducks)
  Meleagris gallapavo (Wild Turkey)
  Family Laridae (Gulls, Terns, and Skimmers)
Class: Mammalia (Mammals)
  Canis sp. (Dogs)
  Procyon lotor (Raccoon)
  Order Pinnipedia (Seals and allies)
  Sciurus carolinensis (Gray Squirrel)
  Tamias striatus (Eastern Chipmunk)
  Sylvilagus sp. (Cottontails)
  Order Artiodactlyla (Even-toed Ungulates)
  Cervus sp. (Elk?)
  Odocoileus virginianus (White-tailed Deer)

Artifact Assemblage

As is typical of Long Island sites, the overwhelming majority of the lithic materials from the van der Kolk midden are quartz or quartzite (approximately 90% of the 782 pieces [11 bifaces including eight projectile points, two unifaces, three cores, and 766 pieces of debitage]). Quartz cobbles are locally ubiquitous and were collected from beaches and other areas where the till of the Harbor Hill Moraine is exposed. Detailed analysis of the quartz tools and debitage indicates that the entire sequence of tool manufacturing took place at van der Kolk (Bernstein 1993b). Decortification pieces are abundant as are small flakes resulting from the final finishing of stone tools.

Virtually all of the non-quartz materials (rhyolite, coarse-grained sedimentary rocks, etc.) could also have simply been gathered from exposed till on the beach just a few meters from the site. The only raw material that is not routinely found in these deposits is chert. Five small pieces of debitage of this material were recovered.

A small ceramic assemblage (165 sherds) was present in the van der Kolk midden. These are all little fragments (few weigh more than one or two grams), most of which are weathered. The small size and often poor condition of these sherds makes it difficult to identify decoration. Six sherds retain evidence for shell-stamping, shell-incising, or punctation. All of the pottery is tempered with grit (29%) or shell (71%). Some of the sherds retain evidence for surface treatment. The techniques represented include cord-marking, smoothing, wiping, brushing, and net-marking. It is not uncommon for more than one technique to be used on a single vessel.

DISCUSSION AND CONCLUSIONS

Since it is possible to determine the approximate length of time in which the deposit accumulated, we are afforded insights into what kinds of resources might have been exploited during the course of a single year. Interestingly, virtually nothing was excavated that suggests long-distant forays of any sort; everything found in the midden was available within a few hundred meters of the site either seasonally or throughout the entire year. Despite the relatively small size of the deposit, a remarkably diverse assemblage of prehistoric materials, representing a broad range of activities, was recovered from the van der Kolk midden. Minimally, seven species of mollusks and 19 of vertebrates are represented at van der Kolk (Table 3.1). As one would expect, the archaeological deposit is visually dominated by shellfish. However, as discussed above, other foods—deer, seal, possibly elk, small mammals, fish, birds, reptiles—also contributed significantly to the diet. It is likely that from a nutritional perspective, terrestrial species were even more important than mollusks. The role of plant foods is difficult to assess. Nearly 80 liters of midden matrix was processed by flotation, but no carbonized macrobotanical specimens (nut shell, seeds, etc.) that can be interpreted as food remains were present.

Food was not only being collected and hunted using the van der Kolk site as a base, but was processed and cooked here as well. These activities are indicated by large quantities of fire-cracked and reddened rocks in the midden, as well as by broken ceramic vessels that were presumably used for cooking. Lithic manufacturing and repair were also important at van der Kolk. Additionally, a bone-working industry is represented in the midden deposit.

The high diversity of materials in the van der Kolk midden is better appreciated when it is remembered that all the refuse was probably deposited during the course of less than a single year. The results of the study of clam growth, the radiocarbon dates, and the seasonal availability estimates are all consistent with the interpretation of deposition occurring over a very short period of time. Despite the small size of the midden and its short use life, this is in no sense a special-purpose site geared towards the exploitation of nearby clam flats. While "shellfish processing locations" dating to late in the prehistoric period are present elsewhere in the region (Lightfoot et al. 1993), at this point they seem to be rare or absent on the shores of Mount Sinai Harbor or at other locales on Long Island's north shore. Shellfishing appears to have been just one segment of a broadly based subsistence strategy that was practiced for thousands of years (Bernstein 1999; Gwynne 1982; Ritchie 1959; Silver 1991; Wyatt 1977). This pattern of the utilization of a broad resource base has substantial time depth on Long Island, extending as far back as at least 4000–5000 B.P. On Mount Sinai Harbor (Figure 3.2), the diffuse subsistence base reflected in the midden at van der Kolk is mirrored in extensive deposits (e.g., Pipestave Hollow, Rudge-Breyer, Tiger Lily) dating to the Late Archaic (Gwynne 1982). Wyatt (1977), in his study of the contemporary occupation at Wading River (Figure 3.1), describes a similar situation at this North Shore locale. For the Terminal Archaic (ca. 3600–2500 B.P.), Ritchie's (1959) well-known study of the Stony Brook site also documented a broad economic focus along with a concentration on locally abundant products. Silver (1991) reports a virtually identical situation for the Middle Woodland site of Henry Lloyd Manor in western Long Island (Figure 3.1). Similarly, Lightfoot et al. (1987), in their regional study of the Middle to Late Woodland occupation on Shelter Island (Figure 3.1), describe a hunting, gathering, and fishing subsistence system in the absence of recognizable settlement mobility. Regardless of the economic role played by agriculture during the late prehistoric period (ca. A.D. 1000–1500) when the van der Kolk shell deposit accumulated, it is clear that an emphasis was placed on maintaining a diversified subsistence base right up to the time of the European arrival in the sixteenth century.

Van der Kolk is but one example of what were for millennia favored settlement locations on Long Island's north coast. The sheltered shores of the region's harbors and coves that were readily accessible to bountiful supplies of food (marine and terrestrial), important industrial resources (especially cobbles for manufacturing stone tools), and transportation routes (canoe) were opulent settings for prehistoric Long Islanders. Settlements similar to those on Mount Sinai Harbor were present on all of the North Shore embayments: from Flushing Bay in modern Queens to Orient on the far eastern end of the island (Figure 3.1). By locating their communities in these attractive locales, native Long Islanders could effectively exploit necessary resources with a minimum of travel and settlement movement. This led them to become more or less tethered to the shore for most, if not all, of the year. Despite their reliance on hunting, gathering, and fishing, they early on established durable communities and territories. This pattern probably originated with the establishment of modern coastal conditions (as far back as five thousand years ago) and continued fairly unchanged until the seventeenth century.

ACKNOWLEDGMENTS

I would like to thank a number of my colleagues and students for their assistance with the research summarized in this chapter. The midden at the van der Kolk site was excavated during a SUNY-Stony Brook field school in 1992. The students participating in the project worked extremely hard during a very hot summer. Robert Cerrato and Heather Wallace of the Marine Sciences Research Center at SUNY-Stony Brook performed the study of clam shells from the van der Kolk site. Curtis Marean, Nicholas Bellantoni, and Frank Dirrigl analyzed the vertebrate faunal remains. Daria Merwin and Michael Lenardi of the Institute for Long Island Archaeology have been working on the shores of Mount Sinai harbor for nearly a decade. Their contributions to our understanding of the region's past are many. Donald and Susan van der Kolk were generous hosts for the field crew from SUNY-Stony Brook during the summer of 1992. Their generosity and friendship are greatly appreciated.

4

Archaeological Investigations at the Lucy Vincent Beach Site (19–DK–148): Preliminary Results and Interpretations

Elizabeth S. Chilton and Dianna L. Doucette

INTRODUCTION

Lucy Vincent Beach is a multicomponent site located in Chilmark, Massachusetts, on the south shore of Martha's Vineyard (Figures 4.1 and 4.2). The site was the focus of the Harvard Archaeological Field School in the summers of 1998 and 1999. The Field School was directed by Elizabeth Chilton, and Dianna Doucette was the Field Director. Lucy Vincent Beach was chosen to be the location of the field school because in 1997, when we started to plan for a field school, we were looking for a site to excavate that was threatened. Our reason for seeking a threatened site was that (1) field schools are not necessarily the most efficient way to excavate a site, since you are training students as you go; and (2) we believe that field schools should have a public education benefit and should contribute to the documentation of the archaeological record whenever possible, especially due to the disappearing nature of that record. Coastal sites are certainly among the most endangered sites in New England because of shoreline erosion and developments pressures (Kerber 1999; Luedtke, this volume), and the investigation of this site provided us with the opportunity to salvage critical archaeological information.

The research value of the Lucy Vincent Beach site turned out to be far greater than we had anticipated. Archaeological evidence from the site provides a unique opportunity to examine the archaeological record

Figure 4.1
Location of the Lucy Vincent Beach Site, 19–DK–148

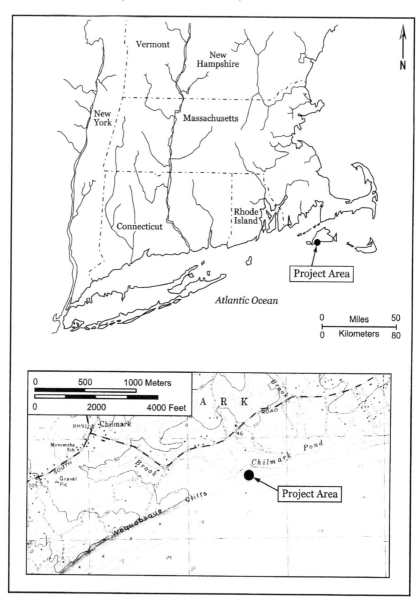

Inset based on USGS 1972. Prepared by Kathryn Curran.

Figure 4.2
Map of Martha's Vineyard

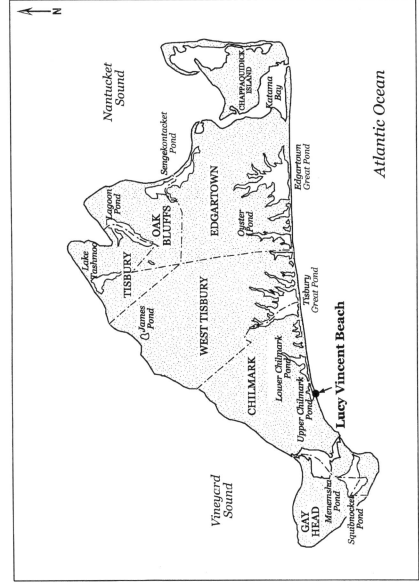

Based on Huntington 1969. Prepared by Kathryn Curran.

on Martha's Vineyard from the Late Paleoindian period (ca. 10,000 B.P.) through the end of the Contact period (ca. 300 B.P.). Further, this information will contribute to our understanding of the complex relationship between environmental change and the lifeways of coastal New England's Native peoples, and it will allow us to investigate the history of the Aquinnah Wampanoag tribe on Martha's Vineyard. In this paper we present an overview of our investigations, and our analyses and preliminary interpretations of the data collected between 1997 and 1999. A more detailed site report is in preparation.

GEOLOGIC AND ENVIRONMENTAL SETTING

The geologic history of Martha's Vineyard is visible in the cliff faces around Lucy Vincent Beach and elsewhere along the southwestern end of the island, where deposits representing a hundred million years have been exposed to the elements (Chamberlain 1964). The more recent glacial activity of the late Pleistocene period (ca. 20,000–10,000 B.P.), however, gave the island its present topography. During the Early Holocene period (ca. 10,000–5000 B.P.), the glaciers retreated, and melting ice created a rapid rise in sea level that eventually separated Martha's Vineyard and Nantucket from the mainland. Sea water flooded the deeper parts of Vineyard Sound approximately 7500 B.P.; and about 6000 B.P. marine waters flooded Nantucket Sound and separated the islands from Cape Cod (Oldale 1992:100) (Figure 4.2).

Chilmark, like the rest of the island of Martha's Vineyard, is located within the band of terminal moraine deposited at the southernmost edge of glacial movement. Glaciers advanced to this point and then retreated, resulting in a complex stratigraphy formed by at least six different glacial episodes. The hilly deposits of the terminal moraine created the "knob and kettle" topography that characterizes this part of the island (Kaye 1964).

Martha's Vineyard is underlain by solid bedrock that ranges from 500 feet thick on the north side of the island to 900 feet along parts of the south shore (U.S. Department of Agriculture 1986). The western part of the island consists of compact sand and clay above bedrock. These clay deposits are close enough to the surface to support a network of streams and running water, unlike the east side of the island, where deep sands and gravel soak up water (Chamberlain 1964:77). In addition, blown sand from the dunes along Chilmark Pond have cut off some of the brooks, causing them to dam up and form poorly drained ponds, bogs, and swamps. Chilmark Pond is closed off from the sea (except during severe storms) by shifting sandbars and dunes.

The Lucy Vincent Beach site is located on a knoll that is approximately 40 feet above sea level (Figures 4.1 and 4.2). It is bordered by a brackish pond to the north (Chilmark Pond, which was likely a fresh water pond until a thousand years or so ago) and the Atlantic Ocean to the south. The upper meter of the knoll is comprised of glacial moraine (clayey sand with pebbles), which overlies outwash gravels. These outwash gravels themselves overlie clays of probable Miocene age and contain quasi-fossilized shark and other remains of probable Miocene age (Conrad Neumann, personal communication, 1998). At some point after the deposition of the outwash, ground waters carrying reduced iron sulfides permeated these gravels and precipitated a ferric oxide cement that makes the bluff red in appearance and semi-consolidated (Neumann, personal communication, 1998). Vegetation on the knoll consists of scrub brush, beach grass, poison ivy, and other low bush plants.

The knoll upon which the site is located is eroding at an alarming rate. In recent years it has been eroding at approximately two meters per year (Chilmark Planning Board et al. 1985) (Figure 4.3). The U.S. Coastal Survey map (1846) shows another knoll between the knoll upon which the site is located and the ocean, and the 1949 topographic map (USGS 1949) shows the flat top of the knoll to be three times its current size. Thus, it is clear that the environment and geographical setting of the site has changed drastically over its long history.

CULTURAL SETTING

Much is known about the Native American history of Martha's Vineyard, particularly in the area of Chilmark. Professional and avocational archaeologists have been conducting research and recording site locations since the early part of the twentieth century. Samuel Guernsey and E.A. Hooten of the Peabody Museum at Harvard University conducted the earliest survey and excavation work along many of the western island ponds and shores. The Lucy Vincent Beach site may be the same site that was tested in 1913 by Guernsey, referred to by Guernsey as Site A (Guernsey 1916). Guernsey's article, however, does not contain enough detail to verify this, and his original field notes could not be located at the Peabody Museum. Nevertheless, Guernsey excavated a "shell pit" at a site at or near this location. The shell pit contained prehistoric pottery fragments, a stone net sinker, scallop shells, and numerous animal bones, including dog (Guernsey 1916).

Figure 4.3
Site Map

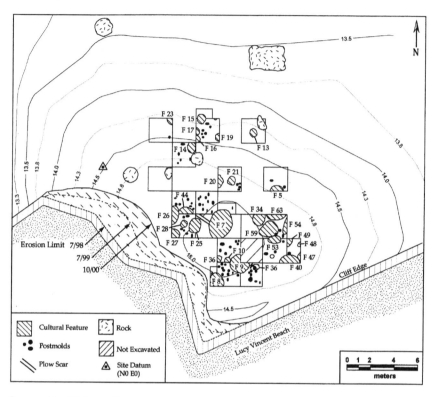

Prepared by Kathryn Curran.

Between the 1930s and 1960s, several professional archaeological surveys were conducted on Martha's Vineyard with the focus primarily on
the large ponds at the southwestern end of the island (Byers and Johnson
1940; Ritchie 1969). Although Chilmark Pond is not specifically identified in these survey works, pre-Contact and early Contact (ca. 350 B.P.)
burial and habitation sites were identified in similar environmental settings around Squibnocket, Nashaquitsa, and Menemsha Ponds (all approximately within a one-mile radius of Lucy Vincent Beach) (Figure
4.2).

In the 1980s, two sites were reported near Chilmark Pond by Richard
Burt of the Martha's Vineyard Archaeological Society. The Allen Farm
site (19-DK-127) is located along the north side of Upper Chilmark
Pond, near Mill Brook (Figure 4.2). According to the site form filed at
the Massachusetts Historical Commission (MHC), large amounts of lithic

materials dating from the Late Archaic (ca. 5000–3000 B.P.) and Late Woodland (ca. 1000–500 B.P.) periods (types of artifacts are not listed) have been recovered from this site by local collectors over the years. A little further to the east, the Beldon's Cove site (19-DK-124) is located just east of the Fulling Mill Brook on the north shore of Upper Chilmark Pond. Many hearth features and artifacts were reportedly exposed in the road cuts and along the shores of the pond. In addition, Middle Archaic (ca. 8000–6000 B.P.) stemmed, Late Archaic small-stemmed, and Late Woodland Levanna projectile points, as well as other lithic materials, have been recovered from the Beldon's Cove site (MHC 1987; Mulholland et al. 1998).

Because the present-day coastline on Martha's Vineyard was not established until approximately 2000 years ago (Oldale 1992:100), it is likely that numerous early sites on Martha's Vineyard are inundated. Nevertheless, there is evidence that the island was occupied as early as the Paleoindian period (ca. 12,000–10,000 B.P.). Although the documented surveys mentioned above have not reported early sites, evidence of diagnostic fluted projectile points from the Paleoindian period and Bifurcated-Base points from the Early Archaic period (ca. 9500–8000 B.P.) have been identified in local artifact collections from the island (Bouck et al. 1983; MHC 1987; Mulholland et al. 1998). In addition, an isolated Bifurcated-Base projectile point was recently recovered from a property in Aquinnah during a cultural resource management survey by the Public Archaeology Laboratory, Inc. (PAL) (Herbster and Cherau 2001).

There is an increase in reported Middle Archaic sites on Martha's Vineyard. Diagnostic Middle Archaic Neville, Neville variant, and Stark projectile points have been reported from at least 28 different sites on the island (Huntington 1959; MHC 1987; Mulholland et al. 1998; Herbster and Cherau 1998, 1999; Macpherson et al. 1999). Ritchie's sequence for a coastal culture really began with the Late Archaic because he found no Paleoindian or Early Archaic components in the course of his excavations (Ritchie 1969). However, Middle Archaic Stark points have been recorded in most island collections from the eastern and central portions of the island (Bouck et al. 1983). More recently, CRM excavations have identified Middle Archaic Neville and Stark projectile points in-situ on the west end of the island (Herbster and Cherau 2001). Although these early point types have not been associated with radiocarbon dates or with more extensive components, they likely represent among the earliest inhabitants of the island whose encampments are now submerged.

The Late Archaic through Late Woodland periods have been well documented on Martha's Vineyard, especially for the Chilmark area (Herbster and Glover 1993; Herbster 1996; Herbster and Cherau 1999; Mulholland et al. 1998; MHC 1987; PAL 1998; Richardson 1985; Ritchie 1969). The Wampanoag Aquinnah Shellfish Hatchery (WASH) site within the Herring Creek Archaeological District on Menemsha Pond in Aquinnah has very well-documented archaeological and historical evidence of Native American occupation from Late Archaic to present day (Herbster and Cherau 1999). The majority of the Late Archaic through Late Woodland sites have been located along the shoreline and around the large ponds where a variety of food resources were exploited, especially fish and shellfish. Many of these sites consist of shell middens or contain shell midden deposits (PAL 1998). In addition, they contain diagnostic projectile points, a variety of stone tools, soapstone bowls, bone tools, pottery, hearths, pit features, and burials.

SITE BACKGROUND

The Lucy Vincent Beach site was first discovered on February 11, 1995, when a pair of individuals walking the beach discovered human remains. The discovery was reported to the Chilmark Police. When the police examined the area, they discovered the rest of a burial eroding out of the cliff face. The coroner and the State Archaeologist were notified, and it was decided that a salvage excavation should be undertaken by the MHC. The salvage excavation was conducted in consultation with the Wampanoag tribe at Aquinnah. By the time MHC archaeologists (Connie Crosby and Leonard Loparto) returned to undertake a burial recovery on February 16, much of the burial had eroded away and many of the human remains had fallen to the base of the cliff. Excavation of a 1×2 m test unit at the edge of the cliff face proceeded through a shell deposit to the top of the burial shaft. The shell feature appears to have been deposited after the burial, but it is uncertain how much time elapsed between the two events. In addition to the shell, the feature contained charcoal, animal bones, a few items of chipped stone, and a broken pottery vessel. The burial shaft itself did not appear to contain artifacts, but most of the grave contents had fallen down the cliff face before they were recovered.

A second human burial was discovered in October 1996. Again, MHC archaeologists undertook a burial recovery, involving the excavation of another 1×2 m test unit at the edge of the cliff face. Another shell pit was found adjacent to the human bone. The shell pit contained fish, bird, and deer bone, chipping debris, and shell. The only artifact in the burial shaft was one piece of worked bone (originally identified by the excavators as a shark's tooth). The archaeologists noted other "pits" or archaeological features in the cliff face, but there was no other human bone apparent. Michael Gibbons of the University of Massachusetts at Boston analyzed both sets of remains, and they were then repatriated to the Aquinnah under the Massachusetts Unmarked Burial Bill.

When we approached State Archaeologist Brona Simon in 1997 for suggestions for a field school location, she suggested the Lucy Vincent Beach site. She felt it was important to salvage important archaeological information before further erosion took place and to develop a long-term plan for the site, rather than continuing to excavate remains on an emergency basis. Before we decided to make Lucy Vincent Beach the site of our field school, we conducted preliminary excavations in the summer of 1997 in order to determine site stratigraphy and to make sure that there was enough of the site left to warrant further investigation. The site is located on private land that is permanently leased to the Town of Chilmark. Thus, we needed to obtain the permission of the Chilmark Board of Selectmen and the Town Conservation Commission, as well as the State Archaeologist. We also submitted a proposal to the Aquinnah tribe and worked very closely with their Natural Resources Department. The tribe was intimately involved in the planning stages of this initial testing, as they were throughout the project.

FIELD METHODS

After receiving the permission and support of all of the above parties, we conducted our initial excavations in 1997 (Chilton and Doucette 1998). Eight 100×50 cm test pits were excavated across the site to identify site integrity and artifact and feature distribution. These excavations showed intact features, including post molds, shell middens, and possible trash pits, that covered the top of the knoll. Recovered artifacts dated to the late prehistoric and early historic periods. Based on these and subsequent excavations, the Lucy Vincent Beach site was determined to be approximately 625 square meters in area (25 m north/south by 25 m east/west) (Figure 4.3). It was also apparent that additional burials were likely to be present at the site. Thus, we sought permission to conduct a field school in the summer of 1998, and then returned again in 1999. There were 14 students and three teaching assistants in 1998, and 10 students and two teaching assistants in 1999. Each summer we had an Aquinnah Tribal member participate in the field school.

The archaeological excavations at the Lucy Vincent Beach site were carried out at a data-recovery level. Based on the data collected from the test pits excavated in 1997, larger units were excavated during the 1998 and 1999 field schools. The primary goals of these excavations were (1) to determine more precisely the horizontal (area) and vertical (depth) boundaries of the surviving portion of the Lucy Vincent Beach site; (2) to investigate the site's internal structure and composition; (3) to identify the temporal/cultural affiliation of occupational episodes; and (4) to identify and excavate features closest to the cliff face because of the threat from erosion. (We did not excavate within two meters of the cliff edge at the request of the Chilmark Conservation Commission and for safety reasons.) The excavation of a representative sample of the site area achieved these objectives. The equivalent of 20 2×2 m units were excavated (80 square meters) or 12.8% of the estimated site area (Figure 4.3).

The excavations were mapped in relation to an arbitrarily selected site datum. This datum served as the N0E0 point of the site grid (Figure 4.3). All excavation units were tied into this site datum and designated according to the datum coordinates. The basic unit of excavation was a 2×2 m unit, which was excavated in 1 m quadrants and in 10 cm arbitrary levels within natural soil horizons. Smaller units measuring 1×2 m were placed as needed to permit the complete excavation and/or mapping of features. Since the site was plowed, we excavated the plow zone by shovel skimming. The site was not stratified; thus, all features were visible in the subsoil at the base of the plow zone. The southwestern corner of each excavation unit was used as a unit datum to plot the horizontal and vertical locations of artifacts and features encountered in situ during excavation.

Following a modified Harris-matrix system (Harris 1989), each soil horizon was given a Harris-matrix number in the field, and all feature soils were given separate Harris-matrix numbers. All non-feature soils were screened through ¼-inch hardware cloth. Feature soils were screened through ⅛-inch hardware cloth, and one- to two-liter samples were collected from each feature for flotation analysis. In addition, one-liter control samples were collected from the plow zone and B1 horizons from each excavation unit. A representative sample of shell was taken from each shell feature, which in most cases consisted of a 10% sample. In the case of column samples, all shell was collected (as with Feature 25), or in some cases when a feature was bisected, one half was screened and the other half was completely collected for flotation analysis (as with Feature 44). When features or concentrations of archaeological material were encountered, plan drawings were completed, and Munsell soil color and texture descriptions were noted. Detailed excavation notes were taken, and profiles were drawn for each feature excavated. Photographs were taken of all features.

Only the most threatened features were excavated during the summer of 1998 (i.e., those located closest to the cliff edge). All features were excavated with a trowel; wooden tools were used to excavate fragile artifacts and bone. In 1998 the unexcavated features were left in situ at approximately the plow zone/B1 interface (which ranged between 22 and 38 cm below surface). All the test units were back-filled with the original topsoil, and grass seed was applied to help mitigate the effects of erosion. The objective for the summer of 1999, then, was to excavate only those features that were left in situ the previous year.

The Discovery of Human Remains

During the summers of 1998 and 1999, human remains were encountered at the site. In both cases, further excavation of the features ceased, the area was secured to prevent disturbance, and the proper authorities were immediately notified: the Aquinnah Wampanoag, the Massachusetts Historical Commission, and the Town of Chilmark. These actions were followed in accordance with the Massachusetts Unmarked Burial Bill. In both cases, excavation plans were established in collaboration with all parties involved, which resulted in the burials being excavated by Elizabeth Chilton, a small group of graduate students, and an experienced osteologist (Ann Marie Mires in 1998, and Catherine Smith in 1998 and 2001). All human remains and associated burial objects were recorded and analyzed in the field and immediately repatriated to the Aquinnah Wampanoag tribe.

Features

A total of 168 features were identified, including 130 possible post molds, 31 pit features, one fire hearth, two human burials, two plow scars, and one charred log (Figure 4.3). We are still in the process of analyzing data from all of these features. Analysis will include comparison of faunal, floral, radiocarbon, and artifactual data. Aside from the site report that is in preparation by the authors, Deena Duranleau, a Ph.D. candidate at Harvard University, will be conducting additional analysis of site materials as part of her dissertation. Thus, we include here only very basic descriptions and interpretations of features.

Most of the 130 possible post molds identified across the site were cross-sectioned. Twenty-five of the feature numbers were designated as post molds, with one feature number assigned to all post molds in one excavation unit (i.e., 6A and 6B, or 50A–50E). All but one of the post molds were round; one was square and obviously from more recent times, probably the remnants of a sign warning people to stay off the beach cliffs (such signs are present to this day). Three of the post molds had tapered bottoms, and three had flat bottoms. Post molds extended from approximately 35–60 cm below unit datum (cmbd), and most were approximately 10–12 cm in diameter. There were no recognizable post mold patterns, likely due to the repeated use of the site over thousands of years.

The 31 pit features encountered undoubtedly served diverse, and perhaps multiple, functions, including food processing, food storage, ceremonial feasting, refuse pits, and human burials. Three of the very small pit features may be large post molds, but they have not been excavated. Pit features ranged in size from 30 to 120 cm in diameter, and extended down to 40 cmbd for the shallow pits and as far as 180 cmbd for the deepest pit (see Figure 4.4 for an example of one of these pit features). The majority of these pits contained mammal and fish bone, charred seeds, shell, charcoal, flakes, and pottery sherds. Five of the pits contained a large quantity of shell (and fish in the case of Feature 44) and can be considered food refuse pits, at least in part (Features 14, 16, 25, 43, and 44). Two of the pit features (Feature 21 and the lower portion of Feature 9, which is likely a separate feature from the upper portion) were essentially empty except for a few flakes, charred plant material, and a small amount of animal bone. Interestingly, radiocarbon dates from these two features were in the vicinity of cal 350 B.C. (2 sigma) (Table 4.1). Because of the size, shape, and depth of both features (160–185 cmbd) and their great antiquity, it is possible that they contained human burials and that the human bone has not preserved. Doucette found there to be high phosphate levels within both features, indicating the presence of organic materials. It is also possible that they were organic refuse features. As part of her dissertation, Doucette is conducting research on these so-called "empty pit features," which are found across New England from many different time periods (Doucette 2001).

One of the two human burials identified was located under a large hearth (Feature 7, Burial 3). This was the only intact fire hearth identified at the site; approximately 100 pieces of fire-cracked rock were collected from the site, but these were predominantly recovered from the plow zone. Burial 3 consisted of a partial human cranium, which was most

Figure 4.4
Profile of Feature 8

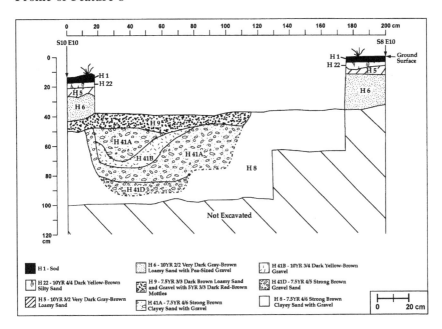

Prepared by Kathryn Curran.

likely a secondary burial (Chilton and Doucette 1999; Mires 1998). No associated funerary objects were evident. The fire hearth above the human remains is apparently in association with the burial. The hearth contained 191 flakes, a side-notched projectile point, one core, a possible grinding stone fragment, 13 pottery sherds, numerous animal and fish bones, shell, and a large amount of charred plant material, including seeds, wood charcoal, and maize kernels. Shell species included quahog, soft-shell clam, bay scallop, and whelk; breakage patterns on the latter suggested use for consumption (Shaw 2001). The large amount of food remains in this fire hearth and the association with a secondary burial suggest that this hearth feature is the result of ceremonial feasting. Three wood charcoal radiocarbon date ranges from Feature 7, including one from the cranium area, were in the vicinity of cal A.D. 1000 (2 sigma) (Table 4.1). However, a radiocarbon date range for maize kernels from the same level as one of these wood charcoal dates was cal A.D. 1325–1467 (2 sigma) (Table 4.1). Possible reasons for the discrepancy between the wood charcoal and maize dates include (1) the wood burned was old wood or heart wood; or (2) the maize is somehow intrusive (although

Table 4.1
Radiocarbon Dates from the Lucy Vincent Beach Site (19–DK–148)

Feature	Type	Material Dated	Geochron Lab #	Depth (cmbd)	Uncalibrated Age[1]	$\delta^{13}C‰$	Calibrated Date Range[2]
5	refuse pit	wood charcoal	GX-25883-AMS	45	670 ± 30	-26.0	A.D. 1281-1391
7	burial 3	wood charcoal	GX-24637-AMS	82	1,010 ± 40	-26.7	A.D. 902-1158
7	hearth	wood charcoal	GX-24636-AMS	61	990 ± 60	-27.1	A.D. 902-1189
7	hearth	wood charcoal	GX-26573-AMS	40	1100 ± 80	-26.5	A.D. 693-1156
7	hearth	maize kernel	GX-26424-AMS	38-48	500 ± 40	-11.2	A.D. 1325-1467
8	refuse pit	wood charcoal (Am. beech)	GX-25884-AMS	23	390 ± 40	-27.3	A.D. 1437-1632
8	refuse pit	wood charcoal (oak)	GX-25885-AMS	66-81	350 ± 40	-25.6	A.D. 1459-1638
9	pit feature	wood charcoal (Am. beech)	GX-25886-AMS	138-148	2,270 ± 40	-28.5	400-206 B.C.
9	pit feature	wood charcoal (hickory)	GX-25887-AMS	70	630 ± 40	-26.1	A.D. 1293-1401
13	refuse pit	wood charcoal	GX-25879	65	225 ± 65	-27.2	A.D. 1524-1950
15	pit feature	wood charcoal	GX-25878-AMS	92	570 ± 40	-26.8	A.D. 1304-1425
20	refuse pit?	wood charcoal	GX-25880-AMS	48	380 ± 40	-24.8	A.D. 1440-1633
21	poss. burial	wood charcoal	GX-25876-AMS	130	2,190 ± 40	-23.9	380-125 B.C.
21	poss. burial	wood charcoal	GX-25877-AMS	88	2,110 ± 40	-25.7	347-2 B.C.
25	refuse pit	wood charcoal (oak)	GX-25888-AMS	46-56	320 ± 40	-27.1	A.D. 1481-1648
25	refuse pit	wood charcoal (oak)	GX-25889-AMS	132	360 ± 50	-25.8	A.D. 1450-1636

1. $\delta^{13}C$-corrected
2. two-sigma date ranges; calibration datasets from Stuiver et al. (1998a, 1998b) and Stuiver and Braziunas (1993)

Table 4.1 Continued

25	refuse pit	wood charcoal (persimmon)	GX-26425-AMS	36-46	320 ± 50	-26.4	A.D. 1464-1655
34	refuse?	wood charcoal	GX-25875-AMS	57	830 ± 40	-23.3	A.D. 1063-1280
44	refuse pit	wood charcoal (poss. Am. beech)	GX-25890-AMS	62	380 ± 40	-27.0	A.D. 1440-1633
44	refuse pit	wood charcoal (oak)	GX-25891-AMS	51	170 ± 50	-24.7	A.D. 1651-1944
59	pit above burial 4	wood charcoal	GX-25881-AMS	58	360 ± 40	-25.9	A.D. 1452-1636
59	pit above burial 4	wood charcoal	GX-25882-AMS	77	280 ± 50	-26.4	A.D. 1475-1941
wooden pipe	none	sample from pipe stem (persimmon wood)	GX-25631-AMS	plowzone	140 ± 50	-27.2	A.D. 1669-1947

there was no evidence for disturbance at the 38–48 cmbd level in which the maize was recovered. This case demonstrates the importance of obtaining direct dates on cultigens, rather than relying on associated wood charcoal dates (Chilton 1999a, 2001).

The other human burial (Burial 4) was discovered at the bottom of Feature 59 in 1999 and was excavated in the summer of 2001. Burial 4 was a primary burial and was nearly complete. The individual was placed at the bottom of a pit in a tightly flexed position. No associated funerary objects were evident. The pit feature above the burial contained faunal remains (including shell), chipping debris, Native American pottery sherds, and charcoal. Radiocarbon date ranges from the pit feature above this burial were (1) cal A.D. 1452–1636 (2 sigma); and (2) cal A.D. 1475–1941 (2 sigma) (Table 4.1). These date ranges and the associated objects most likely place this burial at the end of the Late Woodland period, on the eve of Contact.

A total of 216 flotation samples were collected from features and control areas in 1998 and 1999, including 153 soil samples from features and 63 from non-feature matrix. Column samples were collected from features, as well as from non-feature contexts as a control. The recovered cultural materials and samples are discussed below.

LABORATORY PROCESSING AND ANALYSIS

As part of the field school training, some of the cultural material was processed at the field laboratory that was set up at the Chilmark School in 1998 and the West Tisbury Middle School in 1999. All recovered materials were inventoried, cleaned, and rebagged in clean polyethylene bags. All artifacts and samples were computer catalogued.

After the completion of each field school, all non-burial cultural materials and samples were brought back to the New England Archaeology Laboratory at Harvard University. Analysis of cultural materials recovered during the field school excavations concentrated on categories of information most useful for identifying the temporal/cultural affiliation of occupational episodes and for determining site function(s). Selected carbon samples were weighed, packaged, and sent to Geochron, Inc., for radiocarbon dating. Soil samples collected for flotation were processed by the Public Archaeology Laboratory, Inc., using a 30-gallon flotation tank system. The residues remaining after flotation were analyzed by Tonya Largy for a variety of data classes that included carbonized seeds and nuts, bones, fish scales, charcoal, and microflakes (discussed below). A sample of the shell collected was analyzed by Leslie Shaw of Bowdoin College, and Lucinda McWeeney analyzed a sub-sample of the wood charcoal for species identification. Harvard University is serving as the temporary repository for the archaeological materials until a permanent facility is designated by Aquinnah Wampanoag and the Massachusetts Historical Commission. We are hopeful that all of the samples and collections will eventually be housed at the planned Aquinnah Cultural Center.

PRELIMINARY ANALYSIS AND INTERPRETATIONS

A total of 75 chipped and groundstone tools, 2358 pieces of chipping debris, approximately 100 pieces of fire-cracked rock, 96 pottery sherds, 2746 mammal and fish bone remains, 8912 shells and shell fragments, and floral remains (242 charcoal samples and 26 charred seeds and nuts, not including flotation recovery) were recovered from the site between 1997 and 1999. In this section, we review our analysis and preliminary interpretations of these artifacts and samples.

Most of our interpretations of site chronology are based on the presence of diagnostic artifacts, most of which were found in the plow zone. We recovered one possible Late Paleoindian (Dalton-like) white quartzite projectile point, which likely dates to about 10,000–9000 B.P. This point was broken in two pieces and the halves were found in the plow zone of adjoining test units. The point was likely broken by the plow because the break appears to be relatively recent. The next oldest artifact recovered was a small (reworked) red felsite Neville projectile point, which likely dates to the Middle Archaic period. We recovered a variety of Late Archaic projectile points, including Brewerton Side-Notched (5), possible Brewerton Eared-Notched (2), Squibnocket Triangle (1), and small-stemmed (2); small-stemmed points have also been found in later deposits elsewhere in New England; see Filios 1989; Halligan 2000; Lavin 1984; Ritchie 1969:54). We believe this indicates more frequent use of the site beginning in the Late Archaic period, as is true elsewhere on Martha's Vineyard (see Ritchie 1969:230; Richardson 1985). This coincides with the separation of Martha's Vineyard from the mainland about 6000 years ago (Oldale 1992:100).

Also recovered from the site was a soapstone (steatite) bowl fragment, which likely dates to the end of the Late Archaic period (ca. 3500–3000 B.P.). Because soapstone is not available on Martha's Vineyard, the presence of this object indicates either the movement of peoples to the island or trade between the island and the mainland. Ritchie's (1969) excavations yielded small quantities of steatite from the Hornblower site on Squibnocket Ridge in Chilmark. In addition, several pieces of soapstone with lug handles and drill holes are in the Hornblower collection at Plimoth Plantation (Herbster 1996).

The predominant prehistoric use of the Lucy Vincent Beach site was during the Late Woodland period. This interpretation is based on the presence of what appear to be Late Woodland ceramics, projectile points, and pit features (this is also confirmed by radiocarbon dating of features) (Table 4.1, Figure 4.5). The site was also heavily used during the Contact period (ca. 400–300 B.P.). Artifacts dating to this period include white clay smoking pipes, gunflint fragments, cut brass, and a carved wooden pipe. Very little nineteenth- and twentieth-century materials were recovered from the site, and those that were found were quite small and likely associated with plowing and manuring of the site (e.g., glass, brick, pottery, and metal fragments).

Chipped-Stone Tools

Since the surficial geology of Martha's Vineyard is composed primarily of glacial outwash deposits, the island's prehistoric inhabitants had lithic raw materials available to them in the form of cobbles. Most of the lithic materials used at Lucy Vincent Beach were likely acquired

Figure 4.5
Calibrated Radiocarbon Date Ranges for Features (2 sigma)

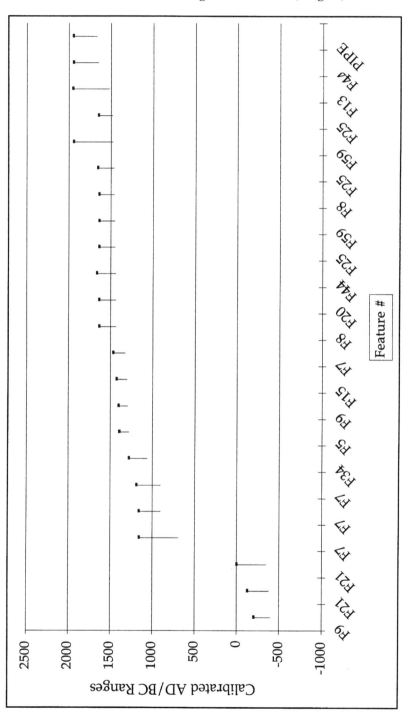

Prepared by Kathryn Curran.

from glacial outwash. Some of the materials, however, were clearly brought in from the mainland. Many of these likely came as finished tools, since very little chipping debris from mainland materials is present on the site.

A total of 23 projectile points was recovered from the Lucy Vincent Beach site, making up 33.82% of the stone tool assemblage. Of these, seven are untyped projectile tips, 10 are mostly complete diagnostic points (base and midsection), and six are complete non-diagnostic points. As discussed previously, the typed points are diagnostic of the Late Paleoindian through Late Woodland periods. All but two projectile points were recovered from the plow zone. The remaining two were recovered from the refuse deposits above each of the burial features (Features 7 and 59). The points were distributed across the site, with no discernable pattern. Lithic materials for projectile points include rhyolite, quartz, and quartzite.

Non-diagnostic chipped-stone bifaces found during the Lucy Vincent Beach excavations make up 10.14% of the stone tool assemblage and include six bifacial tool blades or preforms. The majority of the bifaces are unidentifiable fragments struck off during manufacture or broken off finished tools. Of the six bifaces recovered, five are made of quartz and one of Blue Hills rhyolite; two of the quartz bifaces are likely scrapers. A total of four quartz scrapers (three bifacial, one unifacial) were identified.

Chipped-stone cores and core fragments make up 17.39% of the stone artifact assemblage. A total of 11 quartz cores and one purple rhyolite core were recovered. The majority of the quartz cores are very poor quality, yet contain a high degree of crystal formations. Given the possible ceremonial nature of the Lucy Vincent Beach site, these cores may have been primarily smashed to extract crystals. Two unworked quartz crystals were recovered in the plow zone.

Groundstone and Pecked-Stone Tools

Groundstone and pecked-stone tools (grinding stones, polished groundstone fragments, pestles, net weights, and hammerstones) make up 36.23% of the stone tool assemblage. A total of 25 groundstone and pecked-stone tools were recovered. These include five grinding stone fragments that are also fire cracked, two possible pestle fragments, five net weights, five polished groundstone fragments, seven hammerstones, and one soapstone bowl rim fragment.

Debitage

A total of 2358 pieces of debitage (flakes and shatter produced as part of the lithic reduction process) were recovered. The majority of the chipping debris consisted of various types of rhyolite and quartz, with rhyolite making up 47.75% of the assemblage and quartz 36.59%. The remaining chipping debris consists of chert (4.49%), quartzite (3.90%), chalcedony (2.84%), unidentified material (2.62%), argillite (0.59%), basalt and jasper (0.38%), slate (0.29%), siltstone and mudstone (0.12%).

While a formal lithic analysis has not yet been conducted for this site, a preliminary study by Vargas (1999) of 454 pieces of debitage from primary features revealed that most of this chipping debris consisted of quartz (54%) and rhyolite (33%). Other lithic materials included quartzite, chert, chalcedony, jasper, and basalt. Flake types included primary, secondary, and tertiary, indicating the full range of lithic reduction. Forty-three flakes from Vargas' sample had cobble cortex, including 33 of quartz, seven of rhyolite, and three of chert. Our preliminary interpretation is that most of the lithic material from this site is indigenous, with both quartz and rhyolite available locally as cobbles. Additional lithics of rhyolite, chert, chalcedony, and jasper were likely brought in from the mainland via trade and/or movement of peoples.

Pottery

A total of 686 Native pottery fragments were recovered from Lucy Vincent Beach. Of these, 590 were classified only as "general pottery" but are likely body sherds. Also identified were 86 body sherds, one neck sherd, two decorated rim sherds, six rim sherds with no decoration, and one waster. Coates and Haynie (1999) analyzed 100 sherds, recovered in 1997 and 1998, for minimum number of vessel lots using the method described by Chilton (1996) (a vessel lot constitutes all sherds assignable to a single vessel). This analysis identified 14 minimum vessel lots. The paste of the vessel lots was very similar in color and contained fine muscovite mica, and all vessel lots contained shell or "missing" temper (the latter is most likely shell that has decomposed). Since clay is plentiful on Martha's Vineyard, the pottery was most likely manufactured locally. The most common exterior surface treatment of vessel lots is smooth (64% of vessel lots), followed by smoothed-over cord-marked (50%), wiped (21%), cord-marked (21%), and incised (21%), and dentate-stamped (14%). (These percentages add up to more than 100% because vessels often have more than one surface treatment type.) The modal thickness of the vessel lots analyzed by Coates and Haynie (1999) ranged from 3.6 to 8 mm. In 1999 one nearly complete pot was recovered just south of the Feature 59 burial. This vessel had a smoothed-over cord-marked body and rim, with a dentate-stamped constricted neck, a roughly globular body, and an incipient collar. It measures 15.6 cm in height and 13.5 cm at maximum body width.

Contact-Period Materials

There was an interesting assortment of post-Contact cultural material that was clearly associated with the Native American occupation of the site. This material was recovered from the plow zone and from features, some of which also contained items of Native American manufacture. Artifacts of Euro-American origin consisted of eight very small redware sherds, 13 very small fragments of either redware or brick, three white earthenware sherds, seven pieces of glass, and five buttons (of pewter or lead, ivory, clay or bone, plastic, and metal). Also recovered were 27 smoking pipe fragments including 23 white clay, one wooden, and two Native clay pipes. There is also a light smattering of nineteenth- and twentieth-century materials across the site, such as cartridge casings, coins, coal, and a pencil sharpener.

One whole white clay smoking pipe bowl was recovered, with the pipe maker's initials "LE" (signifying Llewellin Evans of Bristol, England). This bowl was made between 1661 and 1686 (Walker 1977). Ricard (1999) measured the bore diameters of the 11 white clay smoking pipe stems recovered from the site. Five pipe stems had bore diameters of 7/64 inch and six had a diameter of 6/64 inch. Using the Harrington method (1954) gives a date range of 1620–1750. Binford's (1969) formula produces a mean date of 1685. Although one must use caution with such a small sample, taken as a whole these white clay pipe fragments most likely date to the last quarter of the seventeenth century.

The wooden smoking pipe was found in two pieces in the plow zone of adjoining test units and was radiocarbon dated to cal A.D. 1669–1947 (2 sigma) (Table 4.1). The pipe is carved into the shape of a human hand making an "OK" sign. The wood was identified as persimmon (genus *Diospyros*) by Bruce Hoadley at the University of Massachusetts at Amherst. The pipe measures 13.6 cm in length and 2.8 cm in width. The Native clay smoking pipe fragments were recovered from Features 13 and 25. Feature 13 yielded a radiocarbon date range of cal A.D. 1524–1950 (2 sigma) (Table 4.1). Feature 25 yielded date ranges of cal A.D. 1481–1648 (2 sigma), cal A.D. 1450–1636 (2 sigma), and cal A.D. 1464–

1655 (2 sigma) (Table 4.1). Euro-American white clay pipe fragments were also recovered from Feature 25.

Other post-Contact material includes three nails (one hand wrought, one machine cut, and one wire nail), one bifacially flaked, apparently Native-made gunflint (brownish-gray flint), and one flint fragment (same material). Thirteen metal fragments were identified, including three pieces of brass/copper kettle. One of the brass/copper artifacts appears to have been originally cut into a round pendant (approximately 4 cm in diameter), punched with a small hole, then rolled. The second cut object is quarter-moon shaped and measures 3 cm long by 0.5 cm wide. The third is triangular in shape and is scratched in several locations.

Faunal Remains

Data from this section are abstracted from a preliminary report written by Largy and Burns (2001). Fish remains were recovered from flotation of soil from nine features (7, 8, 9, 13, 15, 25, 34, 44, 59). Other remains of vertebrates were collected in situ from six features (7, 8, 13, 15, 34, 59A, 59).

The total analyzed assemblage numbers 2782 specimens (708.9 gm). Bone identified as sub-fossil (number of identified specimens [NISP]=81) comprises 23% of this assemblage. Most of this material is cancellous bone, and some of it resembles sea mammal, but no attempt has been made to analyze this material further. These sub-fossils likely also date from the Miocene and are mixed in with cultural deposits.

The remaining faunal/cultural assemblage numbers 2453 specimens (512.7 gm). Of this total, fish bones and scales number 2225 (91%) and weigh 297.6 gm (58%), while other vertebrates number 228 (9%) and weigh 215.1 gm (42%). Also identified in this analyzed assemblage were 72 stones, one ceramic sherd, two flakes, and two shell fragments. At least 12 fish taxa were identified to species. These include sturgeon and/or ocean catfish (which may strongly resemble each other when fragmented), shad, menhaden, sea bass, cod, drum fish, goosefish, herring, porgies, scup, striped bass, and weakfish.

Other vertebrate fauna from Lucy Vincent Beach include primarily mammal (99%), with turtle (NISP=15; 1%) and bird (NISP=5; <1%) represented to a much lesser extent. Both sea and terrestrial mammal taxa are present in the assemblage. One sea mammal taxon, *Globicephala melaena*, the common blackfish or pilot whale, is represented by one vertebral epiphysis and one phalanx, probably from the same individual since both are unfused, indicating a young animal, and both were recov-

ered from the same level (39–49 cm) of Feature 7. The only terrestrial
mammal taxon is white-tailed deer. Many fragments lack identifying
landmarks and are identified according to size classes such as medium/
large, small/medium, or simply as mammal. One painted turtle is identified based on the reconstruction of 15 fragments of carapace bones.
Three bird taxa are represented by five bones, including *Anas* sp. (duck),
Melanitta [*fusca*] (scoter), and *Diomedea* [*chlororhynchos*] (Yellow-
nosed? Albatross).

Based on percentages of feature contents, it appears the Lucy Vincent
Beach site occupants were exploiting predominantly marine resources
during the Late Woodland and Contact periods. Some of the fish taxa
(goosefish) may have been collected from the beach or by using weirs
in tidal shallows. The presence of a blackfish/pilot whale raises the question of whether Natives were hunting sea mammals in the open ocean,
or whether they exploited a beached whale. As the data continue to be
analyzed and with additional research, more insights can be gained into
fishing methods and technologies, as well as looking at the distributions
of taxa between features and how they might correspond with radiocarbon dates (Largy and Burns 2001).

Shell

Shell samples from five features (7, 8, 9, 25, 44) were sent to Shaw
for analysis. A final report is forthcoming; however, a preliminary report
by Shaw (2001) indicates the presence of a variety of mollusk species.
This section is a summary of Shaw (2001).

Feature 7 contained quahog (*Mercenaria mercenaria*), soft-shell
clam (*Mya arenaria*), bay scallop (*Aequipecten irradians*), and whelk
(*Busycon* sp.). Quahog are found in the subtidal zone in shallow bays
or estuaries; soft-shell clams are found in all tidal levels and subtidal
shallows; bay scallops are found in the lowest intertidal zone and in
subtidal areas with eel grass; and whelk are common in shallow water
with sandy substrate (Shaw 2001). The heavy amount of weathering
evident on shells from this feature, especially on the quahog, suggests
either exposure on the surface after deposition or heavy water leaching
in the soil (Shaw 2001). Feature 8 has a very low frequency of shell,
and the shell present is all heavily weathered and eroded. Based on
shell thickness, the primary species seems to be quahog, but absolute
species identification is difficult. Feature 9 is similar to Feature 8 in
that it has a very low frequency of shell, and species identifications are
limited.

Feature 25 contained soft-shell clam, quahog, bay scallop, and terrestrial gastropod. The variability in the amount of weathering on the shell from this feature suggests that it might represent different disposal episodes, and the surfaces of the dumped materials may have been exposed for variable lengths of time. The presence of terrestrial gastropods also indicates periods of exposure near or on the surface. If this feature had been truncated by erosion in recent times, however, the land snails may be recent intrusions. The fragmentation of the shells within each bag/ stratum is also variable, suggesting perhaps trampling before burial. The fragments of quahog are particularly interesting. Many seem to be smashed, possibly from an impact while on an anvil/rock, that sends a radial fracture through the shell. Shaw (2001) suggests this might represent breakage for tool manufacture or expedient use of the pointed fragments created. The minimum number of individuals (MNI) for quahog is much lower than that for soft-shell clams, and the shells are much harder, so they would not easily be broken by trampling. Shaw (2001) was not able to find any evidence for use of these shells in bead making.

Finally, Feature 44 contained soft-shell clam, quahog, and bay scallop. This feature showed marked differences between levels in terms of species present and the degree of fragmentation. The lower two levels are all soft-shell clam and are not heavily fragmented. This suggests the shell may represent one event (consumption/disposal); the lack of fragmentation indicates quick burial. The shell from these two levels are very well preserved, almost looking fresh, again suggesting quick burial after deposition, and they have slightly thinner shells than seems typical for this species. This may suggest a few warm years with rapid shell growth and limited calcium carbonate in the water. The soft-shell clams from these lower levels also seem to include a full range of ages, from one year to about five years, which suggests that the clam flat where these shells were collected was not over-exploited. The upper levels of this feature show a range in species represented and a more variable degree of fragmentation. Shaw (2001) interprets this as a different/subsequent disposal event (or events). The weathering of shell in these upper levels is low, suggesting a generally rapid burial after disposal. Further analysis of shell remains and correlation with radiocarbon dates and information from the rest of the floral and faunal assemblage will shed light on the consumption and disposal behavior at Lucy Vincent Beach, and it will provide important information about changes in the general habitat over time.

Floral Remains

The majority of the floral remains were recovered through flotation of soil samples collected from features. Although the analysis of the floral material is still in progress, a preliminary assessment has revealed several charred wood, seeds, nuts, and maize. In addition, over 250 charcoal samples were collected, several of which were radiocarbon dated. McWeeney (1999, 2000) analyzed the wood charcoal from seven features (7, 8, 9, 21, 25, 44, 51) prior to radiocarbon dating. Wood species identified in order of quantity include oak (*Quercus* sp.), hickory (*Carya* sp.), American Beech (*Fagus grandifolia*), maple (*Acer* sp.), persimmon (*Diospyros virginiana*), and conifer.

It is clear from this sample that the Native inhabitants of the Lucy Vincent Beach site used a variety of tree species for fuel wood (McWeeney 2000). The presence of hickory, persimmon, and possibly sycamore indicate that Native people were going beyond the immediate area to collect wood (McWeeney 2000). The presence of persimmon wood (smoking pipe and wood charcoal) suggests that either the wood was introduced by Europeans as a trade item or persimmon was part of the local flora; the latter has not been recorded heretofore (McWeeney 2000). Since the site is not presently forested, the charcoal and floral analysis will provide crucial information in our attempts to reconstruct the environmental history of the site.

CONCLUSIONS AND FUTURE PROSPECTS

As Luedtke (this volume) points out, coastal sites often have a wider range of materials preserved than do inland sites; this good preservation is often a source of frustration because there is often little funding to pursue the kinds of analyses that are required. In this case, we were able to conduct flotation on a large number of samples from the site. We were also able to obtain multiple radiocarbon dates from all key features, and we were able to analyze a large sample of the faunal material from the site. There is much work still to be done in our analysis of the Lucy Vincent Beach site. What is mostly sorely needed is research on paleoenvironments and paleo-shorelines of the site area and Martha's Vineyard in general; some of this will be undertaken by Duranleau, as mentioned earlier. The analysis of a larger sample of wood charcoal will provide much needed clues on the forest types represented at Lucy Vincent Beach during different times. A team from the Harvard Forest (directed by David Foster) took a soil core from Upper Chilmark Pond in the fall of

2000, hoping that it would provide evidence for the vegetational history of the immediate area. Although the sediment core was taken to the maximum depth possible, hitting rock at about two meters, it provided evidence for only the most recent storms that breached the pond.

Although it is likely that most of the site was lost to erosion before it came to the attention of archaeologists, we can still offer some tentative interpretations on the basis of the data recovered. It is clear that the site has been important to Native Americans for thousands of years, and it continues to be important to the Aquinnah today. The site obviously served a variety of functions and was most intensively utilized during the Late Woodland and Contact periods (A.D. 1000–1700). There is evidence for at least seasonal settlement at the site; a wide range of plant and animal foods was exploited and consumed at this site, and a number of post molds indicate small seasonal encampments. The lack of a substantial midden or evidence of semi-permanent structures, however, precludes the interpretation of long-term settlement at the site. The presence of fresh water nearby and the proximity of marine resources within the last several hundred years made this an attractive location, most likely during the warmer months of the year. Our preliminary faunal and floral analysis suggests a diverse subsistence base for Native use of the site during the Late Woodland and early Contact periods, similar to what Bernstein (this volume) reports for Long Island. Also, it appears that, like Long Island (Bernstein, this volume), settlement preference on Martha's Vineyard was oriented toward the protected north shore locales (see also Ritchie 1969). Thus, the south shore sites, such as Lucy Vincent Beach, may have been used only on a seasonal basis (perhaps in the warmer months) or for certain ceremonial uses (including burial grounds).

There is certainly a significant amount of shell present at the site, but there is no shell "midden" or mound. Thus, the site was most likely not immediately adjacent to shellfish beds during the period of use. Presently we have no way to reconstruct the location of the shoreline during the Late Woodland and early Contact periods, but it is clear that the shore was quite a distance from the site, and the now brackish pond to the north was likely fresh water during those periods. The patterning of shell pits on this site is similar to what Luedtke (this volume) describes for the Boston Harbor Islands: shell deposits are less than 50 cm thick and take the form of numerous overlapping lenses and features. Luedtke (this volume) suggests that this is what one would expect if shellfish were being gathered as part of a diverse diet during the course of multiple visits spanning hundreds or thousands of years. This is consistent with our current interpretation of the site.

The presence of shells on archaeological sites not only provides us with evidence of subsistence: it is clear that shells were imbued with symbolic meaning and may have held ceremonial significance (see Kerber, this volume). The presence of at least four human burials suggests a ceremonial use of the site, as well. The two burials excavated by the authors (Burials 3 and 4) contained evidence of food consumption in association with the burials (including shellfish), perhaps indicating ceremonial feasting; the analysis of burial feature contents and comparison to non-burial features will help us to test this interpretation. In her paper on the Boston Harbor Islands, Luedtke (this volume) recommends that for future research, archaeologists attempt to investigate the symbolic or ideological aspects of the islands and coast. She suggests we do so using oral traditions, as well as innovative hypothesis testing using archaeological data. We intend to employ both of these sources of data in our exploration of the possible ceremonial aspects of the use of Lucy Vincent Beach and other sites on Martha's Vineyard.

The in-depth analysis of feature contents and site functions also affords us the opportunity to examine the reuse of ceremonial sites on Martha's Vineyard. Ritchie (1969) and others focused on the relationship between coastal ecology and coastal adaptation on the island and whether a coastal culture in general could be defined archaeologically. Although several burial sites on Martha's Vineyard have been identified and documented (i.e., Byers and Johnson 1940; Ritchie 1969; Herbster and Cherau 1998, 1999), they have not been viewed as evidence for the reuse of ceremonial sites on a sacred landscape indicative of the cultural history of the Aquinnah Wampanoag tribe.

The issues that guide our continued analysis of this important site include (1) environmental change and its relationship to subsistence and settlement during the Late Woodland and Contact periods; (2) evidence for trade between mainland and Martha's Vineyard peoples in prehistoric times, and trade with Europeans after Contact; (3) the movement of peoples between the island and the mainland, and the formation of the Wampanoag tribe; and (4) the ceremonial aspects of the site, and how the three above issues relate to such uses. Given the presence of burials at the site and the prominent, beacon-like location of the knoll on the landscape, it is clear that the site was a very special place. We are grateful that we were able to work with the Aquinnah to record such important historical information before the site is completely lost to the ocean.

ACKNOWLEDGMENTS

We wish to thank Jordan Kerber for the invitation to contribute to this volume and for his insightful comments on earlier drafts. We also wish to thank the many individuals involved in this project. Volunteers for the fieldwork in 1997 included Tracy Hoffman, Desiree Martinez, Terry McFadden, and Catherine Smith. Irv and Nancy DeVore provided us with lodging for the 1997 and 2001 field seasons. We are indebted to the field school students from 1998 and 1999 for all of their hard work; excavating a threatened site can be very stressful business, and they handled it gracefully. We also wish to thank the very capable and hard-working Teaching Assistants for the Field Schools: Kit Curran, Christopher Jasparro, and Ninian Stein. Ann Marie Mires and Catherine Smith graciously donated their time and osteological expertise for the excavation of Burials 3 and 4. Siobhan Hart, Deena Duranleau, Kirk Van Dyke, and Gail Van Dyke volunteered their time and assisted in the 2001 excavations. We also wish to acknowledge the work of students who conducted lab projects after the field schools; their work is cited directly in the text.

We wish to thank the faunal analysts for this project, Tonya Largy and Peter Burns, for an inordinate amount of work far beyond our ability to fund them. Douglas Causey, Senior Vertebrate Biologist in the Museum of Comparative Biology, Harvard University, identified the albatross bone. Identifications were made using reference collections housed at the Zooarchaeology Laboratory of the Peabody Museum and the Departments of Ichthyology and Ornithology, Harvard University. Charles Chaff, collections manager, Department of Paleontology, was consulted regarding the sub-fossil mammal bone in the assemblage. Early in the analysis, Largy took several specimens to the 1998 meeting of the Fish Working Group of the International Council of Archaeozoology where they were scanned, enlarged, and the photos shown to fish specialists for help in identification. Dr. Shelton Pleasants Applegate, a shark tooth expert from the University of Mexico, presently a Visiting Scholar in the Department of Ichthyology, identified the shark teeth from the site. Many thanks to our other analysts for this project, Lucinda McWeeney and Leslie Shaw. They were able to extract an amazing amount of data. Tim Kardatzke at the Public Archaeology Laboratory, Inc. was the lab supervisor for the flotation for this project. All radiocarbon analysis was conducted at Geochron, Inc., in Cambridge, Massachusetts, by Alex Cherkinsky, who was extremely helpful and accommodating. Kit Curran created the final graphics; initial scans and earlier drafts of Figures 4.3

and 4.4 were prepared by Tannie Huang and Kim Megdanis. Jessie Halligan, Ivy Owens, and Desiree Martinez were Research Assistants during various stages of this project. We are immensely grateful for their energy, hard work, and initiative.

A ground-penetrating radar survey was conducted in 1998 by Donald Liptack, Jim Turenne, David Skinas, and Rudy Chlanda (U.S. Natural Resources Conservation Service). Donald Liptack also undertook to reseed the site after our 1998 excavations to mitigate the effects of erosion. Our thanks to David Foster, Glenn Motzkin, and other researchers from the Harvard Forest for taking and analyzing a sediment core from Upper Chilmark Pond. We are grateful to Jill Bouck, James Richardson, and Dick Burt for sharing their knowledge of and excitement about Martha's Vineyard archaeology with us. Jill was also very kind in providing our students with a tour of the Martha's Vineyard Historical Society in 1998.

The analysis of faunal and floral remains and the radiocarbon dating for this project was paid for by a grant to Chilton from the William F. Milton Fund, administered by Harvard University (awarded in 1999), and a grant from the Clark/Cooke Fund (Harvard University, awarded in 2000). The Field Schools of 1998 and 1999 were sponsored by the Harvard University Extension/Summer School and the Department of Anthropology at Harvard University. Funding for Research Assistants came from the Faculty of Arts and Sciences Junior Faculty Work Study Program and the Department of Anthropology at Harvard. A special thanks to the Department for temporarily storing the artifacts in the New England Archaeology Laboratory. We wish to thank the Town of Chilmark for allowing us to conduct these excavations. We especially wish to thank Tim Carroll (Board of Selectmen) and Rusty Walton (Conservation Officer). A special thanks to Bret Stearns (Chilmark Police and Natural Resources Department, Aquinnah) for his help and assistance. Our thanks also to the Chilmark School and the West Tisbury School for allowing us to set up our field labs in these locations.

Finally, we offer our most heartfelt thanks to the Aquinnah Wampanoag. Matthew Vanderhoop (THPO) and Mark Harding (Deputy THPO) have been helpful to us throughout this project, but they have also taught us the importance of these kinds of special places on the landscape to the Aquinnah today. Randy Jardin (field school student in 1998 and Aquinnah Tribal Member), educated us, helped us, challenged us, and serves as a staunch protector of archaeological resources on Martha's Vineyard.

5

Small is Beautiful: Tidal Weirs in a Low-Energy Estuary

Dena F. Dincauze and Elena Décima

An opportunity arose in 1985 to expand on earlier investigations of "The Boylston Street Fishweir," a prehistoric facility of legendary size and probably Late Archaic age (ca. 5000–3000 B.P.) encountered below the streets of Boston, Massachusetts (Johnson 1942, 1949). The feature was originally interpreted as a huge current weir involving thousands of stakes over many acres, implying a large organized workforce to build and operate. This prevailing impression was and remains incongruent with the small-scale social groups of the Late Archaic period otherwise revealed by archaeological research in the area. Recent investigations have revealed that the reality was a series of small tidal weirs along an inundating shore, built and used over a period of approximately fifteen hundred years.

Several minimal investigations between 1913 and 1950 of stakes and sticks in marine silts below street level heightened interest in the "fishweir." When new construction was planned in 1985 that would open a city block deep underground, the National Historic Preservation Act required that attention be paid. The case for renewed investigations at the site was presented in the significance statement:

The Boylston Street Fishweir . . . is significant in North American prehistory as the earliest large environment-modifying facility known on the continent. Constructed by communities living a hunting-and-gathering lifestyle, it is surprising for its size and the implications of that size for human labor investment. Regionally, its significance derives from both its uniqueness as a site and for its cultural context—it belongs within the Late Archaic period, a time when the northeastern hunter/gatherer peoples had achieved sufficient population density to support, and perhaps require, an unprecedented level of cultural complexity. Territoriality, subsistence diversification, and ceremonial elaboration characterize the fifth and fourth millennia before the present, yet prehistorians know little about the details of the lifestyles that supported such complexity within societies of temperate-forest wild-food gatherers. The site itself, a coastal facility 30 feet below city streets and offering excellent preservation of a suite of organic remains—is unique in regional archaeology, and is famous for . . . the high quality of the original investigations and the innovative research techniques applied. . . . Research questions appropriate to a site of such significance must involve considerations of the structure's role within the human communities that produced it. Better understanding of the form, size, and function of the feature will lead to understanding the human motives, expectations, and effort that lay behind its construction.

The wooden construction, the estuarine sediments enclosing it, and the plant and animal life that swarmed in the water in which it stood are all preserved in part for examination. A Brown University inventory of a core pulled at the site shows that the classes of data available now include abundant pollen, discontinuously distributed plant macrofossils, diatoms, molluscan shells, some foraminifera and ostracods, and more diversity in the sediment textures than had been expected on the basis of the earlier reports. Thus, we seem to have an opportunity for observing through time and space such environmental conditions as current directions, temperature and salinity of the water, changing shellfish fauna, the kinds of terrestrial plant materials being deposited in the bay, and the plant communities fringing the site. We . . . expect that appropriate data collection techniques will yield fish remains as well. We anticipate retrieval of a rich data set, and expect surprises as one class of data is compared to another and as new questions are [asked]. It is reasonable, also, to hope that within the feature itself, the focus of so much human labor investment, we may find some tangible objects in addition to the stakes and wattles that were brought to the site by the human builders and attendants. (Dincauze 1985)

The 1985 exposure (Figure 5.1) was planned directly south of the first encounter and the major investigations of 1939, incorporating the IBM area that had later provided the first radiocarbon ages. The research design emphasized ecological and cultural data over paleoenvironmental sequences because we respected the earlier work and knew we had the advantage of the radiocarbon dating method. In addition, we would seek evidence for human influence on the vegetation and estuarine fauna in the vicinity, resulting from the large facility (Roberts 1985).

Figure 5.1
Locations of Weir Investigations Plotted on a Street Map of the Back Bay Section of Boston, MA, ca. 1940

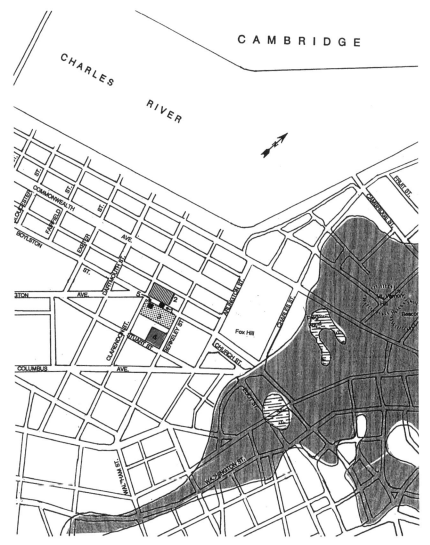

Key: (1) 1913 encounter in subway tunnel; (2) New England Mutual Life Insurance site; (3) John Hancock Tower site; (4) IBM building site; (5) 500 Boylston Street site.

Based on Johnson 1942: Figure 1.

FIELD CONDITIONS AND ENIGMAS

To the surprise of the excavators, observed exposures of stakes in the new location displayed none of the density reported from directly north at the New England Mutual Life Insurance (NEL) site (Décima and Dincauze 1998). Scattered stakes and spotty alignments emerged briefly from the silts, little resembling the thick clusters and long alignments observed across the street. Moreover, the new encounters were at elevations lower than the earlier ones, measured as distance below Boston City Base (the engineering datum defined just below mean low water in 1923 [Kaye and Barghoorn 1964:64]).

Prior to digging, the investigators benefited from an engineering survey of the top of thick glaciomarine Blue Clay that closely underlay all stakes throughout the area. The Blue Clay surface was our best approximation to paleotopography at the several sites; the old land surface on which the sea encroached mostly eroded during transgression. The upper surface of the Blue Clay was weathered, but evidence for soil development or organic remains was missing except for a segment of swamp exposed to the southeast (Johnson 1949) and scattered remnants of "Lower Peat" at NEL and most other sites. The important revelation of the engineering map was the slope of about six feet over a distance of ca. 360 feet from the northeastern to the southwestern corner; all previous maps had shown or assumed an essentially flat plane (e.g., Judson 1949:41). The Blue Clay surface sloped gently westward at the NEL site and dipped to the southwest, south, and southeast at the 500 Boylston Street site (Haley and Aldrich 1985:Figs. 7–10).

Instead of clustered lines of stakes trending roughly north-south toward the Charles River, we found scattered uprights and horizontal twigs in no particular alignment until the digging reached more or less the center of the impact area, where a kind of "fence" configuration (Area A) trended roughly east-west. Weeks of puzzled confusion followed the exposure of Area A, as the digging and recording continued and more short alignments were glimpsed.

The solution appeared as the radiocarbon ages of several weir components came from the lab. Congruence of depth with age is reasonably good, but imperfect; we were hampered by flawed data on elevations and the complications of rotting wood. The oldest dated weir element at the 500 Boylston Street site, from the IBM site down-slope in the northwestern corner of the area, is about 4900 radiocarbon years old; the youngest, in the northeastern corner, is about 3700 years old (Décima and Dincauze 1998:Table 1, 162–163). The features across the street at the NEL site belong, as the Johnson team correctly inferred, to the centuries around 3700 to 3500 years ago, at the end of the weir-building span. The undated deep stakes at the John Hancock site to the southeast we estimate are older than 5000 years. This broad range of time occupied by construction and use of the features confirms irrefutably that they were many, not one, and furthermore, that they were small, not large.

The weir elements were progressively younger up the slope against which the sea level rose, which lay between the weirs and the deeper bay waters to the east. With that insight, we could see that the several orientations of weir segments paralleled contour lines as those changed with depth and position on the shallow conical rise. The stakes did not run out to sea—they were oriented parallel to the shore, a position that varied over time. These ancient marine weirs were not comparable to the freshwater weirs that populate the ethnographic literature, nor to the large commercial coastal-current weirs that Johnson investigated for comparison (Carlson 1985). They were a special case, perfectly suited to their unique situation on a sloping foreshore in a shallow estuary during a time of low tidal amplitude.

PALEOENVIRONMENT

The environment in the ancient Back Bay was unique among paleoenvironments studied on the East Coast of North America—we have no good analogues. The difficulties in realizing the environment explain the problems of interpretation of the site; our advances beyond the earlier efforts are founded on research done elsewhere in the Gulf of Maine (Rosen et al. 1993). Analysis of grain size in the master sediment core (Core 8) supported division into three sedimentary Units representing three contrastive sets of hydrological conditions in the embayment. Sediments, pollen, and diatoms were extracted from this core, and so are directly comparable in terms of provenience. All the dated weir elements, from whatever site, belong to Rosen's Lower Unit, essentially the lowest 2 m of the column with an uncalibrated radiocarbon age span between 5000 and 3500 years ago. The Lower Unit was dominated by clay-rich fine sediments, derived predominantly from the underlying glacial Blue Clay redeposited from relatively quiet brackish waters. The sediment qualities in the weir zone are characteristic of subtidal muds. Interaction of the basin shape of the Gulf of Maine and the rising global sea level produced a low tidal amplitude at this stage of the postglacial inundation—something around a meter at maximum (Rosen et al. 1993). The contrasting conclusions reached by earlier investigators were based on the modern tidal amplitude of ca. 9 feet.

Diatom studies show the first flush of saltwater against the shore in the project area around 5600 years ago. For almost 2000 years, as the sea rose and the embayment expanded in a backwater location in respect to the tidal movement up the Charles River, water remained shallow, brackish, and warm. The diatoms recovered in the weir zone of the sediment column (Lower Unit) confirm brackish water there at weir time (Rice 1988). Subsequent to the weir time (during deposition of the Middle Unit), water deposited less clay, more sand-sized particles, and shell fragments. Gravel was essentially nonexistent in the weir-zone sediments; channel lags (coarse gravel veneers) in sediments above the weirs were composed of shell fragments, especially notable in the coarse shell lags at the NEL site.

Pollen and wood analyses indicated a warm temperate climate approaching modern means—a very good match to the earlier studies. The fairly complacent pollen diagram dominated by hardwoods (Newby and Webb 1994) agrees well with other studies of the regional pollen rain at the time. The low shores of the ancient Back Bay were rimmed by salt marshes and freshwater ponds and swamps with alder and red maples (Newby and Webb 1994; Kaplan et al. 1990). The stakes show preferential selection for young hardwood growth, with no use of the pine revealed in the pollen diagram. Nothing in the micro- or macro-floral data indicates any anthropogenic (cultural impacts on geology and soil formation) stress on the local vegetation, as might be expected from culling of young wood at the rate calculated from the earlier estimates of a gigantic weir.

At the end of the Lower Unit, near the 3-m level below Boston City Base in the sediments, there was a dramatic change in local conditions. Just prior to sediment dated ca. 3500 B.P., the quiet depositional environment was subjected to increased tidal amplitude and energy, elsewhere recognized as a change in the dynamics of the entire Gulf of Maine sea level and tidal system (Rosen et al. 1993). Our investigations in sediments close to Boylston Street implied that the new conditions characterized the sediments at the NEL site as well. Thus, the weir structures at the northern NEL site were larger than the earlier facilities, to resist increased tidal pressures. They were nearing the end of their useful lives as higher tides necessitated more frequent repairs and probably changed the available fish species. The increased amplitude and energy of the tides moved coarser sediment in the bay. In those conditions, the larger weirs at the NEL site probably trapped silt as well as fish. Siltation reduced weir use-life, making them less efficient and more expensive in terms of labor. The facilities were abandoned when continuing use became unfeasible on the original terms.

Shellfish remains associated with the early weirs at the lower, southern end of the area were considerably less abundant than at the NEL site, where oysters clung to stakes in such numbers as to provoke suggestions that the stakes were an oyster farm (Johnson 1942). Stakes would have been the only firm substrate for oyster attachment in the weir zone muds, which were otherwise suboptimal habitat for oysters; it is not surprising that oysters utilized the stakes when both were present. Abandoned stakes in offshore positions would have been the best environments for extended growth of individual oysters, away from human fingers and in clearer, faster water. We observed only three oysters on stakes in the southern area.

Sediment samples from the weir zone at the 500 Boylston Street site revealed a suite of shellfish species limited in comparison to the earlier study. Bivalves near the weir elements included little surf clam, oyster, soft-shell clam, macoma clam, blue mussels, and gem clam. Except for mud snail (*Ilyanassa obsoleta*), univalves were rare in the weir muds, while more diverse elsewhere. There were also barnacles and a few crab claws (Carlson 1988). The most environmentally sensitive of these species live in shallow water, near or below low tide level.

Fish remains were more scarce than we expected, but enough were recovered from sediment flotation to permit identification of about half of the 113 elements and fragments recovered (Carlson 1990). The dominant species in the samples was *Microgadus tomcod*, with vertebrae of flounder, eel, and herring, and one fragment of a sturgeon skute (a specialized skin structure) present. Modern warm, brackish, shallow estuarine waters in southern New England are home to several genera of small fish; prominent among them mummichogs, or killyfish. These little fish move inshore with the tide in brackish, shallow waters. "At ebb tides [they] are often trapped in little pools where they remain until the next tide . . ." (Bigelow and Schroeder 1953:163). No mummichog bones were recovered, possibly because of their small size and fragility. Nevertheless, it is tempting to see the small weir units trapping fish on the ebb tide, as do natural tidal pools. Observant Native Americans could easily create their own versions of tidal pools located conveniently near their dwellings.

CONSTRUCTION AND MAINTENANCE

Stakes for the weirs were collected from living trees in nearby forests during the dormant season, not in the early spring as was the case with the stakes at the NEL site (Kaplan et al. 1990). Deciduous species dominate. Young branches and shoots were selected for straightness, length of a meter or two, and diameter less than 3 cm (smaller than the 5-cm mode at NEL). They were snapped off at the trunk, rarely pointed with tool scars. Axial branches trimmed from the stakes, and probably others as well, were stockpiled with the stakes. The winter cull implies some level of planning for construction and repair of the weir.

Probably during the spring warming, people waded into the shallow near-shore waters to drive stakes into the mud, possibly simply by forcing. Some stones large enough to have served as hammers or mauls were found among the weir elements, but few of the upright stakes showed hammer damage at the upper end. However the stakes were driven, some penetrated the stiff blue glacial clay below the estuarine sediments.

Long lines and bands of upright stakes were driven roughly parallel to the sloping shore. Bundles of branches were forced down among them, to create a low wall of brushwork that probably filled the water column at low tide. Oblique uprights were possibly added after the brushwork, to stabilize it. We found no evidence that horizontal elements were woven around the stakes, as the term "wattling" implies. Instead, we found that many of the horizontal small elements had lateral branches on them. In the northern locations, near the NEL site and close to the time of increasing tidal energy, it was clear that branches had been bundled at their bases, possibly even tied as woody bouquets, before being forced down among the uprights.

Materials for weir building were collected in late winter during the middle and late fifth millennium, in the early spring during the first part of the fourth. None of this gives us solid evidence for the season of construction or use of the weirs, but it does implicate spring. In some places the muds preserved leaf elements, especially stems, indicating that leafy branches were sometimes used in the brushwork. Branches with full-grown leaves may have been used for repairs after summer storm damage; they would not have been available early in spring when weir-building is most efficient.

We found no artifacts in the muds except for the sharpened stakes and broken branches. Stones recovered among the stakes were unmodified and showed no use wear. Despite the most optimistic and dedicated search, the excavators found no trace of basketry, netting, or cordage that could have been part of a trap associated with weir leads. These simple structures were erected for efficient functioning on the model of tidal pools.

STAKES AND BRUSHWORK

Of 218 specimens of recovered wood submitted for identification, 210 could be identified to 16 species. The materials were predominantly hardwood saplings and branches; the only conifers used were hemlock, for about 3% of the samples, and two specimens each of *Juniperus* and unspecified "conifer." The dominant hardwood was beech at 29%, followed by oak, alder, and sassafras, with all other species represented by percentages below 10. The species selected were all present in the pollen spectrum or were expectable in the communities identified through pollen analysis. Selection of alder for stakes increased in frequency toward the north. The discrimination against white pine, an important contributor to the pollen rain, supports attribution of deliberate selection criteria to the builders of the weirs (Kaplan et al. 1990).

The wood chosen for the stakes consisted of straight, slender branches and saplings or sprouts. The great majority showed fewer than 25 annual growth rings (Ulan 1988). The exceptions to this were a few specimens with 25–45 rings, all but one of which were on the north (higher) end of the site. The observation that the largest stakes were on the north is significant; there were more thick stakes, and larger ones, at the NEL site than we found at the 500 Boylston Street site. The correlation of thicker stakes with the latest structures supports the evidence for increased tidal amplitude toward the top of the weir zone. We see the thicker stakes as the builders' response to greater tidal stresses on the structures late in the period of construction and use.

The saplings were normally inserted into the mud in growth position, with the thickest part down, with exceptions. Some few of the upper ends showed a kind of crushing damage, as might develop from pounding with a wooden or stone hammer. None of the tops lacking fresh breaks showed the scouring damage observed at NEL, nor were the tops all at the same elevation in the mud. The stakes that were driven deepest, into the Blue Clay, tended to have split lower ends and crushed tops, as if special effort had been expended to hammer them into the stiff substrate below the silt. A few cobble-sized stones in the silt showed that such expedient tools were available in the area.

Most of the stakes were emplaced vertically, but a notable number were strongly oblique, especially where the oblique stakes leaned with their tops to the east (uphill) at angles approximating 45°. It was not possible to determine whether the obliquity was an original characteristic or a later development created by sediment shifts.

The horizontal elements in the silts were called "wattling" from the

very earliest observations of the structures (Shimer 1918:459; Willoughby 1927), and this terminology was maintained by Johnson despite
his noting that there was no evidence for deliberate interweaving of the
horizontal elements among the vertical. None of the wood pieces lying
horizontally in the silts was bent in the way the vertical stakes were.
Wattling would produce stronger bends in horizontally "woven" smaller
components. Our wider experience with materials in situ led us to aban-
don the term "wattling," with its implications of craft, and adopt the term
"brushwork," which the Johnson team also used occasionally. There is
no evidence of any fastening of the horizontal to the vertical elements.
The picture emerges of lines of brush piles immobilized on the mud by
vertical stakes, perhaps steadied by the oblique stakes. The only artifacts
in the silts were the cut and pointed stakes and the cut and broken
branches, and the structures built with them.

FUNCTIONING OF THE WEIRS

Game fish—the salmon, sturgeon, or even alewives that come to mind
for weir fishing—seem unlikely denizens of the warm, shallow embayment. The traps were not big impoundments; they were artificial tidal
pools bordered by brushwork and the sloping exposed mud at low tide.
As such, they were effective only for small fish that might have been in
such waters in multitudes. Small fish could come in with the tide, swimming easily over the low barriers of brush if those did not reach the high
tide level. As the tide fell, the fish would be held in shallowing water
between the shore and brushwork walls, to make a ready meal for any
hungry human with a basket scoop (Figure 5.2).

Environmental contrasts, not changed social conditions, adequately explain the differences on the two sides of Boylston Street. The impressive
forest of stakes at NEL misled interpreters (cf. Dincauze 1985) about the
size of labor force and the populations supported by the weir fishing.
New insights bring the technology into the known world of the Late
Archaic peoples of southern New England, a world of cooperative extended family units extracting a good living from an environment that
yielded its abundance to their ingenuity and diligence.

The observed differences in the seasons in which the stakes were collected may also reflect conditions of local climate. The latest construc-
tions were built of stakes gathered in early spring; the older ones, in
perhaps a more temperate climate, were built from wood collected earlier
in the year. Exactly when during the year the weirs were erected and
used remains uncertain, but the observation of leaf stems in the north-

Figure 5.2
Artist's Conception of One of the Small Weirs in the Northwestern
Corner of the 500 Boylston Street Site

The emergence of the stakes implies extreme low tide; the size of the largest stakes is
congruent with one of the late weirs, ca. 3500 B.P. The shore behind the impound-
ment is peat marsh, with scrub forest beyond. The hills on the horizon are the Boston
Trimountain. The open ends are speculative; we did not observe any of the ends.

eastern corner implies that, at least there, some of the brushwork was
emplaced after the leafing-out of trees.

Small, low-energy fish traps would constitute elegantly efficient, simple, fully adequate technology for dependable protein collection by small
groups of people. The weirs can be thought of as casual coastal "larders,"
dependably available for gathering fresh fish at least at low tide twice a
day during the warm months. The labor involved in their construction
and maintenance was well within the capabilities of the Late Archaic
populations in New England at the time.

Furthermore, such efficiency and economy suits what we know about
Late Archaic food gathering technology. The Late Archaic period was a
time of maximum population density for non-farming people in southern
New England. During that time span, the archaeological record shows

that people rarely specialized in any classes of food resources. Rather, they learned to gather and hunt, and process and consume, most of the edibles in their various habitats. They were living not only off the fat of the land, but also off the abundance of the lower parts of the food ladders—seeds, shellfish, small animals, and small fish.

The lines of stakes in the Back Bay of the Late Archaic period did not intercept currents; they did not sweep fish into traps. They were passive constructs in the low tides lapping against the sloping shores. The technology and workforce available to Late Archaic societies were adequate to the task of constructing simple facilities to trap small fish swimming with the tide. Especially small bottom or shore feeders, whether schoolers or not, would be carried in with the flood across brush walls that extended little if any distance above mean sea level. At tidal ebb, bottom feeders would be trapped between the slope of the shore and the wall of brush, prey to any person equipped with a scoop, dip net, basket, or other tool for catching a bite of lunch. There was no need for canoes or other large equipment at such sites. Twice a day, the passive trap held a useful, but not overwhelming, amount of living protein food for anyone minded to make use of it. Women and children seem to us most likely to have been the habitual harvesters of such traps—patrons of a natural Automat.

Tomcod, the dominant fish species recovered, are bottom feeders living in shallow, brackish, or even fresh water. In recent centuries their habitats ranged from Nova Scotia to New Jersey. They spawn during the winter in estuaries, and may be numerous year-round. Adult individuals grow to 12–15 inches in length (Bigelow and Schroeder 1953:196–199). They can be taken in weirs or by hook and line. Their habits and size are compatible with the function of in-shore weirs of the sort we postulate. The surprise here is that tomcod are cold-tolerant to a degree unexpected in the Back Bay waters of the fifth and sixth millennia B.P.

Other species no doubt occasionally showed up in the slackwater pools on the shore side of the weirs. Smelt, which feed on mummichogs and sea worms, among other things, we know were present along the Bay (Bigelow and Schroeder 1953:136–137), might have arrived in considerable numbers in spring and fall, but they seem not to spend summer in very warm water. The weirs as we see them would be ideal smelt traps in season, and perhaps they were ready in season. Eels are known to occur in the habitats we have inferred (Bigelow and Schroeder 1953: 151–153). They are not likely to have been easily caught in the weirs, however, given their demonstrable abilities to slither around and through obstacles and to burrow into the mud. The bigger game fish—salmon, shad, and sturgeon—are not at issue in these waters; not even alewives are likely habitués.

There is no obvious reason to imagine that weirs such as we infer here would be limited in their usefulness to merely the warmer months, although the winter take would surely be much reduced. We have no evidence, either, to think that shore ice was a major hazard in the fifth and early fourth millennia B.P., although the low salinity of the Bay waters and the shallowness could have allowed ice to form on and near the fringing marshes. The collecting seasons indicated for the stakes and branches do imply that the weirs were intended to be repaired and rebuilt soon after early spring, and we can agree that such seasonality would put them in shape for their best use at the time of richest harvest—smelt runs are a major social, cultural, and economic event along the Gulf of Maine wherever they are still intact.

Conditions such as existed along the Back Bay 4000–5000 years ago do not exist now. The reconstruction that incorporates all the information we have been able to acquire about the structures in the mud is nevertheless speculative because we have no way to test it in use. No similar fish traps appeared in the literature search of 1985 (Carlson 1985). Since then, comparable structures have been described from the West Coast (Byram 1998:206; Moss and Erlandson 1998). Apparently, similar weirs were in use at Chiloé island off the coast of Chile at the beginning of the eighteenth century. "They were made, according to Father Agueros, by walls made of stakes and interlaced branches; the Chiloé fisherfolk call them "corrals" and they could harvest at a single time of low sea level up to five hundred *robalos*" (Emperaire 1955:208; translated from the French by Dincauze).

Coastal facilities such as these contrast significantly with the construction and function of the freshwater river weirs of the Late Archaic period elsewhere in the Northeast (Johnston and Cassavoy 1978; Petersen et al. 1994). River weirs were built across channels, obstructing currents. They were built with larger stakes, often driven into gravel stream beds, and may well have involved more effort and labor to build and maintain than did the small facilities in the Back Bay muds. If built to intercept spawning runs, such river facilities would have been strongly seasonal, requiring storage techniques for best use.

No prehistoric living sites were identified during the investigations near Boylston Street. However, our perusal of engineering cores curated by the Boston Society of Civil Engineers suggested that a small alley nearby (see Arlington Street in Figure 5.1) may overlie the remains of a midden with shellfish. Black earth with shell fragments is near the shore of fishweir times.

Historically, weirs are important places on the landscape. Their locations were widely known, and people congregated regularly during the appropriate seasons. Beyond their roles as food sources, they were also social nexuses where people could go when they needed to find others or to exchange information. In the seventeenth century, Edward Winslow, traveling with guides from Plymouth Colony in search of Massasoit, was taken to a weir on Nemasket River, as the guides searched for food and information (Heath 1969:60–68).

CONCLUSION

People in southern New England in the Late Archaic period lived prosperously, in terms of their needs, by gathering and hunting wild foods. Their ability to utilize almost everything the environment offered provided a healthy, diverse diet that supplied all essential nutrients. The Back Bay weirs might have supported a larger local human population than would have lived near those shores otherwise, and numbers of people always affect other living things in the neighborhood. However, we found no clear evidence for any increase in local brush and forest fires such as we had expected.

Instead of a single huge structure built to trap large fish, new investigations revealed that the weirs under Boston were built (1) over a long period of time; (2) on a sloping foreshore; (3) as small units that had a relatively short use-life; (4) in a brackish estuary with a low tidal amplitude but rising sea level; (5) parallel to the shore near the low tide line; (6) in ways that required a very small, local labor force; (7) in order to produce a dependable but not dramatic supply of marine proteins; and (8) conformably to what we know elsewhere of cultural values and lifeways characteristic of the fifth and fourth millennia before the present (Dincauze 1998:90).

ACKNOWLEDGMENTS

The study which this chapter reports was funded by Gerald D. Hines Interests, of Dallas, Texas, as part of their development of the building site at 500 Boylston Street in Boston. The archaeological contracting was done by Timelines, Inc., of Littleton, MA. The authors thank especially the crew who endured with reliable good humor the rigors of wet, damp conditions at hard labor: Elena Décima (crew chief), Victoria Bunker, Edna Feighner, Steve Mrozowski, and George Stillson. Brona Simon and Stephen Pendery administered the CRM aspects of the work for the state and the city, respectively. The authors are especially grateful to the consultants whose analytical work teased out meaning from the chaos of the field: Catherine Carlson, R. Bruce Hoadley, Lawrence Kaplan, Paige Newby, Robin Rice, Peter Rosen, Lynn Maybury, Linda Ulan, and significantly, Beta Analytic, Inc. Kerry Lynch provided additional perspectives in a term paper at the University of Massachusetts at Amherst. An earlier version of this chapter, with the same title but different text and lavish illustrations, was presented by Décima at the annual meeting of the Northeastern Anthropological Association in 1995. Elaine Chamberlain prepared Figures 5.1 and 5.2.

PART II

LITHIC ANALYSIS

6

A Petrographic Assessment of Stone Tool Materials in New England

Barbara L.A. Calogero

INTRODUCTION

Some areas of the United States have limited sources of rock, whereas New England has numerous bedrock exposures and glacial deposits with rock cobbles that provided Native American knappers with a variety of materials for stone tools. The complex geology of the region is a result of the tectonic assemblage of island arcs and terranes that formed most of New England. The variety of rocks complicates our task of identifying artifact rock types. It also provides us the opportunity to appreciate knappers' cleverness in finding suitable tool material from many sources, and it offers some clues to trade. A reliable assessment of prehistoric behavior patterns based upon lithic assemblages is possible only if stone tools and flakes are identified accurately.

Archaeologists traditionally identify artifact rock types macroscopically, but geologists consider this method too problematic especially if a rock has been removed from its geological context. They prefer to identify a rock after examining it microscopically in thin section. A thin section is a slice of rock glued to a glass slide and ground to a thickness of 30 microns. At this thickness the rock is sufficiently thin to allow light to pass through it, revealing its crystalline fabric and constituent minerals. With the aid of a petrographic microscope equipped with polarizing lenses, most rock types can be identified and matched to known geological formations. This method, known as petrography, can expose macroscopic misidentifications as well as provide new information about the rocks that tool knappers selected.

In this chapter, I explain the usefulness of petrography before reviewing the geology of New England and its many resources used by prehistoric Native American tool knappers. The regional descriptions will be followed by examples of artifact rocks matched to specific sources through the use of petrography.

ROCK IDENTIFICATION

Before I had learned to prepare rocks in thin section or recognized the value of the technique, I began by simply counting tools and waste flakes by rock type that I viewed as hand specimens in assemblages from central Connecticut. There were far too many "unknowns" or "other" types in each assemblage that I could not identify macroscopically. Many were dark rocks with tan weathered rinds that might be basalt. One looked like a muddy chert. Others were totally unfamiliar to me. I resorted to the non-destructive method, X-ray fluorescence (XRF), to analyze the trace elements of several artifacts for further information that could lead to their identification. The XRF results for the "chert" flake were confusing. It was necessary to make a thin section of the flake to determine its identity as a hornfels, a contact-metamorphosed sedimentary rock (Calogero and Philpotts 1987). I was not familiar with hornfels nor were other archaeologists working in Connecticut (Calogero 1991).

Since that revelation of new information through thin-section analysis, I have relied upon petrography for identifying artifact rocks. There is not sufficient time or resources to examine all tools and flakes so intensively; however, I have found that petrographic analysis of even a small sample of lithic artifacts can provide insight into the diversity of rock types in an assemblage. The method is destructive, and therefore it is preferable to make thin sections of waste flakes. A portion of each flake can be used for thin section and the rest preserved to create a comparative collection of identified rocks for an assemblage.

Some rocks are easily recognizable macroscopically such as quartz, quartzite, and chert, but more can be learned about quartzite and chert when viewed in thin section. For example, the quartzite may have been milled by fault movement and recrystallized into exceptionally fine-grained mylonite. The chert may show bedding and fossils of marine plankton, indicative of its formation in a shallow sea. If chert formed in limestone, it may have rhombic-shaped inclusions of dolomite. Chert deposits in rock rich in minerals will be colored by those minerals. Pulses of silica-rich heated groundwater may have created feathery deposits of chert referred to as chalcedony. What can be learned through petrography of other rocks such as basalt, hornfels, siltstone, or rhyolite? Is the basalt characteristic of local basalt formations? Is it from a flow, dike, or sill? Is the hornfels typical of nearby sources, or was it imported from elsewhere? Is the siltstone like local siltstone sources? Is the rhyolitic rock from a flow, or is it a welded ash flow tuff? Have any of these rocks been altered through regional metamorphism? Questions such as these can be answered through petrographic analysis and in consultation with regional geologists.

In order to appreciate the challenges and opportunities facing prehistoric tool knappers in search of useful tool materials in what is now New England, it is important to recognize the diversity in the resources available to them. I note some of those rocks that have been identified in artifact assemblages, but no doubt there are others. Geological descriptions of the region are drawn from a field guide of the Northern Appalachian terranes of New England compiled by Zen (1989), as well as other field guides compiled by the New England Intercollegiate Geological Conferences.

GEOLOGY OF NEW ENGLAND

During the Paleozoic Era (570–225 million years ago), three continental plates merged to form a supercontinent (Larsen and Birkeland 1982). Ancient North America and ancient Eurasia collided to form Laurasia, which in turn collided with Gondwanaland to form Pangea. New England lay at the juncture of these three ancient continents where beaches, island arcs, and peninsulas were welded together. The estimated boundaries of these different bedrock formations, called terranes, that formed New England are indicated by dashed lines in Figure 6.1.

Western New England periodically experienced marine inundation that created a sequence of sedimentary limestones and cherts east of the Appalachian highlands (Zen 1989). As the Iapetus Ocean between the colliding plates began to close, the coastal beach sands, which now form a strandline of crystalline quartzites, were pushed up onto the shores of continental North America by at least seven exotic terranes (Zen 1989). The massive Cheshire quartzite formation that underlies Vermont's Green Mountains created by this collision has areas of fine-grained quartzites that were quarried prehistorically for tool materials (David Lacy, personal communication, 1993).

The first terrane, the Brompton-Cameron terrane, forms northeastern

Figure 6.1
Map of New England with Terrane Boundaries

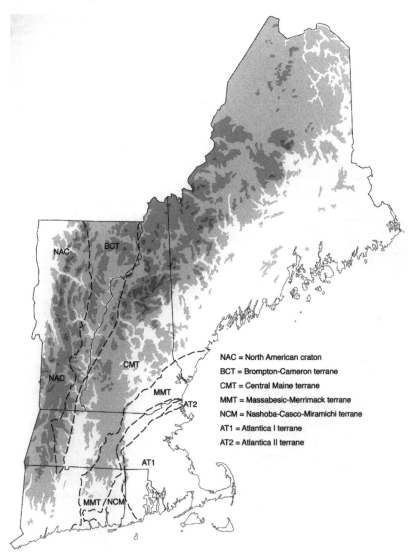

NAC = North American craton
BCT = Brompton-Cameron terrane
CMT = Central Maine terrane
MMT = Massabesic-Merrimack terrane
NCM = Nashoba-Casco-Miramichi terrane
AT1 = Atlantica I terrane
AT2 = Atlantica II terrane

Based on Zen 1989. Prepared by Pietro Calogero.

Vermont and extends south to include Hanover, New Hampshire; Bel-
lows Falls, Vermont; and a narrow portion of Massachusetts and Connecticut. It is believed to be dunite (ocean floor sediments) of the Iapetus
Ocean (Zen 1989). The dunite formations that are now serpentinites and

steatite or soapstone were quarried for bowls during the Terminal Archaic period (ca. 3600–2500 B.P.) (Figure 6.2A).

Much of the Connecticut River valley, New Hampshire, and central and northern Maine are part of the Central Maine terrane (Zen 1989). Part of this second exotic terrane was a volcanic island arc that included Mount Kineo rhyolite, Borestone Mountain's hornfels, and Traveler Mountain's rhyolitic welded ash flow tuff, commonly referred to as ignimbrite (Hanson 1995; Rankin 1995). Mount Kineo rhyolite occurs frequently in Maine's lithic assemblages but not hornfels, according to David Sanger (personal communication, 1995). North of Mount Katahdin and Munsungen Lake are the red, gray, green, and black cherts of Ledge Ridge (Pollock 1987) that were first quarried and used by Paleoindians (ca. 12,000–10,000 B.P.) in Maine (Gramly 1982; Pollock et al. 1995).

The Brompton-Cameron and the Central Maine terranes that napped or overrode and buried the edge of ancient North America were followed by the crystalline rocks of the Massabesic-Merrimack terranes (Zen 1989). These include the coarse-grained Clough quartzite and the finer-grained Plainfield quartzite formations in eastern Connecticut (Calogero and Philpotts 1995). Some areas of quartzite have been mylonitized or milled by movement at fault zones and recrystallized into exceptionally hard, fine-grained rock that knappers used for tools in central Connecticut (Calogero 1991) and elsewhere (Largy and Ritchie 2002; Volmar and Blancke, this volume).

East of the Lake Char-Honey Hill Fault in eastern Connecticut is the Nashoba-Casco-Miramachi terrane that extends from New London, Connecticut, to Newburyport, Massachusetts (Zen 1989). The fifth, sixth, and seventh terranes that comprise the easternmost portions of New England bedrock include the Avalon volcanic arc, called Atlantica I and II, and the Meguma terranes (Zen 1989). The western portion of the Avalon terrane in Massachusetts has a five-kilometer-wide band of sheared crystalline rock of the Westboro Formation quartzites and schists known as the Burlington Mylonite Zone (Skehan et al. 1998). Exceptional examples of mylonite tools and waste flakes have been recovered from archaeological sites in the area (Largy 1979; Largy and Ritchie 2002; Volmar and Blancke, this volume).

The rocks that ring the city of Boston are evidence of the volcanic history of the Avalon terrane before it was welded to North America (Zen 1989). The city of Boston is situated in an ancient caldera of an extinct volcano. The Lynn-Mattapan volcanics north and south of Boston include rhyolite flows and rhyolitic welded ash flow tuff of several ages but similar origins (Hermes et al. 2001; Hermes and Ritchie 1997). They

Figure 6.2
Photomicrographs of Thin Sections of Rock Types from Connecticut

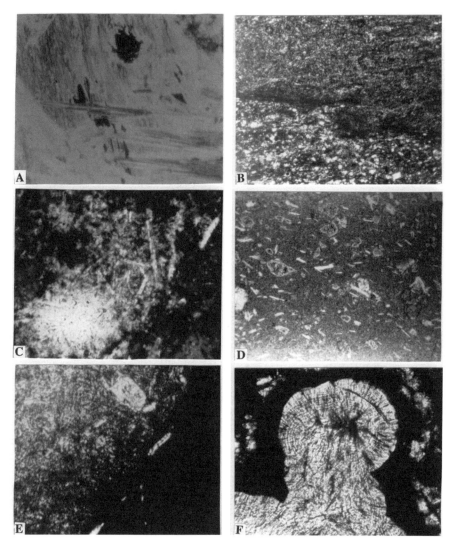

A. steatite, Barkhamsted (crossed polars, 10x); B. hornfels siltstone, Bugbee-Hathaway site, West Hartford (plane light, 10x); C. hornfels sandstone, Canal site, Granby (crossed polars, 40x); D. basalt, Alsop Meadow site, Avon (plane light, 10x); E. buttress dike basalt, Fisher Meadow site, Avon (plane light, 10x); F. chalcedony, Fisher Meadow site, Avon (crossed polars, 40x). Width of the field of view in A, B, D, and E is 1 mm, and C and F is 0.25 mm.

show little deformation from regional tectonism due to their late arrival or last emplacement (Zen 1989). The heat of the rhyolitic lava flows baked the underlying sedimentary rock, metamorphosing the contact margins into hornfels. One prehistoric hornfels quarry is associated with the volcanics in the Blue Hills, south of Boston (Ritchie and Gould 1985).

Atlantica's docking to North America is marked by an assemblage of rocks that include Carboniferous Age coal beds exposed in the Narragansett Basin of Rhode Island. Sedimentary rocks include shale, argillite, and silicified argillite with the more metamorphosed siliceous rocks occurring in southern Rhode Island as a result of regional tectonism (Zen 1989). The Narragansett Basin suite of rocks also include dark red jasper and chalcedony. Luedtke (1987a) noted that those in the modern Conklin quarry may not have been exposed prehistorically but that similar deposits and pebbles may have been available to tool knappers. Undeformed volcanic rhyolites, fossiliferous sediments, and green schists of Atlantica II are preserved in Newburyport, Massachusetts, and along the coast of Maine where the coastal volcanics are believed to be related in age to those of Newfoundland, an island that escaped attachment to North America (Zen 1989). The Meguma terrane is composed of sandstones, shales, and volcanics of Nova Scotia and the Gulf of Maine (Zen 1989).

As Pangea began to break apart during the Mesozoic Era, about 200 million years ago, rifts like those in East Africa today began to tear open; some stopped, leaving the Hudson and Hartford basin alignments (Philpotts and Martello 1986). Others continued to open between North America, Europe, and Africa creating the Atlantic Ocean. With stretching of the earth's crust, the increasing strain allowed the upwelling of magma from the upper mantle to intrude into and through the crust. The magma formed underground sills and lakes of lava called laccoliths. In southwestern New England where fissures extended to the surface, basaltic lava flooded large areas of the region. The first flow of basaltic lava, the Talcott, formed pillows of rock as it flowed into and cooled quickly in a shallow lake (Philpotts and Martello 1986). Two additional flows, the Holyoke and Hampden basalts, were separated by tens of thousands of years during which time meters of sediment accumulated on the previous flows. Molten lava of each successive flow coursing across the sediments baked the underlying sediments, metamorphosing the contact margins into fine-grained hornfels (Philpotts 1990). The hornfels margins are only centimeters thick. Additional rifting caused block faulting of the basalts, hornfels, and sedimentary layers of rock that created a ridgeline extending from Holyoke, Massachusetts, to New Haven, Connecticut (Philpotts and Martello 1986).

There is evidence that the North American Plate passed over two hot spots that caused plumes of magma to create intrusive dikes and batholiths such as Mount Ascutney, Vermont; the White Mountain series batholiths; and the many volcanic ring dikes in New Hampshire, all of which postdate the opening of the Atlantic (Zen 1989). The rock of these ring dikes and associated rocks provided useful tool materials. For ten thousand years, New England tool knappers used the rhyolitic rock from the Mount Jasper ring dike in Berlin, New Hampshire, and other volcanic sources in the state (Dincauze 1976; Gramly 1980, 1984; Luedtke 1980d, 1984b; Pollock et al. 1996) and later the syenitic igneous rock and exceptionally hard, uniformly crystalline hornfels associated with New Hampshire's Moat volcanics (Boisvert et al. 1993; Bunker and Potter 1993, 1994).

Erosion of the landforms was accelerated by glaciation. Bedrock striations indicate the northwest to southeast direction of flow of ice across New England, plucking, dragging, and pushing rocks from their bedrock sources. In this manner, resistant rocks were carried considerable distances southeast from their sources, enriching the glacial till that blankets New England. Cobbles of quartz and quartzite are two examples of rocks that are ubiquitous in the glacial till and streambeds, as well as in the region's archaeological assemblages (Calogero 1991).

Aboriginal people who entered the recently scoured and reshaped landscape approximately 12,000 years ago brought along stone tools of cryptocrystalline cherts with which they were familiar (Snow 1980). Out of necessity and curiosity, tool knappers looked for local sources of hard, fine-grained rock, and found those previously noted above that could provide sharp edges for cutting and piercing, as well as tough, durable rock that could be used for heavier tasks. The discovery and use, through time, of exceptional rock supports the notion that information about the sources of these local rocks was passed on to successive generations. Although cherts were transported or traded from the west, the rocks available in New England continued to be used (Calogero 1991).

SOURCE IDENTIFICATION

Pinpointing the sources of regional rocks that prehistoric Native American knappers used is complicated by New England's varied and complex geology. The same type of rock may have come from more than one bedrock source. Some rock sources are too limited geologically in size or significance to be depicted on the state maps of bedrock geology, but usually they are described in the text accompanying the maps.

Artifact rocks that are not directly associated with quarry sites can be matched to known sources at different levels of specificity, that is, by region, rock formation, or, in rare instances, an extraction point. The following are examples of artifact thin sections from Connecticut assemblages that could be matched petrographically to known sources. These exemplify the challenges and successes in rock identification using thin-section analysis. Of course, many more rock types than these few were used by the aboriginal knappers in the region (Calogero and Philpotts 1995).

Hornfels Siltstone

Hand specimens of fine-grained basalt, siltstone, and hornfels are often difficult or impossible to distinguish from one another (Calogero 1991, 1993). Feldspar minerals in these rocks are particularly susceptible to weathering caused by exposure to moisture and temperature changes. The feldspars alter to clay minerals, creating a tan weathered rind that has a musty odor when moist. The weathered rind, developed over time due to chemical and mechanical alteration, may have an entirely different color, texture, and hardness than the underlying fresh rock. Despite the appearance of tools and flakes recovered archaeologically, those artifacts were once hard fresh rock that knappers exposed and fashioned into tools.

When seen in thin section, many seemingly low-grade lithics turn out to be exceptionally hard, fine-grained rocks, and surprisingly often they are contact-metamorphosed hornfels, a rock type not previously identified in Connecticut assemblages (Calogero 1991; Calogero and Philpotts 1995) (Figure 6.2B). As noted earlier, some of the less-weathered dark, fine-grained hornfels have even been confused with chert (Calogero 1991). Previously mislabeled lithics revealed by thin-section analysis to be hornfels were identified in 18 of 24 sites from the Connecticut and Farmington valleys (Calogero 1991; Tryon and Philpotts 1997). The earliest radiocarbon date of charcoal associated with hornfels at a site in Connecticut is 5970 ± 250 B.P. (uncalibrated) at the Bugbee-Hathaway site in West Hartford in the Connecticut valley, and the most recent in the state is 320 ± 70 B.P. (uncalibrated) at the Whitney site on Avon Mountain ridge situated between the two river valleys (Calogero 1991).

The hornfels is from both local and nonlocal sources. The local sources of hornfels siltstone are the few centimeters-thick contact margins underlying the second and third basalt flows, the Holyoke and Hampden flows (Calogero and Philpotts 1987). The contact margins that may have been exposed at earlier times on the ridgeline are now buried under talus and vegetation, except where rivers and streams have cut down through the ridgeline rocks. Other contact margins are exposed in Tarriffville Gorge between Simsbury and Windsor where the Farmington River has cut through the upper two flows and sedimentary rock, and through most of the Talcott flow (Calogero and Philpotts 1995). The nonlocal sources of hornfels are to the west of New England in the Hudson valley, south of Peekskill, New York (Calogero and Philpotts 1995), and the Lockatong Formation shales in southeastern New York, north-central New Jersey, and northeastern Pennsylvania (Tryon and Philpotts 1997).

Hornfels Sandstone

Most of the hornfels that we have analyzed in thin section from Connecticut assemblages is contact-metamorphosed fine-grained siltstone (Calogero and Philpotts 1995). However, some unusual flakes and cores of hornfels recovered from the Granby Canal site in Granby were unlike any that I had seen previously. The numerous flakes and cores scattered on the site's surface included rough, coarse-grained, felsic or light-colored rock and dark, fine-grained rock, some of which had light tan ellipses. Only one quartz small-stemmed projectile point was recovered, but no charcoal or other diagnostic tools were collected (Calogero et al. 1995).

When geologist Philpotts analyzed the thin sections of 31 flakes and cores from the Granby Canal site, he immediately recognized these rocks as unusual hornfels sandstone from nearby Manitook Mountain. The site is in the lea of the mountain. Twenty-three lithic specimens were identified as hornfels sandstone, eleven had evidence of melting, and nine had needles of tridymite, a high temperature form of quartz (Philpotts, personal communication, 1994). Unlike baked but not melted hornfels, these specimens reflect exposure to a range of temperatures that caused not only heat alteration but also melting (Calogero et al. 1995). Variation in the artifact rocks analyzed petrographically suggests that the quarrier/knappers were chipping toward the most metamorphosed area of contact with the intrusive magma.

Manitook Mountain is a diabase basalt sill and laccolith that intruded into coarse arkosic sandstone and conglomerate during the Mesozoic era.

The contact of the laccolith with the underlying arkose is exposed in the floor of a modern quarry where a series of dikes snakes upward into soft sediment and sand. One edge of the quarry that would have been available to prehistoric quarriers has poorly cemented sedimentary rock baked up to a meter from the contact into a dark, massive hornfels. In thin section, fractured pebbles in the sandstone can be seen suspended in the fine-grained melt underlying the coarse diabase basalt (Calogero et al. 1995).

The hornfels formed under unusual conditions that are not fully understood. The temperature of diabase magma would have been sufficient to bake and metamorphose the arkosic sediments but not sufficient to melt them. However, there is no doubt that temperatures were high enough to cause substantial melting at one contact under the laccolith, possibly as a result of repeated surges of magma that caused the temperature to rise well above the melting point of the coarse, pebble-rich sandstone (Calogero et al. 1995). Melting occurred only where quartz and feldspar grains had come into contact with one another. The evidence is the zones of fine-grained material containing small white tridymite needles between these grains (Figure 6.2C). The melted and recrystallized hornfels sandstone now fractures right through the pebbles rather than around them, making the rock a suitable knapping material.

Basalt Flow

A rock formation such as a basalt dike, lava flow, or sill may be the source of stone tool material. If the formation is extensive, then the tool material might have been collected anywhere along the formation; however, the proximity of a knapping station targets a collection area. One example occurs at the Late Archaic (ca. 5000–3000 B.P.) Alsop Meadow site (4920 ± 250 B.P., uncalibrated), on the second terrace of the Farmington River in Avon, Connecticut, excavated by Feder (1981). More than 10,000 flakes and broken tools of fine-grained rock were recovered. I selected 11 flakes from one excavation unit for thin-section analysis. Two were identified petrographically as hornfels siltstone, and one was hornfels sandstone like that found at Manitook Mountain discussed above. Eight were olivine-bearing Talcott basalt (Calogero and Philpotts 1995). Four of the eight basalt thin sections had a trachytic texture, a description that indicates an alignment of the feldspar phenocrysts in the dark, crystalline groundmass. This texture is a result of a thin layer of lava flowing across dry ground, unlike the rest that tumbled into a shallow lake (Figure 6.2D). The other four basalt flakes were characteristic of the lower chill margins of the flow where the lava cooled quickly and crystallized into fine-grained rock. An exposure of the Talcott flow is visible from the Alsop Meadow site. There are other exposures of the Talcott flow along the north-south trending ridgeline that extends from Holyoke, Massachusetts, to New Haven, Connecticut, but it is reasonable to assume that the Alsop Meadow tool knappers collected the fine-grained material from the source less than a kilometer from their work-shop.

Buttress Dike and Chalcedony

Finding an artifact of another distinctive source of tool material, a buttress dike, was serendipitous. I had been measuring the depth of weathered rind development on hornfels flakes in a number of assem-blages from east and west of the ridgeline that separates the Connecticut and Farmington valleys. One of the flakes that I prepared in thin section was from the Middle Woodland (ca. 2000–1000 B.P.) Fisher Meadow site (1590 ± 100 B.P., uncalibrated) in Avon, also excavated by Feder (1981). It was not hornfels but rather basalt from a buttress dike that was created by a second pulse of magma injected into an earlier dike (Philpotts, personal communication, 1994). A portion of the centimeter-wide thin section is a dark fine-grained basalt with only a few white feldspar phenocrysts against a coarser-grained diabase (Figure 6.2E). A portion of the dike is exposed in the Farmington River in Unionville where it creates rapids in mid-stream. The rock has been identified ge-ologically and mapped as a buttress dike, one of only two that have been identified in the state; the other is in New Haven (Philpotts and Martello 1986). A quarrier/knapper easily could have collected the fine-grained material while in a canoe or by wading into the shallow rapids to collect the rocks to be transported north several kilometers to the Avon site.

The fine-grained flake reflects the tool knappers' curiosity and exper-imentation with new material sources, but this was not the only unusual lithic material in the assemblage. In addition to quartz, quartzite, basalt, hornfels, and imported chert, there was another form of chert, a yellow and reddish-brown chalcedony (Calogero 1991) (Figure 6.2F). A local source of chalcedony is the feathery deposits of silica formed in the interstices of the cooling Talcott pillow basalts by pulses of silica-rich hot water. Fist-sized blocks of chalcedony have been recovered by rock collectors where the Talcott basalt has been disturbed by modern exca-vation for roads and a shopping mall in Farmington (Norman Gray, personal communication, 1988). It is rare in the area's assemblages (Calogero and Philpotts 1995).

DISCUSSION

A number of archaeologists have resorted to petrography and geo-chemical analyses to improve the accuracy of their assessment of lithic artifacts and sources. They include Didier (1974, 1975), Kenyon (1977), Lalish (1979), Lavin (Prothers and Lavin 1990), Luedtke (1976, 1978b, and 1979), Ritchie (Hermes et al. 2001), Strauss (Strauss and Murray 1988), and Volmar and Blancke (this volume). Prothers and Lavin (1990) created a catalogue of macroscopic and microscopic descriptions and photomicrographs of thin sections to facilitate matching cherts with their sources in the Delaware River watershed of New Jersey and New York. Luedtke (1992) created an index of cherts by source, macroscopic and petrographic descriptions, and geochemistry for the eastern United States. Hermes et al. (2001), Hermes and Ritchie (1997), and Luedtke et al. (1998) have expanded upon Luedtke's (1980d) earlier study of New England volcanics by comparing petrographic and geochemical analyses of rhyolitic artifacts with volcanic rocks from specific formations and quarries in southern New England.

As Luedtke (1993) has emphasized, any discussion of lithic resource use and exchange patterns of lithic material requires accurate supporting data. Most siliceous obsidian, quartz, quartzite, chert, and rhyolite can be identified macroscopically, although microscopic analysis of these rocks in thin section may reveal more information about them. For rocks that cannot be easily identified as hand specimens, most can be identified when viewed in thin section. Geochemical data may be necessary to identify the few that cannot be identified petrographically and also to match the specimens to possible rock sources.

Lithic analysis requires correct rock identification before geochemical studies are undertaken. Siliceous obsidian, quartz, quartzite, chert, and rhyolitic rocks usually can be identified macroscopically, although thin-section analysis may reveal more information about these rocks that might be helpful in matching them to sources. For all those rocks that cannot be easily identified as hand specimens, thin-section preparation and analysis is necessary. Once it is known what a rock is, then geo-chemical data may be useful to match the rock to possible sources.

Petrographic assessment of artifacts has revealed that knappers were extremely particular about what they selected for tool materials. Rock sources and formations are not uniform throughout. With few exceptions, the rocks used for sharp-edged tools are extremely fine-grained examples of each rock type indicating selection even within a single rock face or quarry (Calogero and Philpotts 1995). However, many of the rocks that toolmakers chose from New England sources do not fit the criteria of desirable rocks outlined by flint knapper Donald Crabtree (1972). He graded rock suitable for tool knapping using the following desirable and undesirable properties. According to his assessment, a desirable material is "isotropic, cryptocrystalline, homogeneous, elastic, vitreous, and [available in] adequate size"; and an undesirable lithic material has "cleavage planes, inclusions, non-homogenous, vesicular, inherent stress or strain, crystal pockets, fissures, checks, molecular imbalance, and frozen [sic]" (Crabtree 1972:18). Obsidian, most cherts, and some hornfels have the desirable properties he listed. Most New England rocks have less desirable properties: quartz has cleavage planes and fissures; quartzite is granular; rhyolite may have large phenocrysts that interrupt fracturing; basalt may have phenocrysts and gas vesicles that may check or interrupt fracturing; some hornfels may check; amphibolite schist and mylonite have stress or strain; and finally, chalcedony, jasper, silicified sandstone, siltstone, shale, and argillite may include fissures and crystal pockets. Nevertheless, these and a host of other rocks are represented in the lithic assemblages from New England (Calogero and Philpotts 1995). What has been remarkable to note in the hundreds of thin sections analyzed is that knappers frequently chose extremely unusual or rare rock, some of which can be puzzling to identify by even the most experienced geologist (Calogero and Philpotts 1995).

CONCLUSION

New England's geological resources were valuable to people dependent upon stone tools for their daily tasks and livelihood. Unlike some regions where bedrock exposures are rare, such as in the Midwest, prehistoric knappers in New England had much from which to choose. It is evident that petrographic assessment of those tool materials has revealed that knappers used many more and very specific rock types than those identifiable through hand sample analysis alone. Furthermore, matching rocks to their sources requires assistance from geologists familiar with the region's lithics. Whenever I think that I have done enough thin sections for New England, I am confronted with new information from analyzing petrographically yet another group of stone artifacts.

ACKNOWLEDGMENTS

I am indebted to Anthony Philpotts of the University of Connecticut Department of Geology and Geophysics for his collaborative assistance in this research. Pietro Calogero prepared Figure 6.1, and I took the photographs in Figure 6.2.

7

Late Woodland Lithic Resource Use and Native Group Territories in Eastern Massachusetts

Duncan Ritchie

INTRODUCTION

Lithic resource use during the Middle and Late Woodland periods (ca. 2000–500 B.P.) was one of the many aspects of prehistory studied by Barbara Luedtke during her several years of research in the Boston Harbor district in Massachusetts. She was interested in how the distribution of certain lithic materials might reflect settlement systems and group territories of Native Americans in this coastal area during the latter part of the Woodland period. During her study of assemblages from sites on Thompson Island, Luedtke (this volume) found that two large habitation sites at the northern and southern ends of the island had contrasting sets of lithic materials. The northern site contained specific rhyolites (Saugus jasper and Melrose green) from source areas in the Middlesex Fells north of the harbor district, while the site on the southern end of the island had hornfels (Braintree hornfels) from the Blue Hills along the southern boundary of the Boston basin. The presence of lithic materials from sources both north and south of Boston Harbor suggested that Middle and Late Woodland groups based in the Mystic and Neponset estuaries may have shared the use of this island (Luedtke 1997, 1998a, this volume) (Figure 7.1).

In testing this observation with assemblages from other parts of Boston Harbor, Luedtke (1997, this volume) found that sites on islands in the central/northern half of the harbor had higher percentages of Melrose

Figure 7.1
Location of Lithic Source Areas in Relation to Approximate Territories of Native American Groups in Eastern Massachusetts During the Early Historic Period

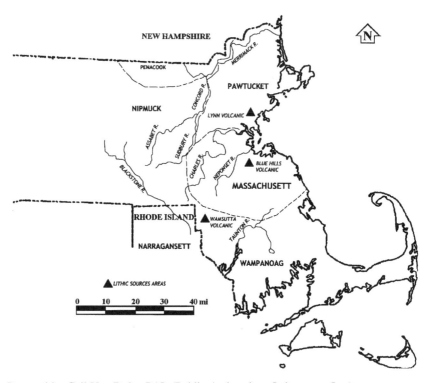

Prepared by Gail Van Dyke, PAL (Public Archaeology Laboratory, Inc.).

green and Saugus jasper rhyolites from sources in the Middlesex Fells area. Sites located on islands in the southern half of the harbor had more hornfels from the Blue Hills source (Luedtke 1997). The hornfels may have had social or ideological importance due to either its appearance or association with the Blue Hills, a major landmark within the former territory of the Massachusett group (Luedtke 1997:17; 1998a:28). The "Saugus jasper" and "Melrose green" rhyolites from source areas to the north of the Boston Harbor district are also visually distinct and could have signified group affiliation or identity for the people using them. The sources of these rhyolites were within an area occupied by the Pawtuck-eog or Pawtucket, a group whose territory extended along the coastal zone and interior uplands north of the Mystic River estuary.

Luedtke (1997:7) made a useful distinction between "generic" and "name-brand" lithic materials. Generic materials have a widespread distribution, or can be obtained from more than one source and are common in lithic assemblages. In the Boston Harbor district, generic materials are mostly gray and black rhyolites from the Lynn volcanic complex, present at outcrops in the Middlesex Fells north of the harbor and also common in cobble form on beaches in this district. "Name-brand" materials such as the Saugus jasper and Melrose green rhyolites, and Braintree hornfels are visually distinct and come from specific, well-defined sources. The sources for Saugus jasper and Melrose green rhyolites are very small and restricted to narrow flows or dikes of fine-grained material within larger bodies of volcanic rocks. Petrographic and geochemical analyses have also shown that these rhyolites, associated with the Lynn volcanic complex, and the Braintree hornfels all have distinct features that allow them to be identified in archaeological contexts (Luedtke 1997:6; Luedtke et al. 1998; Ritchie 1998). The "name-brand" materials have the potential to serve as useful markers of lithic procurement behavior of specific source areas that supplied material to the Native American groups occupying the Boston Harbor Islands.

In this chapter, a sample of Late Woodland projectile points and other data from eastern Massachusetts are examined to pursue evidence for associations between the distribution of certain lithic materials, such as the "name-brand" types described above, and Late Woodland sociopolitical boundaries first noted in the Boston Harbor district by Dincauze (1974:55,56) and Luedtke (1997, 1998a). Another objective is to trace the possible extent of this association or pattern of lithic resource use in areas west and south of Boston Harbor that probably formed the inland sections of Late Woodland group territories based in the coastal/estuarine zone. The potential importance of the proximity of late prehistoric and early historic sachemships to lithic source areas and use of specific lithic materials that could have carried information about group identity is also explored.

River basin territorially has a long history in southeastern New England with evidence for it extending back into the Middle Archaic period to at least 7500 B.P. The focus of settlement within major drainage systems was a pattern continued by Native American populations into the late prehistoric period. In the Late Woodland and Contact periods (ca. 1000–300 B.P.), foraging horticultural groups occupying lowland river valleys focused on arable lands, with the most intensive settlement probably taking place in the vicinity of fishing stations. Inland groups may have been affiliated with others based in the coastal zone, a reflection of the strong orientation of Middle to Late Woodland period settlement to this environmental setting (Mulholland 1988:147,152). By the latter part of this period, sedentary settlement may have taken place in coastal areas with good access to such important resources as shellfish beds, planting fields, and estuaries supporting migratory waterfowl and anadromous fish runs (Bernstein 1990; McManamon 1986). Within inland areas, some semi-sedentary settlement in the Late Woodland period may have occurred at a few specific locations near river or lakeside fishing stations and land suitable for horticulture. Evidence of year-round or sedentary Late Woodland occupation in eastern Massachusetts, however, has remained elusive, and there may have been a variety of dispersed settlement patterns in use across southeastern New England during this period (Luedtke 1988:62–63; Kerber 1988). The controlling positions, centered in coastal/estuarine areas with their high resource density and diversity, may have been maintained through reciprocity from within and outside a core territory. Coastal people had tribute alliances with adjacent inland groups, enabling inland populations to exploit estuarine resources (Mulholland 1988:154,163–164). Movement of some inland resources from the interior to coastal groups could also have been an element of reciprocal tribute alliances.

The long distance transport of lithic materials such as chert and jasper from outside the southeastern New England region, so characteristic of the latter part of the Middle Woodland period, was replaced by increased use of locally available stone in the Late Woodland period after about 1200 B.P. (Luedtke 1987a; Dincauze 1974:55–56). This shift in lithic resource use may reflect such ongoing processes as increased sedentism, decline of long distance interaction, and differentiation of group territories (Goodby 1992:3). There is also evidence that Late Woodland populations developed stronger associations with geographic provinces or smaller units such as drainage basins and their important resources or environmental features. During the Late Woodland and Contact periods, two concentrations or core areas of settlement appear to have been present within the Boston basin and surrounding uplands of the Middlesex Fells and Blue Hills. These core areas were centered on the ecologically diverse environments found within the Mystic and Neponset River estuaries on the northern and southern edges of the Boston Harbor district. From these estuaries, the Neponset and Mystic cores extended inland along these river drainages into the adjacent uplands to include some of the major ponds and tributary stream systems. Those Harbor Islands in close proximity to the Mystic and Neponset estuaries were also apparently part of the core areas of Late Woodland period activity (Massachusetts Historical Commission [MHC] 1982:28–29). These core areas also contained important lithic sources. Within the Neponset core were sources of rhyolite and hornfels quarried at several locations within the Blue Hills. The Mystic core also contained places where outcrops of rhyolite were quarried during the Woodland period.

Large settlements in the Boston Harbor district were at estuary heads on the Mystic, Charles, and Neponset Rivers. They may have functioned as base camps used during seasonal aggregations of people timed to natural events such as spring alewife runs. The groups occupying these drainages made chipped-stone tools with lithic materials from local sources within their own territories. Rhyolites from the Middlesex Fells were used in the Mystic and Saugus basins, and other types of stone (i.e., rhyolite and hornfels) from the Blue Hills were important materials in the Neponset and Monatiquot-Fore River area (Dincauze 1974:53,55–56).

ETHNOHISTORIC DATA

Two primary centers or cores of early historic Native American settlement in the Boston basin and surrounding sections of eastern Massachusetts are recognized by most historic accounts from the early to mid-seventeenth century and recent ethnohistoric research. These core areas are associated with the Pawtuckeog or Pawtucket and Massachusett groups based in areas to the north and south of Boston Harbor, respectively. Presumably, these group territories had some antiquity in this area and also existed in the late prehistoric period.

The major leaders or sachems for these two groups in the early seventeenth century were based in villages located in areas with horticultural land and other important natural resources such as fishweir or trap sites, centered on coastal estuaries and the lower portions of the Mystic, Saugus, and Neponset drainages. The Charles River may have been a recognized boundary between these two related, but differently identified, groups with territories located to the north and south of this drainage (Dincauze 1974:57).

Pawtuckeog/Pawtucket

Pawtuckeog/Pawtucket territory extended across the area north and east of the Charles River and was bounded on the north by the Merrimack River. It stretched along the coastal zone from the Charles and Mystic estuaries north to the Salem Harbor area and Cape Ann into southern Maine (Gookin [1792] 1970:10; Dincauze 1974:57; Salwen

1978). In northeastern Massachusetts, the Pawtucket living along the lower Merrimack River were closely connected through kinship ties with Penacook groups from further north. Seventeenth-century Pawtucket groups in the area near the present town of Chelmsford (Wamesit) and the Concord/Merrimack River confluence were intermarried with Penacook bands from further north in the Merrimack drainage (Leavenworth 1999:277). The Sudbury and Concord Rivers apparently formed the inland limits of Pawtucket territory, with the Nipmuck occupying the area west of these drainages. Further north, the area near the confluence of the Concord and Merrimack Rivers was along the interface between Pawtucket, Nipmuck, and Penacook lands.

Settlements or villages occupied by Pawtucket leaders were located around the mouth of the Mystic River and adjacent estuaries in the 1620s and 1630s. Nanepashemet was the sachem in this area until his death in 1619; authority over traditional landholdings was inherited by his wife, known as Squaw sachem. Their three sons were also sachems with territories centered on coastal drainages from the Mystic basin to the Salem Harbor area. Woenohaquaham, known to the English as Sagamore John, lived at a settlement located in the Mystic River/Alewife Brook area, near present Medford. Montowompate, also known as Sagamore James, resided at a village located on or near the Saugus River, in the Lynn/Saugus/Nahant area. Wenepoykin, or Sagamore George, was a local sachem in the Salem Harbor area (Salwen 1978; Salisbury 1982:183–184). In 1638, the Squaw sachem retained a small reserve of land within the original Pawtucket homeland located along the Mystic drainage, in parts of the present towns of Medford, Arlington, and Winchester (MHC 1982: 45).

English transactions for land in Charlestown, Cambridge, and Concord involving Squaw sachem indicate the extent of Pawtucket lands beyond the Mystic River estuary. A 1635 English land purchase from Squaw sachem for a plantation at Concord shows that this territory extended inland to at least a portion of the Sudbury/Concord drainage. This transaction was witnessed by Jethro, Jehojakim, Tahattawan, and Nimrod, who appear to be local sachems or leaders. Weppacowet, the Squaw sachem's second husband, was also present at this transfer of ownership. A boundary between Pawtucket and Nipmuck lands apparently existed in the middle Sudbury River drainage. When land there was sold to English settlers in the mid-seventeenth century, the vicinity of the fall-line on the Sudbury River, in what is now the Saxonville section of Framingham, was claimed by Native American proprietors based at Nashobah (Littleton), a Nipmuck settlement. In the 1630s, the Nipmuck leader Awassamaug, whose territory appears to have included the middle and upper Sudbury basin, married the daughter of Squaw sachem, and resided for some time at one of the Mystic estuary settlements. Similar connections between neighboring Pawtucket and Nipmuck groups, through the families of sachems or other traditional leaders, probably occurred in the late prehistoric period. Lands described as ancestral holdings by the Awassamaug family when they were sold to new English owners were bounded on the north and southeast by the Sudbury and Charles Rivers, respectively, and extended southwest through the upper Sudbury drainage to the Blackstone River. These land holdings also apparently included the Assabet drainage near the town of Marlborough (Temple [1887] 1988:38–40,48; Leavenworth 1999:282–283).

Massachusett

The area south of the Charles River and north of an approximate boundary in the upper Taunton River basin was occupied by the Massachuseog or Massachusett. The lower Neponset River basin and Blue Hills formed a core area for this territory. A center of political authority or sachemship was based at Moswetusset Hummock, a settlement with an associated fall-line fishing station and planting fields in the Neponset estuary (Clapp 1859; MHC 1982). The western limit of their homeland may have been along the headwaters of the Charles River basin. The early seventeenth-century Massachusett sachem Chickatawbut claimed land between the Neponset and Charles Rivers at the time of establishment of the Dedham Grant by the English in the 1630s (Tilden 1887: 21–22).

The lower Charles River may have been a boundary between adjacent Massachusett and Pawtucket groups. Nonantum, an early seventeenth-century Massachusett village associated with the sachem Waban, was located along the lower Charles River near present-day Newton (Mandell 1996:14). Further upstream, a fishing station at the Hemlock Gorge Rockshelter, in what is now Newton Upper Falls, also appears to have been in Massachusett territory based on ownership claims made in the early eighteenth century (Dincauze 1975:8–9). There is some possibility, however, that the Charles drainage also contained a third group territory or sachemship during the early historic period (Dincauze 1974:57; Salwen 1978:167–170).

In the early seventeenth century, Massachusett territory apparently also extended well into southeastern Massachusetts. Its southern limit was located along the upper Taunton River and probably followed the upper

North River to the coastal zone north of Plymouth Harbor. This boundary was most likely a flexible one, as some parts of the upper Taunton basin were also part of Wampanoag lands. For example, in 1649 the Wampanoag sachem Massasoit sold land to the English in an area known as Satucket, now within the towns of East Bridgewater, and parts of Abington and Hanson (Hurd 1884). The southern edge of Massachusett territory under the control of Chickatawbut and affirmed by other Native American leaders in a mid-seventeenth-century deposition extended from Duxbury southwest to the Titicut district on the upper Taunton River (Bridgewater/Middleborough) and then slightly northwest to Nippenicket Pond (Raynham) and west to Wanamampuke (Wolomonopog) or Lake Pearl in Wrentham (Chaffin 1886:29) This description would place the western limit of Massachusett lands on the upper Charles drainage. Later documents describing ownership claims also indicate a Massachusett presence in the upper North and Taunton River basins in the Titicut district and the Pembroke Ponds district (Mattakeset), in the present towns of Pembroke and Hanson. The Pembroke Pond/Mattakeset area was included in a 1662 deed of land from the Massachusett leader Josiah Wampatuck to Josiah Winslow of Marshfield (Hurd 1884:340; Gardner 1996:19). As late as the 1690s, the Titicut area was still identified as ancestral Massachusett land by descendants of sachem Josiah Wampatuck, a resident of the Ponkapoag area (Mandell 1996:71).

Lithic Source Areas

The core or central areas of the Pawtucket and Massachusett group territories surrounding the Boston Harbor district each contained its own lithic source areas and quarries. These quarries were associated with formations of rhyolites belonging to the Lynn-Mattapan and Blue Hills volcanic complexes and hornfels present within a contact metamorphic zone in the Blue Hills. These quarry sites supplied the Saugus jasper and Melrose green rhyolites and hornfels of primary interest for this study, as well as other rhyolites forming the "generic" category of lithic material. The location of these source areas in relation to the approximate territories of Native American groups in eastern Massachusetts during the early historic period is shown in Figure 7.1.

The Pawtucket core area encompassed the sources for "Saugus jasper" and Melrose green rhyolite. Other outcrops of Lynn-Mattapan volcanic complex rocks in the coastal zone (Revere/Malden) contained dark red-purple rhyolite; nearby uplands in the Middlesex Fells (Wakefield) held dark gray-to-black and light gray weathering rhyolites. A range of other predominantly dark gray-to-gray-brown rhyolites were available at another coastal zone source area further north in Marblehead.

The source of the red-to-pink rhyolite, known locally as Saugus jasper, was apparently a small outcrop located in proximity to the Saugus River. When it was described in the late nineteenth century, the single exposure of this material exhibited signs of prehistoric quarrying, and fragments of worked stone on the surface nearby indicated there were probably lithic workshops in the surrounding area (Haynes 1886). The Saugus Quarry site (19-ES-256) was destroyed or obscured by modern residential development (Grimes et al. 1984:186). Recent attempts to relocate this lithic source area in the town of Saugus have been unsuccessful. It was most likely a small dike or series of dikes with fine-grained, silica-rich material exposed in a very limited area within a section of the Lynn-Mattapan volcanic complex. This fine-grained lithic material was quarried by Native Americans from the Paleoindian through Late Woodland periods (ca. 12,000–500 B.P.).

The Wyoming Quarry site (19-MD-251), the known source of Melrose green rhyolite, was first described in the late nineteenth century (Haynes 1886). Its location was uncertain until the quarry was rediscovered by Luedtke in 1994 (Luedtke et al. 1998). This small lithic source locality is within an area of volcanics belonging to the Lynn-Mattapan group, which includes pyroclastic and mafic rock (Thompson 1985; Thompson and Hermes 1990). Melrose green rhyolite ranges in color from light gray-green-to-blue-green on weathered surfaces; fresh or unweathered material is a dark green. Most material from this source is very fine-grained and uniform in color, though rare phenocrysts, coarse-grained patches, and some flow banding have been seen in pieces of quarry debris at the source area and artifacts from archaeological sites. Petrographic analysis has demonstrated the volcanic origin of the Melrose green rhyolite and that it displays certain features, such as feldspar microphenocrysts, faint flow banding, relict shards of rock, and a set of accessory minerals (epidote, chlorite, calcite) common in rocks of the Lynn-Mattapan volcanic complex (Luedtke et al. 1998; Hermes et al. 2001).

Native American quarrying at the Wyoming Quarry site was based on narrow dikes of fine-grained felsitic rock or rhyolite in an outcrop of pyroclastic tuff and blocks or fragments exposed on a talus slope below the outcrop. Small lithic workshops are located on a hillside terrace adjacent to the rhyolite dikes. A Greene-like projectile point and a Levanna projectile point were found at the quarry by Haynes (1886) when he discovered it. These artifacts are evidence of Middle to Late Woodland period activity at this lithic source. Based on preliminary study of diagnostic projectile points from sites in eastern Massachusetts, Melrose green rhyolite was probably used through the Middle and Late Archaic periods (ca. 8000–3000 B.P.). However, some of the most intensive quarrying may have taken place later during the Middle and Late Woodland periods (Luedtke et al. 1998; Hermes et al. 2001).

Blue Hills

The hornfels so widely used in the Middle and Late Woodland periods within eastern/southeastern Massachusetts was obtained from a series of quarries and related workshop sites located along a contact metamorphic zone in the Blue Hills Range. This material was formed through the alteration of the Braintree argillite by a series of diabase dikes and the Quincy granite. Large sections of the argillite were incorporated into the granite as roof pendants or inclusions. Through metamorphism by heat and recrystallization, the argillite inclusions were transformed into hornfels (Chute 1966; Naylor and Sayer 1976:135,145). A medium-grained, dense and dark gray-to-gray-green variety of hornfels, with rust spots and streaks known as "Braintree Slate," was extensively quarried throughout the Middle and Late Archaic periods. Groundstone tools and chipped preforms of this material were distributed across much of southeastern New England. The finer-grained "Braintree Hornfels" is charcoal-gray-to-black in color on freshly broken surfaces. The weathered surfaces of debitage and artifacts usually have a distinctive speckled brown-to-gray color with occasional black-to-dark-gray bands and rust stains (Bowman and Zeoli 1978; Ritchie and Gould 1985). Limited archaeological survey work in a portion of the Massachusett Hill Quarry complex (site 19-NF-105) recorded shallow pits excavated into talus deposits below outcrops and workshops where hornfels was extracted and reduced to quarry blanks and bifacial preforms (Ritchie 1981).

Hornfels is very common in Middle Woodland contexts and some components from the initial Late Woodland period from the Boston basin west, at least as far as the Blackstone River drainage in central Massachusetts. To the south, it is widely distributed in Middle Woodland contexts across the upper Taunton basin and Narragansett Bay (Ritchie and Gould 1985:46–47). The extraction and distribution of hornfels is estimated to have reached a peak between about 1800 and 1000 B.P., with continued use in the Late Woodland period most evident in portions of southeastern Massachusetts, such as the Taunton basin (Ritchie 1986).

The Blue Hills Range also contains a suite of volcanic rocks consisting of flows of devitrified rhyolite within larger units of granite porphyry

(Naylor and Sayer 1976). The Blue Hills rhyolite appears in archaeological contexts as a fine-grained, dark-to-medium gray material with phenocrysts of tan-to-pink feldspar and clear quartz. This combination of feldspar and quartz phenocrysts is a diagnostic visual feature of rhyolite from the Blue Hills source. Petrographic and geochemical analyses have confirmed that the alkalic rhyolite from the Blue Hills source is enriched in high-field strength trace elements, that it has distinctive textural features, phenocrysts, and accessory mineral assemblages, and that it can be readily distinguished from calc-alkaline Lynn-Mattapan suite rhyolites (Hermes and Ritchie 1997). The Blue Hills rhyolite flows contain fine-grained material that was extensively quarried by Native Americans from the Early Archaic to the Late Woodland periods and widely distributed across eastern and southeastern Massachusetts, particularly in the Neponset and Taunton drainage basins. Rhyolite from this source area was used during the Late Woodland period; Levanna projectile points made of it are known from sites in the nearby Neponset and middle-to-upper Charles drainages, as well as further south in the Taunton basin.

Levanna Point Analysis

A sample of 116 Levanna and Levanna-like projectile points from sites in the combined Sudbury/Assabet/Concord drainage formed the primary data for this study. These artifacts were in both museum and private collections and had been found mostly by avocational archaeologists through informal excavation or surface collecting at the multi component sites well exposed by agricultural activity in fields near these three rivers or tributary streams. The largest numbers of Levanna points were in the Adams Tolman and Benjamin Smith collections at the Concord Museum and the Todd collection, which is curated at the Massachusetts Archaeological Society's Robbins Museum. Tolman, Smith, and Todd all collected extensively in the Concord area from the late nineteenth to the first half of the twentieth centuries. A few projectile points were from excavated contexts at a site in the town of Wayland (Blancke 1978). There are significantly fewer known Late Woodland sites and components in the Sudbury/Assabet/Concord drainage in comparison to the Boston basin and coastal areas, a pattern that has been noted before (Ritchie 1980:86; Blancke 1981:11). Given the limited number of known Late Woodland sites in this area, it was expected there would be a corresponding scarcity of Levanna points. The number of these artifacts found in various collections, however, exceeded initial predictions.

The Levanna points come from a total of 21 sites within this combined drainage basin. Most of the sites (9) are in the middle-to-lower sections of the Sudbury River. Three sites are on the lower end of the Assabet River, just above its confluence with the Sudbury River. Nine of the sites are along the upper Concord River, in the town of Concord. One site (Call/Fordway) was on the lower Concord River in Billerica. The headwater sections of the Sudbury and Assabet drainages are not represented in this sample since they were outside the reconstructed group territories for the Pawtucket and Massachusett. Many of the sites with Late Woodland components are located in clusters within the Sudbury/Assabet/Concord drainage, and they tend to be in or near locations well suited for fishing. Examples are the Heard Pond and Weir Hill/Weir Meadow districts in Sudbury and Wayland. Heard Pond is connected to the Sudbury River, and Weir Hill/Weir Meadow contains a historically documented fishweir location on this river used by both Native Americans and early English settlers. The confluence of the Assabet and Sudbury Rivers at Nashawtuc Hill and Mantatucket Rock in Concord was probably another fishing station. The Nashawtuc Hill/Mantatucket Rock cluster includes at least four sites (Dakin Farm, Beardsel Farm, Old Manse, Mantatucket Rock) with Late Woodland components. Other projectile points came from a few upland sites, situated near streams and springs, that were presumably used for hunting camps. Good examples of small Late Woodland components in upland settings are the Morse Field site, near a spring and tributary stream head on the boundary of the Sudbury and Assabet watersheds, and the Elm Brook and Barthel Farm sites, situated near each other on upper Elm Brook, a Concord River tributary.

The frequency of lithic materials in this sample of Levanna points is shown in Figure 7.2. More than a third of all these points (46) were of various gray-to-black or dark gray-brown-to-purple-gray rhyolites. Based on their general visual macroscopic attributes, these rhyolites are likely to be from source areas north of the Boston Harbor district in the Lynn (Lynn-Mattapan) volcanic complex.

Melrose green and Saugus jasper rhyolites, the two materials of primary interest for their association with the core area of Pawtucket group territory, were represented by only 12 Levanna points (approximately 10% of the total sample). Six were of Melrose green rhyolite and four of typical red-pink Saugus jasper rhyolite. All of these points were from sites in the lower Sudbury, Sudbury/Assabet confluence area, and upper Concord River sections. The 13 points made of hornfels from the Blue Hills source and Massachusett core area made up a larger than expected portion of the study sample. Five of these points could be provenienced to sites in the middle and lower Sudbury and upper Concord drainages;

Figure 7.2
Frequencies of Lithic Material Types in a Sample of Levanna Projectile Points from the Sudbury/Assabet/Concord Drainage

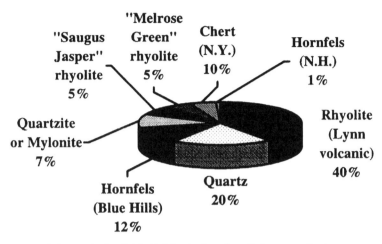

Prepared by Gail Van Dyke, PAL (Public Archaeology Laboratory, Inc.).

the remainder were in the Todd collection and most likely came from sites in the town of Concord. A less frequent, but interesting, material was a gray-to-gray-green metamorphic rock, resembling mylonite or my-lonitized quartzite. Small outcrops that may be source areas for this rock type have been found within upland sections of the Sudbury drainage where sections of the Westboro quartzite formation were altered by meta-morphic processes along the Bloody Bluff fault zone. The eight points made of this type of material, along with 21 others manufactured from quartz, provided ample evidence of local lithic resource use by Late Woodland groups.

Lithic material from sources outside southern New England and in-dicative of long distance transport or exchange networks were also pres-ent in the sample of Levanna points from the Sudbury/Assabet/Concord area. Eleven points had been made from gray-green, dark gray-to-black cherts, representing material probably from various sources in eastern New York. A single point from Concord (Middlesex School site) was of a distinctive gray weathering material visually identical to hornfels from a source area in the Ossipee area of central New Hampshire (Boisvert et al. 1996).

Some Late Woodland sites and components within the estimated boundaries of Massachusett territory have yielded information on the distribution of lithic materials from sources within the core area of that territory. Identified during cultural resource management studies in the Neponset, Charles, and upper Taunton drainage basins, the Late Woodland assemblages on these sites are limited in number, but useful for their contrast with patterns of lithic resource use in the Pawtucket homeland or territory.

A section of the Neponset-Wamsutta site (19-NF-70), along the lower Neponset drainage in Canton, contained important Middle and Late Woodland period components. Within a large collection of material excavated by a group of avocational archaeologists was an assemblage of complete and partially finished Levanna points, triangular preforms, and debitage of hornfels from the nearby Blue Hills source (Ritchie 1987). Hornfels was brought to this site from quarries a few miles away as partially shaped preforms and made into projectile points. Located near extensive marshes and wooded wetlands, this site could have functioned as an inland hunting camp for groups based in the Neponset estuary area. In the middle and upper sections of the adjacent Charles basin, the few widely dispersed Late Woodland components provide other examples of Levanna points. At the Hemlock Gorge Rockshelter, a fall-line fishing station, there was a Levanna point of red rhyolite from an unknown source, chipping debris, and an asymmetrical triangular biface of Saugus jasper (Dincauze 1975:8). This biface may have been a Levanna preform. The presence of Saugus jasper may reflect occasional use of this site by Pawtucket people, given its location near the probable southern boundary of their group territory. It may also indicate the exchange of lithic material across a group boundary. In the middle and upper Charles basin, a few Levanna points of Blue Hills rhyolite and hornfels were in a private collection (Elwyn Chick) assembled mostly from sites in the Medfield/Millis area. Two other examples of Blue Hills rhyolite were found on the Medway 3 site, a single component Late Woodland camp in an upland setting (Rainey 1991:63).

The Bassett Knoll site in Raynham was identified in a cultural resource survey at the headwaters of a small tributary stream flowing into the upper Taunton River. This multicomponent Archaic and Woodland period site is approximately two miles north of the Titicut district in Bridgewater and Middleborough. An archaeological data recovery program on the site revealed a very substantial Late Woodland component. The lithic assemblage included over 150 Levanna points of which about one-third (55) were hornfels. Quartz and gray rhyolite were the other primary lithic materials used to make the remainder of the Levanna points. The rhyolite was not from the Blue Hills, but was visually similar to material from a smaller source area within a section of the Lynn-

Mattapan volcanic complex located in uplands between the Charles and Neponset basins. Evidence of intensive chipped-stone tool production using hornfels was also represented by the 2900 pieces of debitage, 29 bifaces, and seven quarry blanks or cores of this material. The manufacture of Levanna points was an important on-site activity, probably during numerous episodes of occupation by Late Woodland groups. A suite of uncorrected radiocarbon dates of 1240 ± 70 B.P. (Beta 033405), 1190 ± 90 B.P. (Beta 033408), 1060 ± 80 B.P. (Beta 052203), 1020 ± 70 B.P. (Beta 055204), and 520 ± 50 B.P. (Beta 028153) covers the full span of the Late Woodland period. Refuse pit features with Late Woodland ceramic sherds, deer bone, and other faunal remains attest to hunting and related activities carried out by people using this site (Harrison and McCormack 1990). It may have functioned as a staging area or camp connected to larger settlements in the Titicut district.

The Rozenas II site was a relatively small Late Woodland hunting camp on the edge of a white cedar swamp, just south of Nippenicket Pond in Raynham. This site is near one of the landscape features (Nippenicket Pond) defining the southern boundary of Massachusett territory in a seventeenth-century description (Chaffin 1886:29). An archaeological data recovery program yielded Levanna points, bifaces, and debitage of both hornfels and rhyolite from the Blue Hills source areas. In the assemblage of hornfels artifacts were several Levanna points, small triangular preforms, a few ovate bifacial cores or quarry blanks, and over 200 pieces of debitage (Ritchie 1982). A few points similar to the Jack's Reef Pentagonal type, as well as Levanna points with a retouch pattern creating a pentagonal blade outline, suggest the site was occupied in the terminal Middle Woodland or initial part of the Late Woodland period.

DISCUSSION AND SUMMARY

The Sudbury/Assabet/Concord drainage was along the periphery of a territory extending inland from the core area of Pawtucket settlement in the Boston basin. As expected, the majority of Levanna projectile points from sites in this inland area were made of rhyolites most likely derived from sections of the Lynn (Lynn-Mattapan) volcanic complex based on their visual macroscopic attributes. Late Woodland lithic resource use is comparable to other nearby areas such as the Shawsheen drainage, where the Levanna points from several sites were predominantly of "dark felsite," probably a dark gray-black rhyolite and a dark red rhyolite (Bullen 1949:11, 22, 29, 44). The use of Lynn volcanic rhyolites from various source areas was widespread in northeastern Massachusetts throughout the Archaic period, and Late Woodland assemblages appear to show continuity with this older established pattern.

The distinctive Melrose green and Saugus jasper rhyolites were present but not dominant, at least in the sample of Levanna points from the Sudbury/Assabet/Concord basin examined for this study. Their presence, however, demonstrates that lithic materials from small, specific quarry sources in close proximity to known Pawtuckeog/Pawtucket settlements were part of the tool kits used by Late Woodland people in at least a portion of this drainage basin. It is possible that these materials were not as common on the periphery of the Pawtucket group territory in comparison to more central core areas, such as the Mystic drainage or Boston basin. The relatively small amount of Melrose green and Saugus jasper rhyolites may reflect the location of this area on the inland limits of Pawtucket lands along the boundary with Nipmuck territories.

There may also be temporal limits for the quarrying and distribution of these rhyolites in the northern Boston and adjacent Sudbury/Assabet/ Concord drainage basins, with the greatest use occurring mostly in the latter part of the Late Woodland period after about 800 B.P. At the Staiano site in Wayland, a Levanna point of Melrose green rhyolite was associated with a small fire pit, radiocarbon dated to 640 ± 85 B.P. and calibrated to A.D. 1307 ± 89 (Blancke 1978:176). At present, this is the best indication for when Melrose green rhyolite was used in the Sudbury/ Concord drainage.

The 13 Levanna points of hornfels formed slightly more than 10% of the sample, a larger than expected amount of this southern Boston basin material. This contrasts, however, with the hornfels-dominated Late Woodland assemblages from former Massachusett territory in the Neponset and upper Taunton drainage, which were described above. The points of hornfels from the Sudbury/Assabet/Concord drainage may reflect larger scale processes. This material was widely distributed across parts of southern New England in the Middle Woodland period as shown by the geographical spread of certain projectile point and biface styles (Jack's Reef, Fox Creek) made of this material (Ritchie and Gould 1985; Strauss 1992). Research in other areas of southeastern Massachusetts has indicated that the most intensive use of hornfels from the Blue Hills source was during the Middle Woodland and initial Late Woodland periods, from about 1600 to 1000 B.P., based on radiocarbon-dated contexts from sites in the Taunton and Neponset drainages (Ritchie and Gould 1985, Ritchie 1986).

After about 1000 B.P., local lithic materials may have become dominant, concurrent with establishment of defined Late Woodland group territories as described by Dincauze (1974), particularly in parts of eastern Massachusetts farther from the Blue Hills. In the Sudbury/Assabet/Concord drainage, use of hornfels may have ended around this time as Late Woodland groups relied more on other materials such as the Lynn volcanic complex rhyolites, or local quartz, mylonite, and quartzite. Use of hornfels in the Sudbury/Assabet/Concord drainage may also mean that lithic materials occasionally crossed the boundaries of Late Woodland group territories defined by drainage basins and other landscape features. The southern part of the Sudbury drainage shares a boundary with the adjacent Charles basin and is less than 20 miles west of the hornfels source in the Blue Hills.

It may be significant that no Levanna points of Blue Hills rhyolite were in the sample from the Sudbury/Assabet/Concord drainage. The absence of this type of rhyolite gave some support for the prediction that a southern Boston basin material would not occur in Late Woodland assemblages from the area historically documented as Pawtucket lands. Levanna points of Blue Hills rhyolite are known to occur in Late Woodland assemblages from sites in the Neponset, Charles, and upper Taunton drainages that formed the Massachusett group territory.

The relatively strong representation of chert Levanna points in the sample may be related to the proximity of the Sudbury and Assabet drainages to the central Massachusetts uplands. Chert from sources in eastern New York is more common in central Massachusetts even in older, Late/Terminal Archaic period lithic assemblages. The Sudbury and Assabet drainages were most likely part of the route along which chert as preforms or finished tools travelled as it was moved from interior uplands to other parts of eastern Massachusetts. Like hornfels, there may be a temporal aspect to the use of this material, with chert most prevalent in the first part of the Late Woodland when some vestiges of the exchange networks that distributed non-local materials during the Middle Woodland could have persisted.

Late Woodland assemblages from outside the limits of the historically documented Pawtucket and Massachusett territories contrast with patterns of lithic resource use within both of these areas. They also demonstrate that there are potentially informative sub-regional differences in the sets of lithic materials used by Late Woodland groups occupying drainage basins across eastern and central Massachusetts. Local quartzites and quartz were the primary materials for Late Woodland groups in central Massachusetts; rhyolites and hornfels are rare or absent. The Bear Hollow site in the middle Blackstone drainage contained an assemblage with a Levanna point and triangular preforms of quartz and fine-grained tan-gray quartzite. The Late Woodland component forming this site was radiocarbon dated to 425 ± 150 B.P. (GX 9215) and 340 ± 150 B.P. (GX 9215) or about A.D. 1550 (Thorbahn and Cox 1983:91). Debitage of fine-grained gray-green quartzite also appeared with chert in a Late Woodland context within the nearby Hartford Avenue Rockshelter, dated to 740 ± 80 B.P. (Beta 008929) and 610 ± 70 B.P. (Beta 008928) (Ritchie 1985). These distinctive quartzites are probably derived from a section of either the Westboro or Plainfield formations, which extend from northeastern Connecticut across the southern Worcester plateau area (Zen et al. 1983).

In the lower Taunton River estuary and upper Narragansett Bay area, beyond the southern limits of the Massachusett homeland, the relative scarcity of Boston basin rhyolite and hornfels in Late Woodland assemblages is also apparent. Most of the 34 Levanna points in a collection from the Read Farm site in Seekonk, at the head of Narragansett Bay, were of white quartz, and there were only a few of rhyolite and one of hornfels (Johnson and Mahlstedt 1985:60). Reliance on quartz is also apparent in many other assemblages of Levanna points from the lower Taunton estuary and throughout the Narragansett Bay area.

In summary, materials like Melrose green, Saugus jasper rhyolite, and hornfels that are distinctive in terms of their macroscopic attributes and other features such as petrography and geochemistry have the potential to serve as markers of Woodland lithic resource use within reconstructed group territories. Analysis of ceramics from the coastal zone indicated that there were relatively stable microtraditions in areas not very far apart (Luedtke 1986b:132). Kenyon (1983) also found evidence of distinct Woodland period ceramic style zones along sections of the Merrimack basin that coincide with geographic provinces. Late Woodland lithic resource use within eastern Massachusetts and other parts of southern New England may have also been defined by localized microtraditions or patterns as group territories became more clearly defined in the late prehistoric period.

ACKNOWLEDGMENTS

Barbara Luedtke's studies of lithic resource use were an inspiration for this chapter. Don Hermes also provided valuable insights into the geology of the Boston basin rocks. I would like to thank Shirley Blancke for her assistance with collections research at the Concord Museum. The Massachusetts Archaeological Society was also generous with access to collections at the Robbins Museum. Gail Van Dyke prepared Figures 7.1 and 7.2.

8

Landscape Interpretation on the Microscopic Scale: Case Studies in Southern New England

Michael A. Volmar and Shirley Blancke

INTRODUCTION

Luedtke (2000) expressed a desire that new techniques like soil microstratigraphy be applied to Massachusetts coastal archaeology, and indicated how increased knowledge of lithics could add to an understanding of the social landscape. The interpretation of the landscape with respect to archaeological processes is usually thought of in macroscopic terms such as settlement patterns or long-distance trade. In the Precontact and Contact Periods archaeological record in coastal southern New England, evidence of these cultural products is largely represented as "soil stains" or features, durable artifacts like lithic flakes and other stone tools, and pottery fragments. With the notable exceptions of flotation analysis and radiocarbon dating, and to a lesser extent neutron activation analysis, few of the technological innovations in the field of archaeology have been adopted by practicing archaeologists. Two techniques that are relatively new to American archaeology, soil micromorphology and lithography, have the potential for allowing microscopic interpretations that would not be possible from the macroscopic remains alone.

Lithography examines thin sections of rock under magnification to classify more accurately the rock type. It is a very effective technique to examine debitage or stone tools to specify a geological source. Thus, lithography links an artifact or site into a wider cultural framework. Soil micromorphology examines thin sections of soil collected in situ using

Figure 8.1
Map of Southern New England, Showing the Locations of Block Island and Concord

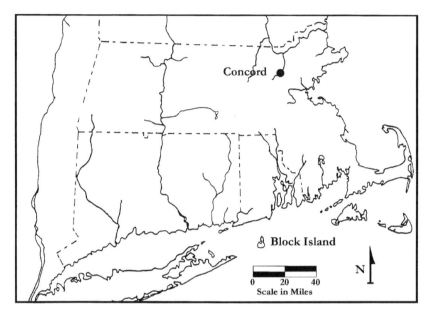

a rigid container. During the microscopic analysis, the character of the soil is determined, described, and documented. The arrangement of the fine (smaller than silt) and coarse (silt-sized and larger) material and any textural features are interpreted in light of field observations during excavation. This allows the researcher to challenge field observations, and to analyze site formation processes and feature deposition. Both lithography and soil micromorphology can add to the geological, pedological (soil development), and anthropological understanding of the past.

In this chapter, we present evidence from the Sleepy Hollow site in Concord, Massachusetts, and Fort Island on Block Island in Rhode Island (Figure 8.1) to demonstrate how the microscopic scale enables archaeologists to refine their interpretations and augment field observations with previously unidentifiable data. In both examples the field interpretations and questions were addressed with these techniques, expanding our understanding of site depositional history by identifying the geological source for lithic debitage and the microscopic evidence of site and feature formation processes. The evidence presented adds to a small but growing visual lexicon of microscopic observations from southern New England archaeological sites that can assist in classifying inter- and intra-site activity areas elsewhere.

LITHOGRAPHY AND MICROMORPHOLOGY

Lithic analysis is typically conducted with no more than 10x magnification by many archaeology laboratories. By examining lithic microstructure at greater magnification, petrographic characteristics can be matched with known geological formations (Calogero, this volume). Recent research by Calogero (this volume, 1991) and Pretola (2001, 2000, 1995, 1994) on New England archaeological and mineralogical collections has advanced our understanding of microscopic evidence in lithics and its relevance to archaeological interpretation.

As discussed previously, soil micromorphology is the visual interpretation of in situ soil microstructure. The microstructure is made up of mineral and organic components of fine (clay-sized) and coarse (silt-sized and larger) materials and the associated spaces between them or void structures. Macroscopic observations of soil made by archaeologists typically include color and texture delineations. Texture assessments made in the field typically involve a qualitative physical estimate of the sand/silt/clay in a soil. Color is described based on the Munsell soil color charts or by more idiosyncratic delineations. This method also provides "witness blocks" of soil that can be reanalyzed by other archaeologists to evaluate interpretations, inferences, and conclusions.

On the microscopic scale, all soils examined in this study had coarse material made up of primarily quartz, with lesser amounts of feldspar, mica, schist, and other rock types. The fine material included organic residues and clay. The soil colors we see and report on in the field are related to the color and density of fine material components. Many observations of soil characteristics made during excavation of macroscopically different colored feature lenses or soil horizons can appear microscopically as essentially the same coarse material, with differing concentrations of fine material of varying hues.

Anthropogenic (cultural impacts on geology and pedology) deposits typically have gone through less mechanical sorting when compared to a soil that developed on sediments that were deposited by wind or water. Bullock et al. (1985) suggest that descriptions of soil microstructure include coarse and fine materials, their mineral and organic components, and any apparent pedofeatures. Coarse material texture is determined by estimating or counting rock particles of differing sizes to determine the amount of sorting. Fine materials also have various textures. Pedofeatures are discrete fabric units within the sample recognizable from the surrounding groundmass (coarse and fine material) by a difference in one or more components (Bullock et al. 1985:19, 95–138). There is a variety of clues in the distribution of organic and mineral components of soil that micromorphology exposes. Direct and indirect actions to soil by human agents change the coarse and fine material distributions, creating a distinctive soil or pedofeature. Other materials are often unconsciously transported by a human agent and added to a given soil horizon or feature.

LITERATURE REVIEW

Several recent efforts demonstrate the relevance of soil micromorphology to archaeological interpretation (Currie 1994; Goldberg 1992; Volmar 1998). Archaeological site formation processes include geological, pedological, and anthropogenic processes. Interpretations of these three processes help define contextual constraints on archaeological interpretation (Goldberg, Nash, and Petraglia 1993:x).

Researchers argue that there are recognizable micromorphological signatures in soil that relate to the human use of space (Courty et al. 1989, 1994; Goldberg 1992). For example, micromorphological studies provide detailed information about anthropogenic accumulations relating to firing processes (Courty et al. 1989; Ulery and Graham 1993) and the identification of the charred remains of parenchymous tissues or tubers (Hather 1991; Volmar 1998). Other research has focused on the micromorphological evidence of cultivation practices (Courty et al. 1994; Macphail et al. 1990; Macphail and Goldberg 1990; Sandor and Nash 1995) and soil fabric alterations induced by human compaction of occupation surfaces (Ge' et al. 1993; Davidson et al. 1992; Goldberg and Whitbread 1993). Also, in a recent study (Tipping et al. 1994) soil micromorphology and pollen analysis are used to interpret ancient evidence of turf stripping. Research is also being conducted on the effects of earthworms on carbon in soil (Zhang and Hendrix 1995) and on the distribution of artifacts (Armour-Chelu and Andrews 1994), including excrement pedofeatures and structural alterations of the soil fabric (Volmar 1998).

THE EXAMPLES

In this section, we present the field observations, historical research, and microscopic evidence from the Sleepy Hollow site and Fort Island. In each case, the field observations present interpretive challenges that can be addressed using microscopic techniques. The microscopic analysis of lithic types led to inter-site connections being made, and feature interpretations based on standard field techniques were changed by the results of soil micromorphology tests.

Concord

Archaeological surveys and two phases of data recovery were conducted in a field in Concord, Massachusetts (Figure 8.1), due to the expansion of the Sleepy Hollow cemetery. This area, close to the Concord River, was thought to be the general location of Native American planting fields just prior to the founding of the town in 1635. The field had been plowed since the seventeenth century. These "planting fields," together with a fishweir, were given in exchange for wampum, tools, and clothing by the Native people of the Musketaquid River to the first settlers in Concord, according to a 1637 deed (Shattuck 1835:6). In 1853 the cemetery expansion area was bought by the trustees of the Middlesex Agricultural Society who erected livestock pens and an exhibition shed in the area. Projectile point finds from the 1997–1999 seasons indicated that Middle and Late Archaic components (ca. 8000–3000 B.P.) had once existed at the site, and three ceramic sherds pointed to a Woodland presence (ca. 3000–500 B.P.). Edge tools, perforators, and gouge fragments, as well as historical finds such as part of an eighteenth-century decorated clay pipe bowl, came out of the plow zone within areas designated 19-MD-100 and 19-MD-101 (Blancke 2001, 1999, 1998; Waller and Ritchie 1997).

Concord Lithic Analysis

Macroscopic inspection of the lithics from Sleepy Hollow indicated that many varieties of stone had been used by toolmakers. Lithography provided some precise identifications, and pointed to some source areas and inter-site connections. The three main lithic types represented in the debitage from the plow zone loam at Sleepy Hollow were gray and black rhyolites that together made up half the total, and a black hornfels that represented one-third of a total 1106 flakes, chunks, and cores. Also represented in small quantities were gray or tan quartzite, gray argillite, and white quartz; and in minute quantities, mylonitized rhyolite, gray amphibolite, slate, purple rhyolite, gray quartz, black schist, red rhyolite, and chert (Blancke 2001, 1999, 1998, 1988, 1987, 1981; Waller and Ritchie 1997). Most of these lithics are local or from the Boston basin.

The gray and black rhyolites that occur frequently on Precontact sites in eastern Massachusetts have long been considered to belong to the

Lynn volcanics that are exposed along the coast north of Boston (Din-cauze 1968). Thin sectioning has confirmed this and identified the stone as rhyolite rather than felsite, a previously used generic term (Duncan Ritchie, personal communication, 2001). By contrast, hornfels has been recognized relatively recently (Calogero, this volume). The thin section-ing of a hornfels flake from Sleepy Hollow showed an exceptionally fine-grained groundmass full of black opaque minerals with relict bedding from the original argillitic rock baked by molten lava into a contact-metamorphic rock (Calogero and Philpotts 2001). This hornfels is characteristic of the Ossipee mountains of New Hampshire, and is found on sites along the Merrimack River of which the Concord River is a tributary (Duncan Ritchie and Victoria Bunker, personal communi-cation, 2001; Bunker 2001). This kind of hornfels, identified by thin section, also occurred at the Pine Hawk site in Acton, Massachusetts, on the Assabet River, a tributary of the Concord River (Waller and Ritchie 2001).

Two rare stone types identified by lithography at Sleepy Hollow, my-lonitized rhyolite and amphibolite, also allowed inter-site comparisons to be made in the Concord-Sudbury-Assabet River valleys. Macroscopically identified "mylonite" was shown by thin section to be a mylonitized rhyolite or mylonitized rhyolitic silicified ash flow (Calogero and Phil-potts 2001). "Mylonite," viewed macroscopically, is a very hard, fine-grained and well-laminated lithic that is light gray or greenish in color with the look of quartz, but lithography demonstrates that it may vary in mineralogical composition, and the term has been used to cover more than one lithic type. Mylonites are formed in ductile fault shear zones in continental and oceanic crusts, and outcroppings in Sudbury are a likely source that requires confirmation through lithography (Largy and Ritchie 2002; Waller and Ritchie 2001; Ritchie 1979). At Sleepy Hollow we recovered what may be a broken perforator of a gray lithic with sparkling crystals identified by thin section as amphibolite with green amphiboles, plagioclase, and minor magnetite (Calogero and Philpotts 2001). Amphibolites occur in the bedrock of the Concord area scattered as lenses or beds among the various gneisses and schists, but also as a formation (Hansen 1956).

There is thin section evidence that mylonitized rhyolite was used in the Middle (ca. 8000–6000 B.P.) and Late Archaic (ca. 5000–3000 B.P.) periods and amphibolite in the Middle Archaic period (Largy and Ritchie 2002; Alfred Hosmer and Benjamin Smith collections, Concord Mu-seum) from two sites in Wayland, Castle Hill and Sherman Bridge (Fig-ure 8.2), both located close to the Sudbury River that flows into the

Figure 8.2
Neville-Variant and Small Triangle Projectile Points of Mylonite from
Sherman Bridge, Wayland

The projectile point at the lower left may be a Levanna type. Prepared by Shirley Blancke, Concord Museum, Alfred Hosmer Collection.

Concord (Largy 1979) (Figure 8.1). At Pine Hawk, Acton, Massachusetts, a small "mylonite" workshop was located where mylonite (identified by thin section as quartzite derived from sandstone or siltstone)
was being reduced primarily into bifacial tools, but no diagnostic points
were found. An age of 3150 ± 60 radiocarbon years B.P. (charcoal, Beta
141124, δ^{13}C corrected) from a nearby hearth in direct association with
mylonite debitage appeared to relate this site with the Late Archaic
Stemmed Point tradition (Waller and Ritchie 2001). A recent study has
identified many more sites where both mylonite and amphibolite have
been found in the Concord River drainage (Largy and Ritchie 2002).
    Since no diagnostic artifacts of mylonitized rhyolite or amphibolite
were found at Sleepy Hollow, their use cannot be assigned a cultural
context. However, the presence of two Stark-Like projectile points and

two possible Stark-Like base fragments of gray quartzite and gray-brown argillite indicates a Middle Archaic component once existed, and there are also Late Archaic remains (Blancke 1999; Waller and Ritchie 1997).

Concord Feature Interpretation

Soil micromorphological testing was applied to the results of standard excavation technique to evaluate the conclusions reached about the nature of two principal features. These features include a "fire pit" and a "black platform." The fire pit extended 10 cm into the sandy subsoil below 24 cm of plow zone loam and had a radiocarbon age of 3820 ± 85 B.P. (charcoal, GX-24954, δ^{13}C corrected), placing it in the Late Archaic period. About 50 meters to the north, on the edge of a bank above a swamp, there was an extensive blackened area, 2 cm thick at the top of the subsoil below approximately 40 cm of loam. A sample from near the center of this feature was dated 550 ± 50 B.P. (charcoal, GX-25983, δ^{13}C corrected), and another from the edge, 470 ± 60 B.P. (charcoal, GX-26646, δ^{13}C corrected), indicating the end of the Late Woodland period (ca. 1000–500 B.P.).

The fire pit charcoal was identified as white oak with one fragment resembling the red oak group. Many samples had narrow rings indicating "stressed" wood (Blancke 2001, 1999). No other macroscopic plant or bone remains or artifacts were recovered. The fire pit was interpreted as a likely cooking fire, and a microscopic bone fragment identified in a soil thin section reinforces this conclusion (Volmar 2000).

The interpretation of the oval black platform, 7.5 m in length and 4 m in width, was more challenging. The area was blackened by what appeared to be charcoal dust, but there was very little actual charcoal. In the center there were very small fragments of charred wood, but no other macroscopic finds were made. The wood was identified as conifer, comprising pine, spruce, and larch or tamarack (Blancke 2001). Initially it was thought that if post molds were found, the black platform might be a wigwam floor. Since none was uncovered, the platform was instead interpreted as the result of a brush fire for field clearance. Subsequently, soil micromorphology results indicated the black platform was a living floor of some kind, but presumably an uncovered one because of the lack of post molds (Volmar 2000; Blancke 1999, 2001). Without the soil micromorphology tests, this possibility would never have been entertained.

Block Island

The Manisees first made Fort Island, on Block Island (Figure 8.1), into a palisaded defensive encampment some time between 1636 and 1661. In 1636 their island was "conquered" by the English after two "plantations" of about 60 wigwams were destroyed. After this attack, the Manisees built a more formidable defensive structure. The first map of Block Island that was made by the English colonists in 1661 divided the land into 16 farm lots. It does not incorporate Fort Island but does list it in its present location on the southeastern side of the Great Salt Pond. (The map is currently in the collection of the Block Island Historical Society.) Bellantoni (1987) and McBride (1986) suggest that Fort Island was used year-round during the seventeenth century, on the basis of the presence of sturgeon, seal, and white-tailed deer. Presumably, this year-round occupation supported wampum production (Ceci 1990a; McBride 1995). Ethnohistoric information also suggests that Block Island was a well-known source of wampum (Gookin [1792] 1970:18). As an English possession, the Manisees were required to send a yearly tribute to Boston of 10 fathoms of wampum, requiring its steady production at least from 1637 onwards. Excavations in 1994 revealed a tiny European flint drill, used to drill wampum before metal varieties became available, and wampum in several stages of production, blanks, finished pieces, and waste material (Volmar 1998:94).

Block Island Feature Interpretation

The soils at Fort Island can be described as Montauk series soil (Veneman 1994). These consist of very deep, well-drained soils on glacial moraines, forming in glaciofluvial or ablation deposits underlain by a firm sandy till. During excavation, we observed that Fort Island soil development occurred on a basal till, which contained substantial amounts of pebble-sized gravel and concreted nodules (Volmar 1998: Appendix D).

Originally, we had no idea what the concreted nodules were. This prompted us to sample them and examine them in thin section and using microprobe analysis. We thought they might be the residual effects of pottery manufacture at the site. The many nodules that we encountered during excavation can be generally described as very hard, small light brown concretions. Physical tests revealed that they do not slack (disintegrate) in water. Thin section analysis revealed that some nodules had clearly defined clay coatings forming the primary cementing element and that some are hollow. Microprobe analysis indicates that the primary cementing agent is kaolinite, with approximately 1% iron oxide (45/40 Si/Al; Jercinovic 1997a:1). Constituent minerals of the kaolinite nodules are predominantly quartz, K-feldspar, plagioclase feldspar, and minor amounts of ilmenite. In contrast, microprobe analysis of one pottery fragment recovered from Fort Island (S5E0 NW quad, 56–60 cmbll, incised design) indicates that it is composed of illite or illite/smectite (Jercinovic 1997b:1). Thus, we conclude that the nodules are not the remnants of pottery manufacturing at the site and are more probably geological in origin (Volmar 1998:288–289; Volmar 1999).

Fort Island contains many types of anthropogenic features. The primary goal of the excavation in 1994 was to identify site formation processes within large areas of dense anthropogenic deposits to sequence depositional events, dividing the strata between Native and English occupations. Features sampled for micromorphological examination are summarized in Table 8.1.

Feature 66 appeared during excavation as a fire-reddened soil. Microscopically, the feature appeared to be two distinct kinds of soil loosely mixed together (Volmar 1998:Fig. 25). This indicates that, after the burning activity occurred that caused the reddening, the soil was partially disturbed by some other activity.

Feature 1 is interpreted to be a wigwam floor; it is a clearly recognizable black lens, probably the result of seventeenth-century Native food preparation activities (Volmar 1998). Microscopic observations revealed that the different feature lenses did not demonstrate differential layering or compaction one would expect from a living surface. This lack of any layering or compacting seems primarily due to the attractive nature of organic residues to earthworms, cicadas, various insects like spiders, and other soil creatures. These biota are drawn to and feed on the rich organics in anthropogenic deposits, resulting in disruption of the soil microstructure (Volmar 1998:Figs. 21, 26, 27, and 34). Despite these inconclusive results, we still believe this is a wigwam floor. However, our initial assumption that it was "undisturbed" was revised since the soil was heavily reworked by soil organisms.

Unusual mineral components can also be found and can impact site interpretation. For example, Feature 71 was interpreted as "ash" in the field. Microscopic details revealed that it is composed of quartz and feldspar sand-sized particles in a single grain structure (Volmar 1998: Figs. 40 and 41). In effect, this feature was filled with clean sand. Its interpretation as a large post hole suggests that the "large post" was removed and then "the hole" was rapidly filled in with clean sand. The

Table 8.1
Fort Island Soil Micromorphology Summary

Feature #	Field Description	Microstructure Summary	Interpretation
1	Intact stratified black and gray lenses identified as a wigwam floor or living surface.	The distinctiveness of the individual lenses became much less pronounced microscopically. Microstructure showed nearly ubiquitous evidence of bioturbation.	Wigwam floor or living surface.
64	Sheet midden with faunal remains.	Fish scale, burned and unburned bones, ash, organic residues in loose microstructure.	Intact seventeenth-century sheet midden.
66	Fire-reddened soil.	Microscopically, the feature appeared to be two distinct kinds of soil loosely mixed together.	After the burning activity occurred that caused the reddening, the soil was partially disturbed by some other activity.
71	Large post hole that underlies Feature 1, post remains may be ash, possibly burned in place?	Perfectly sorted sand.	Large post removed and infilled during a single depositional episode of clean beach sand, possible aeolian event. Predates intensive occupation of the site.
100	Bell-shaped pit.	Homogeneous unstratified microstructure with some evidence of food remains.	This bell-shaped pit was rapidly filled in during one depositional episode.

question remains whether Native people chose to fill in the hole with clean sand, or whether it was wind blown material from some natural event.

One pit feature was uncovered during excavations at Fort Island, F 100 (Volmar 1998:Fig. 14), a small bell-shaped pit (with a volume of approximately 5 gallons). It contained a homogeneous dark brown soil, which had microscopically identifiable particles of burned bone and shell, pottery, and other evidence of burning (Volmar 1998:Figs. 44 and

45). This suggests that the feature was used for storage and then filled in with domestic refuse, presumably to clean up a particular surface.

Feature 64 was interpreted in the field as a sheet midden. Numerous sturgeon plates, fish remains, shell, and other faunal remains were observed during excavation of the black organic-rich soil. Microscopic details revealed the presence of ash (Volmar 1998:Fig. 43), a material that only preserves archaeologically in basic (pH > 7) conditions. The large number of shells, as well as the salt-rich estuarine environment, contribute to the preservation of ash at this site.

SUMMARY AND CONCLUSION

The identification of lithics through thin section allows for a greater degree of confidence when trying to determine inter-site connections, particularly when the quantity of a particular type of stone is very small. Without it we would not have felt confident identifying the presence of amphibolite or mylonitized rhyolite at the Sleepy Hollow site in Concord. These two rare lithics support finds from other sites in the Concord-Sudbury-Assabet River valley, Massachusetts, where these materials were used in Middle and Late Archaic contexts. In addition, the type of hornfels found at Sleepy Hollow connects the site with others in the Merrimack River drainage area and the Ossipee mountains of New Hampshire.

The accumulated knowledge of recent soil micromorphology projects is beginning to construct a lexicon of signatures in the micromorphological record for specific human and animal behaviors and soil processes. More work needs to be done to describe adequately the wide array of archaeological features, especially for open-air sites and subsoil features (Volmar 1998). Archaeological interpretation often can proceed without employing soil micromorphology. However, micromorphology can provide detailed interpretive information that other methods cannot. Therefore, microstructural analysis is a useful tool that enriches archaeological interpretation by gleaning cultural information contained in the nature and arrangement of coarse and fine components of soil and pedofeatures.

Sleepy Hollow provided a test case for the application of soil micromorphology in data recovery to test models proposed by standard excavation. A sample taken from a 4000-year-old feature identified as a cooking fire pit showed a microscopic piece of bone that reinforced the inference of human activity. An area of blackened soil with occasional fragments of charred wood 500 years old was initially interpreted as a possible wigwam floor, but subsequently, due to lack of post molds or other macroscopic finds, as a bonfire for field clearance. A soil block sample taken from this area pointed rather to its being a living floor of some kind.

The Fort Island samples revealed major differences between field observations and soil microstructure. Field observations of "intact" features failed to recognize subtle alterations to soil fabrics, in particular poor preservation of the soil microstructure in "wigwam floor" areas. This was surprising, considering the macroscopically observable stratified deposits at the site. A major factor in the loss of intact fabrics was rootlets, earthworms, and cicadas. These kinds of disturbances are present at most sites in this region. Also, in several features (64, 71, and 100), microartifacts were identified in thin section that influenced site interpretation. The ash identified in the midden deposit (Feature 64) does not usually preserve in the acidic conditions of southern New England. However, at this coastal site, a combination of the proximity to salt water and the large amounts of shellfish remains may provide exceptional conditions for the preservation of organic materials. Future excavations at this well-preserved site may reveal more unusual materials.

There are a few lessons we learned from this study. Samples are more effective when they are taken to answer specific questions. It is hard to justify the time and expense if there is no real question that these types of analyses can answer. Also, at many sites clastic sediments (like pottery fragments), charred botanicals, phytoliths, and micro debitage were evident in the micromorphology samples. One other lesson is that we underestimated the ubiquitous impact of bioturbation (the impact of biological organisms on soil fabric) as a mechanism that disrupts soil microstructure. What looks intact macroscopically may not appear microscopically so homogeneous. Bioturbation should be factored into archaeological interpretations.

The southern New England landscape retains information relevant to better understanding the geological, pedological, ecological, and anthropological past. It is contingent upon the archaeologists to discriminate between these differing effects by employing sensitive methodologies to aid interpretation. Microstructural analysis of lithics, soils, and sediments is a useful tool that can resolve some questions, and may suggest possible areas of inquiry into the region's past. These analyses provided more detail to site interpretation, and sometimes surprising answers to unasked questions.

ACKNOWLEDGMENTS

Volmar acknowledges the guidance, thoughtful criticism, and editorial insights offered by H. Martin Wobst, Peter Veneman, Arthur Keene, Kevin McBride, and Dena Dincauze during the course of his Ph.D. research. Paul Goldberg and Doug Currie offered helpful discussions on micromorphology and the use of their microscopic equipment. In addition, Volmar wants to thank Jordan Kerber, Shirley Blancke, and Barbara Luedtke for their interest in soil micromorphological analysis. Blancke wishes particularly to thank those who undertook the microscopic analyses for the Sleepy Hollow site: Barbara Calogero and Anthony Philpotts for the lithics, Michael Volmar for the soil micromorphology, and Tony Largy for the wood. Figure 8.1 was created by Volmar, and Figure 8.2 was photographed by Blancke.

PART III

CERAMIC ANALYSIS

9

Reconsidering the Shantok Tradition

Robert G. Goodby

INTRODUCTION

Approximately 50 years ago, Irving Rouse introduced the concept of the Shantok ceramic tradition to New England archaeology, which he defined as a distinct ceramic tradition associated with the historically known Pequot-Mohegan people of southeastern Connecticut (Rouse 1947). Since that time, the belief that Shantok ceramics were a distinct ethnic or cultural marker has gone largely unchallenged and unexamined, and when comparable ceramics have appeared in adjacent areas occupied by other tribal groups, their occurrence has been attributed to the diaspora that followed the Pequot War of 1637. This paper presents a critical analysis of the Shantok tradition concept, drawing on contemporaneous ceramics from adjacent areas of southeastern New England to demonstrate that Shantok ceramics did not function as ethnic or tribal markers during the seventeenth century, and that the ethnicity or tribal identity of particular potters cannot be inferred from either the stylistic or technological attributes of these vessels.[1]

THE SHANTOK CERAMIC TRADITION: ITS ORIGIN AS AN ARCHAEOLOGICAL CONCEPT

Rouse's (1947) Shantok tradition was formulated on the basis of ceramic assemblages from the seventeenth-century Mohegan village at Fort

Figure 9.1
Tribal Territories and Sites with Seventeenth-Century Ceramic Sherds Discussed in the Text

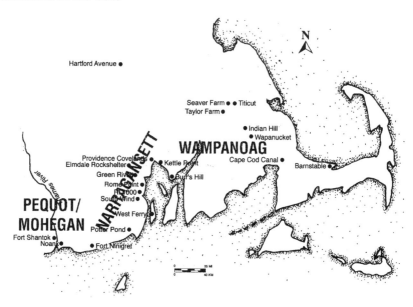

Prepared by Dennis E. Howe.

Shantok on the Thames River near Norwich and a second site in Noank, Connecticut (Figure 9.1). While lacking the time depth normally associated with ceramic traditions, Shantok ceramics were judged to be so different from Windsor ceramics that Rouse placed them in their own tradition. Shantok ceramics were described as shell-tempered, thin-walled vessels with round bases, distinct shoulders and necks, and collars with prominent triangular lobes (Figure 9.2). Castellations were common, and collars and castellations were decorated with "bands" and "plats" of incised lines and punctations. Small effigies of human or animal heads were present on some castellation points. Other nodes were present on castellation points or beneath them on the base of the collar; these either had "... a phallic appearance ... [or] ... resemble ears of corn" (Rouse 1947:16).

The origins of this tradition were held to be "obscure," and Rouse suggested that the Pequot-Mohegan people were themselves recent immigrants to the region, bringing with them a mix of exotic ceramic traits that became incorporated into Shantok pottery (1947:22–23). Rouse very explicitly linked the ceramic style with an ethnic group:

Figure 9.2
Ceramic Sherds from Fort Shantok

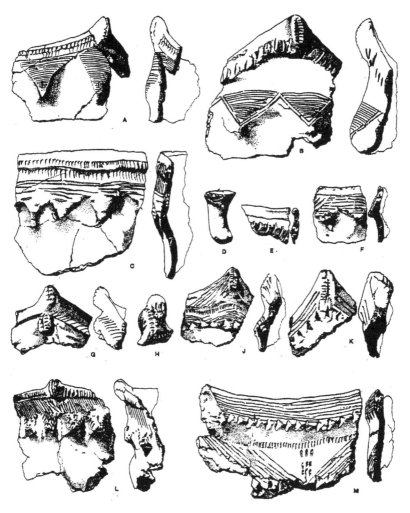

Irving Rouse. "Styles of Pottery in Connecticut." *Bulletin of the Massachusetts Archae-
    ological Society*, 7 (1945): 1–18, Figure 2, 3.

Alone of all the local traditions, *this one coincides in distribution with a tribal
group*. Its type site, Fort Shantok, was a historic Mohegan village and in Connecticut it is limited in distribution to the area occupied at the time of historic
contact by the Mohegan-Pequot. To be sure, the tradition also occurs on eastern
Long Island; this may indicate the tradition spread to other tribes or it may be
the result of Pequot flight across the Sound during historic times (1947:22–23;
italics added).

In adjacent areas of southern New England, according to Rouse, ceramics of the Niantic phase of the Windsor tradition (ca. 3000–450 B.P.) predominated (1947:21) during this period. If this pattern was correct, then the assertion of Rouse and later archaeologists of the limited distribution of Shantok ware and its association with the Pequot-Mohegan would be supported. More recent interpretations of Windsor tradition ceramics, however, indicate that Niantic ceramics originate in the beginning of the Late Woodland period (ca. 1100 B.P.) (Lavin 1988b), and that their association with Contact-period sites by Rouse is unsubstantiated (McBride 1984:147). It now appears that Rouse's understanding of the spatial distributions of seventeenth-century ceramic styles was based in part on erroneous temporal information, reopening the question of what other ceramic styles might exist at this time, and what the true distribution of Shantok ceramics was.

Subsequent archaeological research in southern New England did not question, but merely elaborated on, the association of Shantok ceramics with the Pequot-Mohegan. Carlyle Smith's (1950) study of ceramics from Fort Corchaug on Long Island included a number of vessels he assigned to the Shantok tradition. His description is essentially similar to Rouse's, although he notes the use of clamshells to create both incised and stamped lines (1950:112). He explains the presence of Shantok ceramics on Long Island by noting that "in 1637 or 1638 impetus was given to the adoption of the Shantok culture by the migration of a group of Pequot to eastern Long Island after the Pequot War," and that ". . . Shantok pottery . . . was introduced into eastern Long Island from Connecticut just prior to the middle of the seventeenth century" (Smith 1950: 109–110). Smith also shared with Rouse the idea that the creators of Shantok were recent immigrants to the area, suggesting that "in about 1600 the Mohegan-Pequot invaded Connecticut" (1950:109). With regard to Rouse's original definition of Shantok ceramics, Smith noted that "because Rouse based his definition of the Shantok tradition on the pottery from the site, it is per se Shantok" (1950:112). The reification of this ceramic type based on the serendipity of this particular assemblage being available continues to affect archaeological interpretations of ceramics in southern New England. It is tempting to speculate on how interpretations might have differed if the Fort Corchaug assemblage were described first and the assemblage from Fort Shantok interpreted as a derivative of it, or if a ceramic assemblage from the heart of Narragansett country in what is now Rhode Island had been the focus of Rouse's efforts.

The noted archaeologist Ralph Solecki conducted his own study of

Fort Corchaug in light of Rouse's original definition (Solecki 1950, 1957). Noting the basic similarity of Fort Corchaug ceramics to those from Shantok, while also noting more subtle differences in technology and design, he asked ". . . are the variations in technique on a foreign pottery (Shantok) local in character, or are these techniques also exotic?" (1950:5). Solecki (1950:8) shared the view of Rouse and Smith that the Pequot-Mohegan were recent invaders, coming into the area in the early 1600s. The distribution of the Shantok ceramic style he also attributes to the effects of the Pequot diaspora, noting: "It is not improbable that the germ of Shantok pottery originated with the Pequots who were conquered and dispersed among the several neighboring tribes, spreading the idea of a new ceramic style or at least making some innovations in the pottery of their own milieu" (Solecki 1950:9). Unlike his contemporaries, Solecki does note the paucity of good ceramic data from adjacent tribal areas, and stated that it would be significant to ". . . note what pottery type the Narragansetts then had, as they also received their share of vanished Pequots" (1950:35).

The work of Rouse, Smith, and Solecki helped fix in the archaeological literature the notion that Shantok ceramics originated with the Pequot-Mohegan, were diagnostic of that cultural group, and that the appearance of these ceramics outside the Pequot-Mohegan homeland was due to diffusion resulting from the Pequot War and the subsequent diaspora. These interpretations were taken up by other archaeologists to explain away the frequent occurrence of Shantok-like ceramics appearing elsewhere in southeastern New England. Contact-period vessels from a grave at the Taylor Farm site in North Middleboro, Massachusetts, were classified by Fowler (1974) as belonging to the Shantok tradition. He explained their presence at this site as reflecting "captured Pequot women" living among the local Wampanoag (Fowler 1974:17). Similarities with Shantok ceramics were noted at other Wampanoag-area sites including Wapanucket in Massachusetts (Robbins 1959:64; 1980) and Burr's Hill in Rhode Island (Johnson 2000a:130), and when contemporaneous vessels from Narragansett sites were discovered, they too exhibited a strong similarity to Shantok ceramics (Simmons 1970:110–113; Mayer n.d.).

Many of the problems involved in interpreting the meaning and distribution of ceramic styles in New England stem from Rouse's essentializing description and the lack of comparative data from adjacent regions. Subsequent studies have increasingly emphasized the diversity within the Shantok assemblage. Williams (1972) reanalyzed the ceramic assemblage from Fort Shantok and reported that it was far more heterogeneous than implied by Rouse. She subdivided an assemblage of 107 vessel lots into six "classes" based primarily on vessel profile (a vessel lot constitutes all sherds assignable to a single vessel). Of these 107 vessel lots, only 35 vessels were sufficiently complete to permit classification, and no class had more than seven vessels. Two of the classes had only three examples of each. In addition, five of the 35 vessels were "so distinctive [as] to be unclassifiable" (Williams 1972:346–352). Williams acknowledged the "wide range of variation in Shantok ware" and suggested that this variation

makes it seem unlikely that all subtypes are directly associated with the Mohegan. Undoubtedly somewhere within the . . . classification is the Mohegan's "Shantok ware," but, on the basis of the present sample alone, it cannot be positively identified. Other types may be associated with surrounding Indian groups, *about whose pottery little is known.* (Williams 1972:347; italics added)

Williams' depiction of the Shantok assemblage as surprisingly small and heterogeneous might have given pause to archaeologists assuming these ceramics were an ethnic marker, but her findings did not change the prevailing consciousness about the nature of Shantok ceramics as a marker of Pequot-Mohegan identity.

In sum, the Shantok ceramic tradition was formulated by Rouse on the basis of a small, heterogeneous sample dominated by vessels from a single site. Assumptions about its relationship to other ceramic traditions, phases, or types were skewed by a lack of chronological control and little worthwhile comparative data on seventeenth-century ceramics from adjacent areas, and by a naive assumption of a rigid association between ceramic styles and ethnic groups (cf. Stark 1998b). As more archaeological data became available, and it became clear that Shantok-style vessels were widely distributed outside the Pequot-Mohegan homeland, they were explained as the result of diffusion from the Pequot War. It was never suggested that, perhaps, Rouse's original formulation had been in error, and the highly diverse ceramics given the Shantok label were not the original, exclusive products of any one ethnic or tribal group.

THE SHANTOK TRADITION: MODERN USES

In recent decades, the Shantok tradition construct has shown surprising resilience, with many archaeologists furthering and promoting the assumptions and conclusions of Rouse. The steadily accumulating body of ceramic data from southeastern New England has, however, imposed increasing strains on the Rouse interpretation. One of the first to question it was McBride, who argued that Shantok was best conceived of as a "horizon style with various local and regional expressions," rather than a product of a single ethnic group (1984:261). Instead, he proposed a Hackney Pond ceramic phase, representing a Contact-period continuation of the Windsor ceramic tradition, which contained many different pottery types, including Shantok Incised (McBride 1984:155; cf. Lavin 1987: 35). Subsequently, McBride argued for a variation on the older school of thought, arguing that Shantok ceramics were the distinct product of the Mohegan people, manufactured only after the defeat of the Pequot by the Mohegan, Narragansett, and English in 1637 (McBride 1990:99). Hackney Pond ceramics, in contrast, were associated with the Pequot homeland between the Thames and Pawcatuck Rivers (Lizee 1994a; McBride 1990:99), although it is admitted that they are "not as precise as an ethnic marker as Shantok" (Lizee et al. 1995:518).

Lizee (1989, 1994a), while supporting the association of Shantok ceramics with the historic Mohegan, also presents data indicating how uncertain the relationships between ceramic "traditions" and specific communities really are (Lizee et al. 1995). In a comparative compositional analysis of Niantic, Hackney Pond, and Shantok ceramics, Lizee et al. (1995) argue that the Shantok ceramic tradition derived from earlier Windsor tradition ceramics, but that "Windsor and Shantok tradition ceramics in southern New England show a considerable geographic overlap," and that Hackney Pond ceramics, elsewhere attributed to the historic Pequot, actually "have been recovered from a wide range of sites and ecozones in southern New England" (Lizee et al. 1995:516–520). Specific data presented in this analysis indicate that Hackney Pond ceramics were recovered from the Mohegan site at Fort Shantok, and at least one Shantok vessel was recovered from the Pequot fort at Mystic, Connecticut. While it is acknowledged that "Shantok decorative practices were followed in several zones" and that the decorative traits of Hackney Pond ceramics "were also disseminated widely," Lizee et al. attempt to preserve Rouse's original construct by arguing that the "main focus of Shantok production" was in the Mohegan homeland west of the Thames River (1995:516–520). As in almost all previous interpretations of Shantok, little effort is made to consider ceramics to the east of this area from the Narragansett and Wampanoag homelands.

Current interpretations of ceramic style have been shaped by the realization that stylistic behavior is complex, subject to many variables, and that style may express many aspects of individual and social identity and are often not direct reflections of social or ethnic identity (Conkey

1990:11; Wobst 1977; Stark 1998b; Hodder 1986). Wiessner (1983) has distinguished "emblemic" style, which signals group identity, from "assertive" style, which is expressive of individual identity. The use of style to signal group affiliation is likely to occur only in specific contexts (Hodder 1979, 1982) and with particular types of material culture that are suitable for such expressions (Wobst 1977). While interpretations from Rouse and Smith to McBride have argued that Shantok is an example of Weisner's "emblemic" style, it has become increasingly necessary to explain why ceramics would have been used to express group identity by examining both the social and historic contexts in which ceramics were used and the motivations of individual potters.

THE POLITICS OF POTTERY

The most ambitious attempt at an updated defense of the Rouse-Smith interpretation of Shantok ceramics as markers of tribal identity has been developed by Johnson (2000a, 2000b). According to Johnson, Shantok ceramics are the distinctive product of the historic Mohegan people, produced after the Pequot War. The motivation for the production of an emblemic ceramic style lay in the tensions of the Contact era and the need to forge and maintain a distinct Mohegan identity as increasing numbers of refugees from other groups arrived in Mohegan villages. These stresses created the need for the "production of material culture with new, distinct design elements that expressed messages of community solidarity" (Johnson 2000a:122). As emblemic markers, Shantok ceramics ". . . should be distributed predominantly within the Mohegan homeland" west of the Thames River (Johnson 2000a:126).

Johnson first attempts to identify which stylistic characteristics define Shantok pottery. Although acknowledging the diversity in this assemblage and the fact that many of the decorative attributes present in the assemblage are found outside the Mohegan homeland, he argues that Shantok ceramics "are so distinct they are their own type" (Johnson 2000a:127) and "can be distinguished by certain decorative characteristics" (Johnson 2000a:129–130):

Specifically, the applied or extruded lobes or notched rings along the base of the collars are considered to be almost entirely unique to Shantok wares. Prominent castellations and their occasional modeling are also most often associated with Shantok ware . . . although other northeastern pottery styles occasionally exhibit these attributes. (Johnson 2000a:129–130)

According to this definition, then, the presence of lobes is the only definitive attribute of Shantok ceramics.

In attempting to show that Shantok ceramics are indeed restricted to the Mohegan homeland, Johnson, like archaeologists before him, employs little comparative data to make this case. While Shantok is held to be distinct from Hackney Pond based on an analysis of very small ceramic samples by Lizee (1989, cited in Johnson 2000a:131), Johnson cites only a single site to the east, Fort Ninigret, to buttress his argument. The Fort Ninigret assemblage has been analyzed by Mayer (n.d.) and by the author (Goodby 1994:72–73, 127–129). As Johnson acknowledges, the ceramic assemblage from the site is small, consisting of only five vessel lots attributable to the Contact period. These five vessel lots include only six rim sherds among them, most of which are very small and none of which is sufficient to determine overall decorative motifs or vessel forms. Thus, the Fort Ninigret assemblage cannot be held to be "significantly different" from Shantok ceramics (Goodby 1994:127–129, cf. Johnson 2000a:138).

An analysis of Contact-period Narragansett and Wampanoag ceramics and comparison of these to published descriptions of Shantok tradition ceramics by the author (Goodby 1994, 1998) is to date the only effort at the sort of regional comparison needed to evaluate the "emblemic" status of Shantok pottery relative to assemblages to the east. Data from this study can also be used to evaluate claims about the distribution of Shantok ceramics, especially when a single decorative trait, the presence of lobes, is held to be definitive of the type. At the Contact-period Narragansett cemetery RI-1000, one of three vessel lots had lobes (Goodby 1994:140), and at the Narragansett cemetery at West Ferry, also in Rhode Island, three of four vessels had lobes. Lobes also occur frequently further to the east in the Wampanoag homeland. All three vessels from the Taylor Farm site in North Middleboro, Massachusetts, have lobes, as do two of three vessels from the Titicut site in Bridgewater, Massachusetts (Goodby 1994:171–176). Two of the four vessels from Burr's Hill in Rhode Island have closely-spaced punctates along the base of the collar that resemble lobes (Mrozowski 1980) and contribute to their "Shantoklike" appearance (Johnson 2000a:130).

The distribution of "prominent castellations and . . . occasional modeling" also extends into the homelands of adjacent peoples and are commonly encountered on a variety of Narragansett and Wampanoag sites (Goodby 1994, 1998). Even the modeled figures on the peaks of castellations are identical to those from Fort Shantok, including the "ear of corn" effigy that is widely encountered (Figure 9.3). Likewise, the bands

Figure 9.3
Wampanoag Ceramic Vessels with "Corn Ear" Effigies

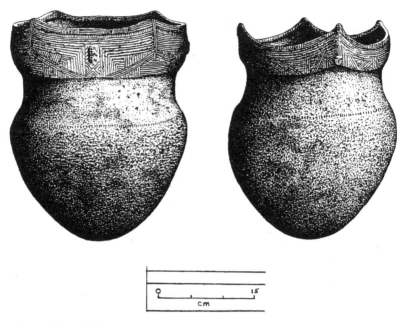

Left: Seaver Farm, Bridgewater, Massachusetts. *Right*: Cape Cod Canal Pot.

William S. Fowler, revised by Curtiss R. Hoffman. *A Handbook of Indian Artifacts from Southern New England*. Middleborough, MA: Massachusetts Archaeological Society, 1991, 90.

of incised lines on collars and castellations noted by Rouse are commonly encountered on vessels from Narragansett and Wampanoag sites. In sum, what has been proposed as the only true diagnostic attribute of Shantok tradition ceramics, lobes, are not confined to the Mohegan homeland, and no other attribute or set of attributes can convincingly distinguish Shantok ceramics from contemporaneous ceramics to the east.

Finally, while Johnson provides a clear explanation for why the Shantok tradition emerges (to promote Mohegan identity), he does not explain who among the increasingly diverse community at Fort Shantok was promoting this ideal, and why the women producing ceramic vessels would choose to express this ideal in their art. The Mohegan themselves, under the politically ambitious sachem Uncas, had only recently split from the Pequot (Weinstein 1991:10; Johnson 2000b:162), and the Mohegan community at Fort Shantok included "Mohegans, Pequots, refugees from eastern Massachusetts, individuals from Long Island, and people from other southern New England communities" (Johnson 2000b: 163). While it is clear that "Uncas and those who had an interest in maintaining his position" (Johnson 2000b:164) had an interest in promoting a consciousness of Mohegan unity, it is not at all clear why individual women in this community would have followed his lead, especially if this would have required that they turn away from their natal communities and their own identities. Instead, the diversity of the Fort Shantok community is mirrored in the diversity of the ceramic assemblage from that site noted by Williams (1972:347), and many of the most overt stylistic attributes of these ceramics are encountered across the different tribal homelands of southern New England (Goodby 1994, 1998).

THE SHANTOK TRADITION RECONSIDERED

A number of serious problems exist with the Shantok tradition concept as defined by Rouse and employed by three generations of archaeologists in New England. First is the high degree of diversity within the Fort Shantok assemblage and within seventeenth-century ceramic assemblages generally (Luedtke 1985, 1986b). This diversity frustrates attempts to formulate clear definitions of ceramic types (Chilton 1998, 1999b; Pretola, this volume), resulting in descriptions that can include many ceramic vessel lots from the Narragansett and Wampanoag homelands to the east. A second problem, derivative of the first, is an uncertainty about which attribute or combination of attributes is definitive of Shantok, as the definitions have shifted continually over the years. A third problem is the lack of comparative data from tribal homelands to the east, and the misinterpretation of that data when they have become available. A fourth and related problem is explaining the remarkable frequency with which "Shantok" ceramics occur in other tribal homelands (see Lavin, this volume). Attributing this to the diaspora of Pequot women following 1637 begs the question of where the "local" (non-Shantok) ceramics are, and why the wares of the Pequot refugees should be so widespread and conspicuous.

An alternative interpretation developed elsewhere (Goodby 1994, 1998) is that ceramics did not function as tribal or ethnic markers during the seventeenth century. Instead, in the context of an ongoing debate about Native identity and responses to English "divide-and-conquer" tactics, many Native people chose to emphasize the shared bonds of kinship and culture that crossed the "tribal" boundaries of the seventeenth century, boundaries that themselves may have been of recent origin (Robinson 1990). This emphasis on a common, shared identity and interests resulted in the production of ceramic styles whose distributions did not, and do not, correspond to tribal boundaries but instead were used to blur those boundaries. While the promotion of collective tribal identities by Uncas and other sachems was part of the reality of seventeenth-century Native politics, these male sachems were not the makers of ceramic vessels. The women who did make and decorate pots may well have dissented from the theme of division in Native politics, following instead the views of those like the Narragansett sachem Miantonomi who was actively urging the unification of all Native people in a common effort to survive in the face of English colonial aggression (Goodby 1994:210–212; Simmons 1989:42).

Nor should it be thought that questions of tribal identity are the only, or even the most important, "meaning" expressed in the styles of these pots. The elaboration in form and decoration seen in seventeenth-century ceramics reflects an artistic renaissance in a traditional technology that defies the trend toward a rapid loss of traditional culture in the seventeenth century. Native women, presented with European brass and copper kettles that were far more durable than their clay pots, responded not by abandoning their traditional wares but producing them in increasingly more elaborate and expressive forms. One of the meanings of these pots, then, is a preference for "traditional" Native culture, a meaning whose importance transcends tribal boundaries.

In the face of rapid acculturation, war, disease, and a myriad of stresses on "traditional" culture, ceramic vessels became an icon of cultural resistance to colonialism (Handsman 1988, 1990; Rubertone 1989). This is seen not only in the ceramic renaissance of the seventeenth century, but also in the creation of a new class of ceramic vessel, miniature vessels whose distribution is limited to graves (Luedtke 1985:221–226). Present in a small number of graves in Narragansett cemeteries at RI-1000 and West Ferry, and in Wampanoag cemeteries at the Burr's Hill and Taylor Farm sites, these pots indicate that the meaning of ceramics was important enough to include them in the most sacred of contexts, and that this was done in a way that did not respect tribal boundaries.

Problems with interpreting the nature and meaning of stylistic variability in this area are exacerbated by the use of the Shantok assemblage as a reference. The notion that Shantok ceramics themselves are distinctive is an artifact of archaeological history and not an inherent feature of the ceramics themselves. The Fort Shantok assemblage became the touchstone and main point of comparison only because it was excavated prior to most other contemporaneous sites, because the ceramic assemblage from the site was seemingly distinct from Windsor tradition ceramics, and because of the erroneous assumption that the Pequot-Mohegan people were a recently arrived migrant population. There is nothing in the stylistic variability from the Fort Shantok assemblage, however, that can justifiably be called "classic" or "archetypal" relative to ceramics from adjacent areas to the east. The Shantok construct itself, by equating a single, heterogeneous assemblage with a particular cultural-historical entity (the seventeenth-century Mohegan), has impeded the recognition of both variability and similarity in regional ceramic assemblages. In addition, acknowledging basic similarity by applying the term "Shantok" to any given vessel or assemblage does little to explain or illuminate that similarity. Shantok tradition ceramics are not a "type" or "tradition" coterminus with the Mohegan people, but (as has been suggested by both McBride [1984:161] and Simmons [1970: 46–47]) part of a widespread stylistic sphere encompassing people throughout southeastern New England and Long Island. If the notion of a Shantok ceramic tradition is to be maintained, then it seems it must be extended well to the east and across the boundaries of deeply estranged communities. The utility of extending the geographic boundaries of the Shantok tradition, however, is questionable. Instead, the concept should be abandoned.

ACKNOWLEDGMENTS

The author gratefully acknowledges the following individuals and institutions for providing access to data discussed in this chapter: Carol Barnes and Pierre Morenon, Rhode Island College; Paul Robinson, Rhode Island Historic Preservation and Heritage Commission; James Bradley and Malinda Bluestain, R.S. Peabody Museum of Archaeology; the late Nanepashemet, Plimoth Plantation; William Taylor, Middleboro, Massachusetts; Ronald Dalton, Ruth Warfield, Tom Lux, and Curtiss Hoffman, Robbins Museum of Archaeology; Ned Dwyer, Rhode Island School of Design; Mary Minor, Jamestown Historical Society; and Deborah Cox, Alan Leveillee, and Duncan Ritchie, Public Archaeology Laboratory, Inc.

Figure 9.1 was prepared by Dennis E. Howe. Permission to reprint the illustrations in Figures 9.2 and 9.3 was granted by the Massachusetts Archaeological Society, and their cooperation is gratefully acknowledged. Sharon MacCartney of the Division of Behavioral Science, Franklin Pierce College, provided invaluable assistance in editing and preparing the manuscript. Jordan Kerber is thanked for his editorial advice and for his almost limitless patience. Inspiration and guidance for my research on seventeenth-century ceramics was provided by Patricia Rubertone, Brown University, Paul Robinson, Russell Handsman, and the late Nanepashemet. Finally, the late Barbara E. Luedtke is thanked for her insights into ceramic variability and for her unfailing generosity and collegiality.

NOTE

1. Many of the ceramic vessels from seventeenth-century Narragansett and Wampanoag sites were removed from graves. Illustrations and photographs of these sacred items are not included in this paper out of respect for the wishes of many Native people.

10

Those Puzzling Late Woodland Collared Pottery Styles: An Hypothesis

Lucianne Lavin

INTRODUCTION

The middle-late Late Woodland period in New England, the Hudson valley of eastern New York, and the upper Delaware valley of New Jersey is marked by the appearance of collared pottery with incised decoration virtually identical to Iroquois ceramic types. Specifically, pots tend to resemble early Mohawk types such as Chance Incised and Deowongo Incised, as described by MacNeish (1952). Chance phase styles contain rather finely applied incising in a band about low to medium collars, often with incised or linear punctate neck decoration (MacNeish 1952:78). Chance Incised lacks basal collar notches, while Deowongo Incised exhibits small basal notching (Lenig 1965). The time frame for this incised-collar horizon style appears to be from about A.D. 1350 to 1500. After this, the collared pottery becomes more regionalized.

Brumbach (1975) first addressed this phenomenon in her innovative statistical analysis of ceramic attributes from Iroquois sites in the Mohawk valley of eastern New York and from supposed Algonquian sites in the Hudson valley. Brumbach performed tests based on the frequency distribution of decorative and metric attributes. The tests failed to distinguish two discrete ceramic groups, and so Brumbach concluded that the Mohawk Iroquois and the Hudson valley Algonquians had shared a common ceramic tradition. She hypothesized that this tradition was the result of an "interaction sphere," "possibly an exchange network of raw materials and foodstuffs, which was subsequently disrupted by the European-oriented fur trade" (Brumbach 1975:28).

Pretola (this volume) recently has shown that microscopic identification of ceramic manufacturing techniques of pots from Mohawk and Algonquian homelands can demonstrate some basic differences in Iroquois and Algonquian technological styles. This breakthrough in archaeological method, however, does not explain why the decorative style of those groups was indistinguishable. Brumbach (1995) recently revisited this subject, and hypothesized on the kind of interaction sphere that caused the phenomenon. She suggested that the spread of Iroquoian-like pottery styles into Algonquian territory was due to the diffusion of maize horticulture and an accompanying corn ceremonial complex, such as the historically known Green Corn Ceremony, from Iroquoian groups to the west and south of the Hudson valley.

This hypothesis is not easy to test, given the difficulties of uncovering religious/ceremonial activities in the archaeological record. Further, radiocarbon dates between A.D. 850 and 1020 have been associated with maize remains at six New York and New England sites (Bendremer 1993:Table 13-3). They indicate maize horticulture predates by several hundred years the earliest known occurrence of collared-incised pottery in the Northeast (ca. A.D. 1200–1250) (Lenig 1965:66–67; Niemczycki 1986:36).

I believe Brumbach is partially correct in her assessment that an interaction sphere is responsible for the similarities in collared-incised pottery, but the situation is a bit more complicated than her hypothesis indicates.[1] Consequently, I propose a more expansive, more testable hypothesis that concerns associated language groups or dialects, the dynamics of inter-group relations, and stable settlement patterns. Each of these social entities acted upon one another in a dynamic feedback situation that modified the material cultures of the societies in question.

Ethnohistorical documents show that neighboring Native villages who spoke the same language and shared similar economic and political needs forged socio-political links through marriage, social events, and loose political coalitions to help meet those needs. Kith, kin, clan, and other social and economic relationships connected each neighbor to the settlements of its neighbor, and so forth. These social links down the line formed an intricate communications network along which goods and ideas quickly traveled. This would include notions of ceramic function and design. Such sharing of the rather limited decorative techniques and geometric designs found on Northeastern pottery would result in geographically expansive ceramic horizons like the middle-late Late Wood-

Figure 10.1
Map of Study Area, Showing Location of Sites Discussed in the Text

land incised-collar pottery horizon. To convince readers of this hypothesis, a short review of ceramic sequences in New England is essential. The map in Figure 10.1 shows the localities and sites mentioned in the text.

NEW ENGLAND CERAMIC HORIZONS

During the early Contact period (ca. 450–400 B.P.), the geographic area presently known as New England and easternmost New York (i.e., the portion of the state east of the Hudson River) was inhabited mainly by Algonquian-speaking Indian societies (Snow 1980). In this relatively small geographic expanse, the presence of a broad ceramic horizon style is not confined to the Late Woodland period (ca. 1000–500 B.P.). We find virtually identical pottery styles in the Early Woodland (ca. 3000–2000 B.P.) and in the Middle Woodland (ca. 2000–1000 B.P.) periods, as well. In fact, greater New England prehistory includes four such major ceramic horizons: (1) a cord-marked interior horizon; (2) a dentate and rocker-stamped horizon; (3) a cord-wrapped stick or paddle-edge decorated horizon; and (4) an incised-collar horizon.

Cord-Marked Interior Ceramic Horizon

The first ceramic horizon dates to the Early Woodland and early Middle Woodland periods (ca. 1000 B.C.–A.D. 500). It is represented by the type Vinette Cord-Marked Interior. These pots are characterized by cord- or fabric-wrapped paddle impressions on both the interior and exterior surfaces of an undecorated wide-mouth pot with a conical base. Variants of this type include partially-smoothed interior or exterior surfaces, or both, or rare decoration in the form of simple incision, punctation, or cord stamping.[2] Neither the type nor its variants appear to be confined to any specific geographic region (Brumbach 1979; Fowler 1966; Goodby 1995; Lavin 1987; Lavin and Miroff 1992; Lizee 1994a:48–50; Lopez 1957:23–32; Petersen and Sanger 1991:126–131; Ritchie and MacNeish 1949; Rouse 1947; Smith 1950:195; Wiegand 1987).

Dentate and Rocker-Stamped Ceramic Horizon

The standard time marker for the early Middle Woodland period is dentate and rocker-stamped decorated pottery (Figure 10.2). Dentate pottery is decorated with a series of rectangular or square "toothmark"-like impressions similar to the impression made when one bites into a chocolate bar; hence the term "dentate." Rocker-stamping refers to the application of a toothed or toothless tool in a rocking motion across the wet clay to produce a series of curved V-shaped impressions. The stamping often was applied in an overall pattern to both the upper and lower body of the vessel. This style of pottery is called by several type names, depending on the geographic locality in which it was found: Vinette Dentate, Vinette Complex Dentate, and Point Peninsula Rocker-Stamped in New York and western New England (Ritchie and MacNeish 1949); Matinecock Point Stamped, Clearview Stamped, Linear Dentate, and Rocker Dentate in southern New England and coastal New York (Smith 1950; Lavin 1984, 1987; Lizee 1994a; McBride 1984; Wiegand 1987); and Wheeler's Punctate-Dentate in northeastern Massachusetts (Barber

Figure 10.2
Dentate Stamped Pottery from Connecticut Sites

1982). In parts of northern and eastern New England, pots exhibiting similar dentate styles were untyped (Childs 1984; Dincauze 1975; Fowler 1966; Goodby 1995; Petersen 1980, 1985; Petersen and Sanger 1991).

The attribute clusters characteristic of each dentate type or style, however, are virtually identical: usually smoothed exterior surfaces, although cord-impressed exteriors sometimes occur; interior surfaces are usually smoothed, but cord-impressed and channeled or brushed interiors also occur;[3] bases may be conical or bag-like; rims may be straight-sided or slightly flaring; and the dentate and rocker-stamping decorative techniques are sometimes combined with punctation in a variety of motifs, the most common of which are parallel horizontal rows of stamping often underlain and/or overlain by diagonal, triangular, or rocker elements (Barber 1982:46; Cassedy 1998, esp. Fig. 41; Childs 1984a, 1984b; Goodby 1995:49–53; Lavin 1987; Lizee 1994a, esp. Figs. 9–12; McBride 1984; Petersen 1985; Petersen and Power 1985; Petersen and Sanger 1991:131–136; Ritchie and MacNeish 1949; Rouse 1947; Smith 1950: 195–196; Wiegand 1987). Again, these attributes and attribute combinations are widely dispersed throughout the research area.

Figure 10.3
Cord-Wrapped Stick Stamped Pottery from Connecticut Sites

Cord-Wrapped Stick Stamped Ceramic Horizon

The third ceramic horizon includes Point Peninsula-like cord-wrapped stick decorated pottery, often exhibiting punctates as a secondary decoration. The Point Peninsula tradition was originally ascribed by Ritchie to Middle Woodland Native American groups in interior New York and Ontario (Robert E. Funk, personal communication, 2001; Ritchie and MacNeish 1949). Researchers in those regions traditionally believed that the early Late Woodland Owasco tradition derived from that of Point Peninsula (Ritchie 1980; Funk 1976), a belief that has been challenged recently by Snow (1995). Snow's hypothesis has been strongly opposed by other New York and Ontario researchers at subsequent local and regional archaeology meetings. In any case, Point Peninsula- and Owasco-like ceramics have been recovered from New England sites (Figures 10.3 and 10.4). The cord decoration was produced by impressing a cord-wrapped stick or paddle edge into the soft clay. Pots with similar forms and designs occur throughout New York and New England. Familiar styles include parallel horizontal or vertical rows encircling the rim, often bordered above and/or below by opposing rows; herringbone design; parallel plats (Cassedy 1998, esp. Fig. 16; Childs 1984a, 1984b;

Figure 10.4
Cord-Wrapped Stick Stamped Pottery from the Apponaug Site, Rhode Island

Fowler 1966; Goodby 1994:58–61, 1995:54; Lavin 1987, 1997, 1998; Lavin and Miroff 1992; Lavin et al. 1993; Lizee 1994a, esp. Figs. 16–17; Luedtke 1980a, 1985, 1986b; Petersen 1980, 1985; Petersen and Power 1985; Petersen and Sanger 1991:142; Ritchie and MacNeish 1949; Smith 1950:137–138, 191–192; Wiegand 1987). In northern New England, the pottery has been dated between A.D. 600 and 1500 (Petersen and Sanger 1991:Tables 7.5–7.7). The few dates from southern New England place the style between A.D. 940 and 1070 (Lizee 1994a:Table 6).

The traditional hypothesis presented for the wide distribution of these three early ceramic horizon styles has been the itinerant nature of Native American societies during the Early Woodland and early Middle Woodland periods. The emphasis on settlement pattern archaeology and regional archaeological surveys in the past 15 years, however, has shown this to be untrue in southern New England, at least. Surveys by McBride (1984; McBride and Dewar 1981; McBride et al. 1979, 1980; Feder 1981) and others indicate a semisedentary seasonal round within a fairly circumscribed area for these groups. Nor does the presence of these pot styles seem to be a sporadic result of trade. Large sites that appear

Figure 10.5
Collared-Incised Pottery from Eastern New York

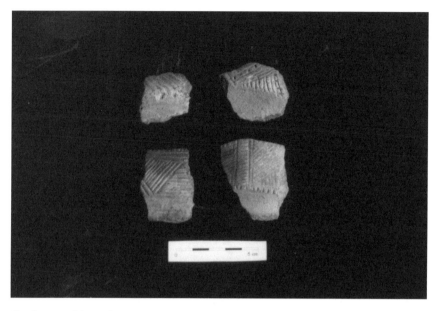

Confluence of Roelof Jansen Kill and the Hudson River.

to be base camps contain significant percentages of pots representing these styles (Lavin and Miroff 1992; Luedtke 1985; Petersen and Power 1985), all of which suggest their manufacture by local residents.

Collared-Incised Ceramic Horizon

It is no surprise that the collared-incised wares manufactured in New England ca. A.D. 1350–1500 cannot be distinguished from the contemporary New York Iroquoian pottery types, particularly Chance Incised and Deowongo Incised (Figures 10.5–10.7). They exhibit mainly smoothed, but sometimes impressed, exterior surfaces; interior surfaces are usually smoothed but channeled, or brushed interiors also occur. Bases are bag-like. The pots exhibit shoulders, necks, and collars. Collars are incised with a band of geometric designs such as chevrons, triangles, rectangles, and/or a series of opposed diagonal lines. Sometimes the band is bordered above and/or below with a row of diagonal notches or small punctates, or one or more horizontal lines. Castellations sometimes occur. Necks and shoulders may exhibit simple design motifs such as a row of diagonal or straight incised lines, plats of horizontal/diagonal

Figure 10.6
Collared-Incised Pottery from Various Connecticut Sites

incised lines, or a row of punctates. Lower bodies are undecorated. Again, these attributes and attribute combinations are not concentrated in specific river valleys or microenvironments. They are found throughout New York, New Jersey, and New England (Brumbach 1975, 1995; Cassedy 1998, esp. Fig. 25; Fowler 1966; Kraft 1975a; Lavin 1988b; Lavin et al. 1993; Lavin et al. 1996; McBride 1984; Petersen and Sanger 1991:151–154; Puniello 1980; Werner 1972).

An important point here is that this phenomenon of geographically widespread ceramic horizon styles is not new. It is just more visible in the late prehistoric period because there were more people on the landscape, making more pots. Additionally, Iroquoian studies, with its concomitant emphasis on Iroquoian collared pottery and its social meaning, has been a major focus of archaeological studies for the past 30 years (Bradley 1987; Chapdelaine 1990; Foster et al. 1984; Hayes 1980; Kuhn 1996; Kuhn et al. 1993; Niemczycki 1984, 1986, 1991; Pendergast 1996; Pratt 1976; Prezzano 1996; Richardson and Swauger 1996; Smith 1987; Snow 1991; Tooker 1970; Trigger 1981; Tuck 1978; Warrick 1988). As yet, the published literature contains not one article professing to demonstrate definitive regional distinctions among any of the pottery types/ styles comprising each of these four ceramic horizons, except in the vaguest manner.[4]

Figure 10.7
Collared-Incised Pottery from the Upper Delaware Valley

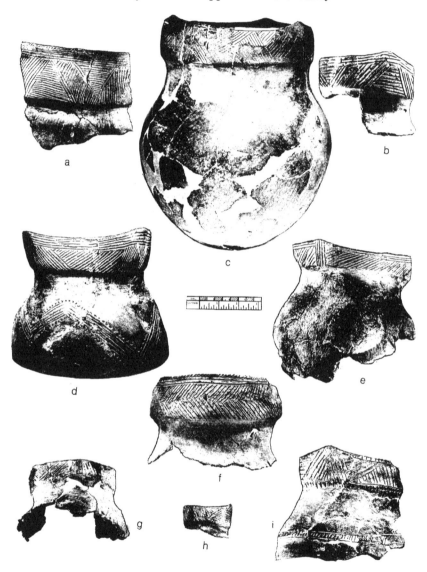

Herbert C. Kraft. *The Archaeology of the Tocks Island Area*. South Orange, NJ: Seton
Hall University Museum, 1975b, 135, Figure 8.

METHODOLOGY IN POTTERY ANALYSIS

In order to develop ceramic sequences and generate cultural interpretations based on ceramic assemblages, one needs to classify the pottery sherds. The two main systems of classification are attribute analysis and typology. Attribute analysis involves the comparison of classes of artifact features, such as incising or dentate-stamping as classes of decorative techniques. In the last 10 years or so, a number of local researchers have concentrated on classification and comparison of technological attributes (Chilton 1996, 1999b; Kuhn 1987; Pretola, this volume). Typological studies involve comparison of classes of artifacts, such as rim sherds or whole pots (Rouse 1972; Lavin 1986; McBride 1984; Lizee 1994a; Wiegand 1987).

As I noted 15 years ago, attribute analysis and typology are often depicted, erroneously, as diametrically opposed ways of standardizing archaeological data (Lavin 1986:3). Twenty-five years earlier, Rouse (1960) demonstrated to opposing camps of analysts that attribute analysis and typology are really complementary stages in the ordering of archaeological data. Because a type consists of a recurring group of attributes, logic demands that attribute analysis must be the first step in a ceramic study. The result of such a study leads to the generation of sherd lots, which may (or may not) represent types. A sherd lot is further divided into vessel lots (a vessel lot constitutes all sherds assignable to a single vessel). A truly "cultural" type exhibits a combination of attributes that was consistently produced, consciously or unconsciously, by members of a particular social group at a given time and within a given spatial range.

Rouse (1960) also demonstrated how attribute analysis and typology could provide different, yet complementary, forms of cultural information. Attribute analysis has been used to discern cultural change within a group, as well as cultural diversity among groups (Chilton 1996, 1999b; Luedtke 1985, 1986b; Pretola, this volume). Because types consist of attribute complexes, a typology may conceivably mask artifact variation (Lavin 1986:3). Alternatively, their relative complexity makes types more reliable in discerning cultural stability and cultural sharing. Typology has been most helpful in establishing time periods (Lavin 1987; Lenig 1965; Lizee 1994a; McBride 1984; Ritchie and MacNeish 1949; Smith 1950), and in delineating socio-cultural units across the landscape in both New York and New England (Lavin 1998; MacNeish 1952; Niemczycki 1984, 1986, 1991; Puniello 1993).

Both systems of classification have enjoyed periods of alternating popularity throughout the twentieth century (for historical examples, see Rouse [1960, 1972]). Attribute analysis is presently enjoying a popularity surge among some New England archaeologists, particularly in central Massachusetts. Typologists have become the straw men for graduate students wishing to make a stronger case for their attribute classification studies of cultural diversity.

As noted above, I and others before me conceded long ago that types are not conducive to such studies, and frankly, I am not interested in exploring prehistoric societies from that end of the theoretical continuum. I am interested in artifact similarities because they imply sustained human interactions. As an anthropological archaeologist, I am most interested in what kinds of socio-cultural behavior promoted the sharing of ceramic attribute clusters through time and space. To that end, I have used both attribute analysis and typology (Lavin and Kra 1994; Lavin 1998; Lavin et al. 1993).

THE REGIONALIZATION OF CERAMIC STYLES

During the very late prehistoric and early historic periods (ca. A.D. 1500–1550), we do begin to see some geographic patterning of what Goodby (this volume) and Pretola (this volume) refer to as "emblemic" styles of pottery. Goodby notes that "emblemic style signals group identity." The key word here is the rather amorphous term "group." As Goodby and Pretola show, New England archaeologists have often interpreted emblemic style as an ethnic or tribal marker. However, an emblemic style might also represent a socio-political alliance, a social (e.g., marriage pool) or economic (e.g., exchange network) interaction sphere, or a language group. All of the latter could include the exchange of ideas and/or women.

Southeastern New England

An example of such an emblemic style is Shantok ware. Sites in southeastern New England and easternmost Long Island contain large amounts of Shantok Incised pottery, which is normally characterized by smoothed exterior and interior surfaces, pronounced necks, round bases and globular bodies, applied rings, nodes, and bosses with anthropomorphic and "corn" designs, and thick, castellated collars with bands of incised lines (Goodby 1994; Lizee 1994a; McBride 1984; Rouse 1947; Smith 1950; Williams 1972).[5] Although the major decorative technique appears to be incision, Smith (1950) and Williams' (1972) extensive analyses of vessels

Figure 10.8
Shantok Incised Pottery from Fort Shantok in Uncasville, Connecticut

from Fort Shantok, a seventeenth- to eighteenth-century Mohegan for-
tification along the lower Thames River in Connecticut, and other sites
led both to conclude that the design was produced by stamping and
dragging the edge of a clam shell (Figure 10.8; see also Williams 1972:
Plates 49–71 and Lizee 1994a:Figs. 60–84). Site 75–6 in southeastern
Connecticut and site RI 118 in Rhode Island have provided radiocarbon
dates of A.D. 1520 and 1750, respectively, for Shantok ceramics (Lizee
1994a:Table 8).

Many researchers have attributed Shantok ware to the historical Mohegan Tribe. Goodby (this volume) details this history, and uses ceramic
data from Rhode Island and eastern Massachusetts to help refute that
theory. Goodby believes that Shantok ware was a stylistic sphere that
cut across ethnic boundaries and included Narragansett and Wampanoag,
as well as Mohegan peoples. More ceramic assemblages are required to
test this hypothesis. However, if Goodby is correct that Shantok pottery
is not a marker for the Mohegan ethnic group, it does not necessarily
follow that Shantok ware is not an emblemic style.

Shantok ware does not appear to represent a language group. Masthay
and Siebert (1997) report that Mohegan-Pequot members spoke a y-
dialect of Algonquian, while Narragansett and Wampanoag members

spoke an n-dialect. Goodby (this volume) suggests that Shantok ware is inter-ethnic and gender specific, representing southeastern New England Native women's promotion of a pan-Native identity/unity. Another possibility is that Shantok represents an interaction sphere of the various southeastern New England and eastern Long Island ethnic groups created and continued by inter-group marriage and resultant kin networks. Documentary evidence demonstrates that political hostilities in eastern New England did not preclude intermarriage. Rather, the loose form of political alliances forged by seventeenth- and eighteenth-century New England Native American societies (Salwen 1978:167–168) necessitated other socio-economic relationships such as marriage and kin ties to help stabilize the fragile political relationships. For example, the 1679 account of the genealogy of Uncas, sachem of the Mohegan, showed descent from Pequot, Narragansett, and Long Island Indian societies (Salwen 1978:167–168). Perhaps the distribution of Shantok ware and, ultimately, those ceramic styles characterizing the other regions, discussed below, represent the geographic extent of a Native marriage pool.

Upper Delaware, Hudson, and Housatonic Valleys of Western Connecticut

Sites in the upper Hudson valley and westernmost New England tend to exhibit Garoga-like pottery styles, with an incised band of interlocking plats of verticals, horizontals, obliques, or triangles underlain by a row of large, deep, distinctive punctates at the base of the collar (Funk 1976; Lavin et al. 1996, esp. Fig. 8; MacNeish 1952).[6] The lower-mid Hudson valley and upper Delaware valley sites contain a majority of Munsee and Kingston Incised styles, characterized by high collars with intricate incised designs with ladder and "dot" elements and effigy faces (Cassedy 1998, esp. Fig. 24; Diamond 1994; Werner 1972; Kraft 1975a, 1978; Puniello 1980). Kraft (1975a) dates the Munsee and Kingston Incised types to A.D. 1500–1700. He subsumes Kingston Incised pottery within the type Munsee Incised, although Diamond and Ritchie consider both styles to be separate types (Lavin et al. 1996:122). Figures 10.9 and 10.10 depict examples of these regional styles.

Middle Connecticut Valley

Researchers in south-central Massachusetts and central Connecticut have identified a distinctive style that was originally referred to as Guida tradition ceramics, after the Guida Farm type site in Westfield, Massa-

Figure 10.9
Garoga-Like Pottery from the Goldkrest Site in East Greenbush, Upper Hudson Valley

chusetts (Byers and Rouse 1960; Lizee 1994a; McBride 1984). This tradition is characterized by globular vessels of very fine paste with shallow constricted necks, very low collars without castellations, and finely drawn and finely incised or stamped, closely spaced designs in a horizontal band about the collar. Nodes, bosses, and modeled figures are absent. Modeling occurs in the form of a ring around the vessel below the rim. Small lobes sometimes occur that are incised rather than applied.

Byers and Rouse (1960) identified Guida as a distinct ceramic tradition. Based on her analysis of one of the collections from Guida Farm, Chilton interpreted the Guida tradition ceramics as "nothing more than a residual category" (Chilton 1999b:101). She suggests that the type ceramics are simply a localized phenomenon (Chilton 1999b:100–101). Nevertheless, McBride (1984) and later Lizee (1994a) identified "Guida-like" ceramics from several sites in the Connecticut valley of central Connecticut. I have seen similar pottery in amateur collections from central Connecticut as well, particularly those of the late Ray Marin (Figures 10.11 and 10.12). McBride (1984) has suggested that some of the pottery I identified as Niantic Stamped in my analysis of the Ben Hollister assemblage from Glastonbury, Connecticut, as a graduate student in the

Figure 10.10
Munsee Incised Pottery, Feature 239, Faucett Site, Bushkill, Pennsylvania,
Upper Delaware Valley

From Moeller 1992:35.

1970s (Lavin 1980) may have been Guida-like. For the record, I believe
he is correct; a few small rim sherds have very low (ca. less than one
inch) collars with little neck.

McBride placed the Guida-like pottery in the Hackney Pond phase,
the final phase of the Windsor tradition (McBride 1984:155–159). Lizee
(1994a) reclassified the ceramics in a new type, Hackney Pond. He
placed this type within the Hackney Pond phase, which he believed was
characterized by three ceramic types: Hackney Pond, Niantic, and Shantok (Lizee 1994a:87–89). He cites two radiocarbon dates for Hackney
Pond ceramics, A.D. 1680 and A.D. 1770 (Lizee 1994a:Table 8). Lizee
(1994a:91) does not consider Shantok a separate tradition, but rather a
part of the historic Windsor tradition. For good depictions of the Guida/
Hackney Pond style, see Lizee (1994a:Figs. 54–58) and McBride (1984:
Fig. 4.24).

Figure 10.11
**Two Guida-Like Hackney Pond Phase Vessels from Marlborough in
Central Connecticut**

Northern New England

Petersen and Sanger (1991:157–160) describe distinctive fabric-paddled, incised-collared vessels, and uncollared fabric-paddled vessels with no decoration or with cord-wrapped stick decoration dated between A.D. 1550 and 1750 from sites in southwestern Maine and adjacent New Hampshire and northern Massachusetts. They note that "few, if any of these latter ceramics closely resemble Proto-Iroquoian or Iroquoian specimens and therefore, a non-Iroquoian horizon style or styles can be postulated for most of eastern New England, Maine, and the Maritimes" (Petersen and Sanger 1991:157–160, Figs. 7.14–7.19).

South-Central Connecticut, Long Island, and Lower Connecticut Valley

There is an exception to the sequence of inter-regional horizon styles. It is the Windsor ceramic tradition, originally described by Rouse (1947) and Smith (1950) over 50 years ago. I believe that this exception was created by the northeastern movement of people from Delmarva into the

Figure 10.12
Guida Incised Vessel, Hackney Pond Site, Haddam, Connecticut

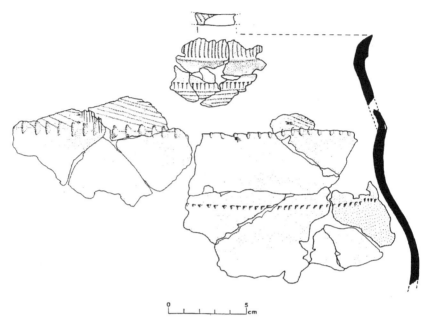

Kevin A. McBride. *Prehistory of the Lower Connecticut River Valley.* Storrs, CT: Ph.D.
   dissertation, Department of Anthropology, University of Connecticut, 1984, 191.

Long Island Sound area sometime during the middle Middle Woodland
period. The Windsor tradition is characterized by the pottery techniques
of brushing, net impression, fabric impression, and shell stamping (Rouse
1947; Smith 1950; Lavin 1980, 1987; Lavin et al. 1993; Lizee 1994a;
McBride 1984). In its final Woodland phase, it was characterized by
collared, scallop-shell-stamped vessels with smoothed or impressed bag-
like bodies usually typed as Niantic Stamped, Niantic Stamp and Drag,
or Clason's Point Stamped (Figure 10.13).

   The Windsor ceramic tradition is a discrete tradition, with pottery
types quite distinct from the surrounding dentate and cord-stamped ceramic horizons into which it spread, forming a wedge that practically
divided the present state of Connecticut in half. I have discussed elsewhere this hypothesized population movement from the Delmarva, the
geographic distribution of Windsor pottery, and its probable affiliation
with one of the major language groups of southern New England (Lavin
1998). In sum, the distribution of the Windsor ceramic tradition along
the Connecticut coast, lower Connecticut valley, and adjacent Long Is-

Figure 10.13
Niantic Stamped Vessels from Various Sites in South-Central Connecticut

land corresponds with that of the Quiripey-Unquachog language group. The tradition suggests sustained social interaction among its speakers that probably included kin visits, intermarriage, economic assistance, and other socio-political events as documented for early historic Connecticut Native American societies (see below).

Puniello's (1993) study of the late Windsor type, Niantic Stamped, supports this theory. He concluded that the type's distribution was not a marker for the Niantic ethnic group but rather for some more geographically extensive social group. Niantic Stamped pottery has been dated as late as A.D. 1690 ± 100 (Lizee 1994a:Table 8).

SOCIAL CORRELATES

What are the social mechanisms behind these material patternings? Why do we find the same ceramic styles ranging widely throughout New England and eastern New York during most of the Woodland period? Why do they only form geographic clusters during the very Late Woodland and early historic periods? In other words, what do these trends in material culture tell us about the people who made the pots?

The semi-sedentary nature of Algonquian social groups, the intensity of interaction among such groups, and the ease in which members were able to change their group alliances is a scenario described by various researchers in early historic Algonquian studies (Binzen 1997; Bragdon 1996; Frazier 1992; Johnson 1993; Salwen 1978). I hypothesize that the broad, sequential ceramic horizons are the result of stable long-term socio-economic forces operating within Algonquian societies during these time periods. Grumet reported such intensive socio-economic relationships among the seventeenth-century upper Delawaran Algonquians: "Alliance insured survival, and was cemented by kinship ties, proof of military competence, and gifting. Kinship was constantly reaffirmed by the presence of relatives in the households of allies, and continually validated through the claims to kinship-defined rights and obligations made upon each other" (Grumet 1978:268).

My recent studies of eighteenth-century Moravian missionary records of Native American village life in northwestern Connecticut and northeastern New York support these findings (Lavin 2001). The Moravians were an evangelical Protestant sect with headquarters in Bethlehem, Pennsylvania. In the 1740s they established mission villages at the Indian settlements of Shekomeko in eastern Dutchess County, New York; Wechquadnach in Sharon, Connecticut; and Pishgatikuk (Schaghticoke) in Kent, Connecticut. The missionaries kept extensive and detailed records of their Native flocks that included diaries, letters, baptismal records, and other vital statistics. They document that members of these mission villages and other nearby Indian settlements consistently visited one another for mutual economic and political reasons, and to participate in kin-related activities. Marriages between members of adjacent villages were common (Moravian Church 1743–1760, 1751–1758). Additionally, missionary records show that adjacent groups spoke similar dialects of Algonquian so that they easily understood one another's Native tongues from the Mahikan territory along the Hudson valley east to Stockbridge, Massachusetts, and south down the Housatonic as far as present-day Newtown. The linguistic similarities and the aforementioned social processes would certainly have contributed to a free exchange of ideas on ceramic manufacture, aesthetics of design, and symbolic imagery.

Of course, this scenario describes Native American societies at Contact, at which point their cultural characteristics may already have been altered by Euro-American influences. However, in regard to the regions in question (western Connecticut, eastern New York, and western Massachusetts), these geographic areas were the western frontier at the time period in question. Because of the French and Indian War (1754–1763) and earlier eighteenth-century French-English conflicts, few settlers ventured into the area for fear of Indian attack (Trumbull and Hoadley 1850–1890). Also, boundary disputes between New York, Connecticut, and Massachusetts made this region undesirable for English settlement until the mid-eighteenth century (Connecticut Resolves and Private Laws 1837). Consequently, the Native settlements there were less affected by English colonialism than were their Native contemporaries to the east and south. Moravian documents note that in the 1740s and 1750s, Native societies in northwestern Connecticut were still practicing their seasonal round and other traditional economic activities (Moravian Church 1751–1758; Binzen 1997:68–87).

Moreover, archaeological evidence supports this scenario of small, fairly mobile groups of Algonquians in southern New England and eastern New York during the Woodland period. Settlement pattern studies show that Early and Middle Woodland sites tend to be small, nonsedentary, and diffuse in artifact contents. Dietary studies based on floral, faunal, and flotation analyses show that the occupants practiced a mixed hunting, fishing, and gathering economy within a semi-sedentary seasonal round (Feder 1981; Funk 1976; Handsman 1989; Lavin et al. 1996; McBride 1984; Petersen 1980; Snow 1980). In some areas, Late Woodland base camps become larger through time and contain greater amounts of artifacts and biological remains, reflecting population growth and increasing sedentism that appear to be associated with the adoption of horticulture inland and the growth of marshlands along the coasts (Bendremer 1993; Bernstein 1987; Bragdon 1996; Lavin 1988a, 1988b; McBride 1984). The data, however, suggest a continuation of earlier Woodland seasonal round and semi-sedentism. This social fluidity continued to foster the swift exchange of ceramic functional and stylistic attributes and culminated in the incised-collar horizon.

The increasing population and increasingly sedentary behavior indicated by the regional archaeological surveys discussed above may have interacted in a feedback system, eventually creating the need for some terminal Late Woodland/Contact Native societies to protect their economic resources from other groups, whether these be productive marshlands, important anadromous fish camps, or fertile horticultural fields. Or possibly they were protecting hunting territories for fur pelts, wampum shell territories, or strategic bays or coves in which European traders could set anchor. Such protection eventually may have led to territorial circumscription and the regionalization of material cultures (or groups of cultures). Specifically, constricted social liaisons in the form of marriage, kin visits, and ephemeral political alliances created the geographic clustering of emblemic styles during terminal Late Woodland and Contact times.

CONCLUSIONS

Widely dispersed ceramic horizon styles among Algonquian-speaking societies in greater New England were not confined to the middle-late Late Woodland period. Rather, broad ceramic horizons were shared throughout the Early Woodland and Middle Woodland periods as well. The four ceramic horizons discussed above reflect the social mobility, social fluidity, and intensive interrelationships that characterized the small, semi-sedentary, politically decentralized, yet economically stable, Algonquian societies.

Both Goodby (1994) and Pretola (this volume) point out that Native American socio-cultural groups were open and fluid systems. Linguistic similarities and habitual intermarriage among these social groups served to intensify system fluidity (group interactions); i.e., the free exchange of ceramic-making ideas and ceramic-making women that culminated in the incised-collar ceramic horizon. Positive feedback between gradual population expansion and the increasingly intensive exploitation of marshlands, fertile farmlands, or environments related to European trade, however, may have fostered territorialism among later Algonquian groups. Geographic constriction instigated the regionalization of Native societies and their material cultures, as exemplified by the geographic clustering of emblemic ceramic attributes during the final Woodland and early historic periods.

ACKNOWLEDGMENTS

This chapter and the accompanying graphics are the result of the generosity of the many persons who allowed me to study and photograph their ceramic collections. The late Barbara Luedtke, John Pretola, Dena Dincauze, Elizabeth Chilton, and Fred Dunford kindly provided access to various Massachusetts collections. I thank Carol Barnes and Pierre Morenon for allowing me the opportunity to study ceramic assemblages from Apponaug and other Rhode Island sites. Roger Moeller kindly provided access to ceramics from Faucet and other upper Delaware valley sites. Robert Funk and Lynne Sullivan, Joseph Diamond, and Hetty Jo Brumbach generously allowed me to peruse New York ceramic collections from their respective institutions. Ralph Solecki at Columbia University, and the staffs at Garvies' Point Museum and Preserve and at the Suffolk County Archaeological Association's museum and research center kindly allowed access to Long Island collections. Several amateur archaeologists graciously allowed me access to their Connecticut collections, especially Jeffrey Tottenham, the late Ray Marin, the late Andy Kowalsky, the late John Dorso, and the Albert Morgan Archaeological Society. David Thompson provided access to the collections of the Greater New Haven Archaeological Society. The Connecticut Office of State Archaeology allowed access to the Bull collection. Kevin McBride has always been most generous in allowing me access to his collections and unpublished work. Irving Rouse of Yale's Peabody Museum and staff at the Institute of American Indian Studies provided access to their institutions' collections. An earlier version of this chapter was presented in 1997 at the 64th annual meeting of the Eastern States Archaeological Federation at Mount Holly, New Jersey. The present version profited from subsequent conversations with Northeastern ceramic specialists in the audience, particularly Jim Petersen. I thank Robert Funk and Roger Moeller for their critiques of draft versions of this chapter. I thank Jordan Kerber for his constructive editing and helpful suggestions. They enhanced the final version of this chapter. Figure 10.1 was drawn by the author, who also took the photograph in Figure 10.11. The remaining photographs that appear in this article were taken by the author with assistance from Marina Mozzi (Figure 10.4), Susan DiPiazza (Figures 10.2, 10.3, 10.6, 10.8, and 10.13), Noel Coonce-Ewing (Figure 10.5), and staff of Archaeological Research Specialists (Figure 10.9). Roger Moeller took the photograph in Figure 10.10. Permission to reprint Figures 10.7 and 10.10 was granted by the Archaeological Research Center at the Seton Hall University Museum and Archaeological Services, respectively. Also, I am grateful for permission from Kevin McBride to reprint Figure 10.12.

NOTES

1. In this context, "interaction sphere" is a very loose term that merely means sustained human relationships, the important word being "sustained."

2. Radiocarbon dating suggests, tentatively, that the variants may be time-sensitive; i.e., the type changes through time. Partial smoothing and simple rim decoration appear to be an early Middle Woodland phenomenon that may have a functional basis; e.g., smoothed interiors were easier to clean, which improved flavor and hygiene (see Luedtke [1985]). At the Wicker's Creek site in Westchester County, New York, Vinette I and partially smoothed and/or decorated

interior cord-marked vessels were recovered from the same levels. A radiocarbon date of 10 ± 100 B.C. suggests a terminal Early Woodland date (Lavin 1988c; see also Lopez 1957, who also hypothesizes that the cord-marked interior ceramic horizon occurs in later contexts). Ritchie (1959) found a Vinette I-like pottery with smoothed interiors associated with Orient phase habitation sites on Long Island.

3. Ceramic surface treatment that exhibits parallel horizontal grooves is usually called "channeling" by New York archaeologists, "scoring" by workers in the Delmarva region, and "brushing" by New England archaeologists.

4. I do not mean to imply that the Native cultures participating in these ceramic horizons were not dynamic. Within each horizon there was variability as well as overlap of types and attributes through time. For example, dentate-decorated pots were produced side by side with undecorated modified Vinette Interior pots. Owasco uncollared corded types were produced side by side with corded collared types. The horizons appear to reflect a more or less continuous development of northeastern cultures over 3000 years.

5. These design elements have also been referred to as "caterpillars" and women's genitalia, depending on each individual's interpretation of what the design represents.

6. Lenig (1965) includes the Iroquoian types Garoga Incised, Otstungo Incised, and Cayadutta Incised within this category. Wagoner Incised is a similar type also found in the upper Hudson valley. Although they occur in earlier contexts, the majority of these pottery types occur between A.D. 1500 and 1600 (Lenig 1965:66–67).

11

An Optical Mineralogy Approach to Northeastern Ceramic Diversity

John P. Pretola

INTRODUCTION

For generations, American archaeologists have used ceramic typology to construct chronology and culture history. Overall, typologies enable archaeologists to organize data for various purposes, to describe, and to communicate with their peers, but typology also has its limitations. Hodder (1986:49) points out that typology requires us to assume that artisans are passive, share the same set of rules and norms, and assign the same meanings to corresponding behavior. Hodder insists that this view does not acknowledge the individual's active social role. Artifact diversity cannot be understood by a method that fails to allow for individual agency (Hodder 1986:49).

Despite its utility elsewhere, typology has not been successfully applied in the Northeast where ceramic trait diversity defies typing. At times, Northeastern archaeologists have been guilty of ignoring that diversity and forcing the typological method on their data, creating overgeneralized types and confusing our understanding of prehistory. Relying upon these typological misconstructions, many archaeologists view New England Algonquians as passive cultural receivers. The southern New England ceramic typology (Smith 1947; Rouse 1947) strives to make pots equivalent to people, creating a false picture and ultimately giving the impression that southern New England prehistory had much less cultural dynamism than was the case.

By contrast, researchers in eastern New England have refused to apply the typological method to diverse ceramic assemblages there. Dincauze (1975) summarized the situation when she concluded that ceramic traits circulated widely and were differentially selected and recombined throughout the Northeast. Taking a similar stance, Luedtke (1986b) also saw ceramic diversity and regional differentiation in eastern New England coastal zones. Although Luedtke did not assume that this pattern was typical of all New England, the record for the upper Merrimack valley (Kenyon 1983) supports her findings of a series of small "micro traditions" (Luedtke 1986b:132). These clusters of differing pottery production coincide with geographic provinces within the coastal plain and its river valleys. These eastern New England studies show that when archaeologists avoid typology-bound methods, the pattern that emerges is one of extreme diversity in ceramics. While all assemblages and traditions display many of the same forms and styles, these are often recombined in geographically specific ways that defy typological classifications.

In this chapter, I adopt a non-typological approach to investigate and explain the ceramic diversity of southern New England. Specifically, I examine the puzzling existence of "Iroquoian" ceramic traits in southern New England. This study explores the use of technologic stylistic analysis to explain Iroquoian ceramic traits in terms of ceramic production and culturally determined choices. To do this, I formulate four hypotheses phrased in terms of ceramic composition and manufacturing technology that are testable using symbolic and technologic stylistic analysis. My methodology relies upon ceramic petrography and uses optical mineralogical analysis with polarized light to study plastic (i.e., pliable ceramic paste elements such as clay and impurities) and aplastic (i.e., nonplastic paste elements such as temper and inclusions) ceramic constituents. Ceramic petrography involves the systematic description and classification of rocks and minerals, present as inclusions in ceramic pastes, by means of microscopic examination of thin sections. Ceramic petrography relies upon the polarizing microscope in which light is changed by passage through a prism, or other polarizer, so that its transverse vibrations occur in a single plane. By observing the behavior of crystals in polarized light, it is possible to identify accurately the aplastic constituents of ceramic pastes in order to establish origin of ceramic manufacture (Williams 1983:301). I also examine construction techniques with traditional macroscopic analysis, as well.

CENTRAL NEW YORK TRAITS IN SOUTHERN NEW ENGLAND

Superimposed over this puzzle of diverse micro traditions and bounded entities is the problem of "Iroquoian" traits in southern New England. Because the Rouse/Smith model equates ceramic traditions with social groups, some archaeologists have continued an outmoded line of study following Willoughby (1909:93), who first attributed the spread of "Iroquoian" traits to warfare and tribute relationships. He, like many others of his day, thought that the Iroquois "exerted a strong influence on the arts of the less cultured Algonquians" (Willoughby 1909:94).

Like their southern New England counterparts, some archaeologists in New York State and southeastern Canada also have equated ceramic styles with societies. Iroquoianists, for example, continue to judge differences in the quality of material culture, dubbing "superior" and "well made" ceramics Iroquoian, and "crude," "rudely" decorated pots, Algonquian. They ignore the possibility that Iroquoian-like pottery could be made by Algonquian-speakers.

Archaeologists developing the paradigms in southern Ontario and elsewhere constructed dichotomous Iroquoian and Algonquian trait lists that they used to classify sites (Griffin 1946; Parker 1923; Ritchie 1932; Skinner 1919b, 1921, 1923; Wintemberg 1931). None thought the variability could be due to diachronic indigenous development (Trigger 1985:60). They explained the variability in terms of Iroquois migration, following the lead of French Jesuit missionaries who, in the sixteenth century, used migration to explain northern Iroquois origins (Thwaites 1896, 21:193–195). Parker (1916), himself a Seneca, contended the Iroquois homeland was in the southeast. He based this on Iroquois tradition and linguistic data linking their language to Cherokee.

By 1939, some archaeologists began to question the migration theory. Flannery (1939) noted that the Iroquois and Algonquians shared many traits, and Griffin (1944) questioned the lack of hard evidence for migration. Fenton's (1948) review of Northeastern anthropology emphasized cultural similarities, while reaffirming the idea that Owasco culture represented prehistoric Iroquois. Fenton also observed that archaeologists had ignored the direct historic approach in constructing their culture histories. It was not long before MacNeish, under Griffin's encouragement, made the direct historic approach the methodological cornerstone for his "In Situ Hypothesis" of Iroquois development (MacNeish 1952). MacNeish compared historic Iroquoian, "pre-Iroquoian" Owasco (ca. 1000 B.P.), and Point Peninsula (ca. 1900 B.P.) ceramics (Ritchie and

Figure 11.1
Map Showing the Location of Sites in This Study

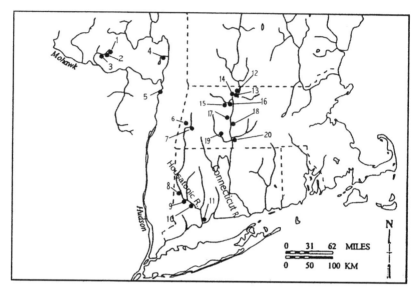

Key: (1) Smith; (2) Garoga; (3) Klock; (4) Winney's Rift; (5) Goldkrest; (6) Chassell; (7) Hop Brook #1; (8) Boulder Home; (9) Whitlock; (10) Lover's Leap; (11) Milford, CT; (12) Bennett Brook; (13) Gill; (14) Falls River; (15) Stillwater Bridge; (16) Acorn Squash; (17) Bark Wigwams; (18) Hockanum; (19) Guida Farm; (20) Springfield Fort Hill.

MacNeish 1949), to show the three were related. He interpreted this to mean that local Point Peninsula ceramics, which archaeologists had previously associated with Algonquian cultures, were prehistoric Iroquois.

More recently, Starna and Funk (1994) have questioned our ability to distinguish between Iroquoian groups and Algonquian cultures based on their material culture. Starna and Funk now think that distinguishing between Iroquois and Algonquian ceramics is difficult due to the number of shared types that appear distributed in a clinal manner. These clines, or geographic gradients of shared morphological traits, extend beyond New York State, and many "Iroquoian" ceramic traits are found far beyond Iroquois geographic limits. Brumbach (1975) was unable to distinguish between Mohawk (Iroquoian) and Mahican (Algonquian) pottery in the Hudson River valley, claiming both groups' pottery was indistinguishable morphologically and stylistically. Subsequently however, Brumbach and Bender (1986) identified ceramics from the Winney's Rift site, in the upper Hudson River valley, as Mahican (Figure 11.1). They relied upon X-ray fluorescence to analyze trace elements in ceramic pastes to show the use of Hudson River valley clays rather than those from the Mohawk River valley (Kuhn 1986). The evidence, however, is not strong. To the south, the upper Delaware River valley sequence is a long continuum from Point Peninsula through Contact (ca. 1900–500 B.P.), and we know these historically Algonquian speakers appear to have made "Iroquoian" pottery (Kraft 1975a). Starna and Funk (1994) argue that Northeastern ceramic traits do not correlate with tribes or ethnic groups, and that MacNeish's study has not stood the test of time.

The overlapping and clinal distributions of "Iroquoian" traits pose a dilemma for both southern New England and Iroquoian archaeologists. Northeastern archaeologists who equate cultural groups with specific ceramic types and deny ceramic diversity have entered a theoretical cul de sac. They can only rely upon migration, trade, and manufacture by immigrant potters to explain the ceramic diversity they see. Many anthropologists know that cultural interactions are more reciprocal and dynamic than this paradigm allows. The world is, and has been, a totality of interconnected processes and cultures, not a series of bounded entities. Societies have always been open systems involved with others near and far in complex sets of interrelationships. Traditional taxonomic approaches have produced a false model of reality that makes nations, societies, and cultures appear internally homogeneous and externally bounded so that in contact situations, entities repel each other rather than encounter, respond, and adapt to each other. Human societies are linked through ecological, demographic, economic, and political connections. It was true in the past, as it is true today (Wolf 1982).

Eastern Algonquians have not been studied as open systems interacting with their neighbors in a complex set of relationships. Instead, they have been viewed as morally inferior and manipulated to supplement interpretations of Iroquois culture history as in this passage:

The eastern [Algonquian] tribes probably equaled the Iroquois in bravery, intelligence, and physical powers, but lacked their constancy, solidity of character, and capability of organization. . . . [The Algonquians were] incapable of combining in large bodies even against a common enemy. (Hodge 1906:43)

This thinking has its archaeological counterpart in the extension of Ritchie's (1946) New York classification to New England. Even Bullen (1948), who favored interpretations stressing cultural continuity for southern New England, thought in terms of borrowed central New York ceramic traits. Fowler's (1948) four "stages" of ceramic development

continued the tendency for New England archaeologists to compare findings with New York State and to assume a unidirectional flow of innovation. As late as 1969, Young (1969) commented that the general
prehistory of the central Connecticut River valley followed the prehistoric outline for New York. Although Dincauze (1969) rightly stated that
should be tested, not assumed, the New York scheme continues to dominate New England prehistory.

TESTING A MODEL OF STYLE

Recent theoretical advances that view style as the product of symbolic
behavior suggest that technological traits such as clays, tempers, and
manner of construction can be indicators of group affiliation (Chilton
1996, 1999b; Plog 1990; Sackett 1990; Wiessner 1990). Wiessner (1990:
107) defines style as "a form of non-verbal communication through doing
something in a certain way that communicates information about relative
identity." This can include asserting group affiliation (Hodder 1982,
1987; Wobst 1977). Style can reside in both functional and decorative
attributes, and its expression can be active or passive, shifting as the role
of the artifact changes. Sackett (1985, 1990), Wiessner (1985, 1990) and
Plog (1990) have developed the idea that style exists as manifestations
of symbolic, iconographic, and technologic behavior. This triad was pos-
ited by Binford (1962), who, inspired by White (1959), first described
his technomic, socio-technic, and ideo-technic artifact categories.

Symbolic style is personal expression manifested as either assertive or
emblemic styles, or a combination of both. Assertive style conveys information about individual identity and self-image, but is culturally and
historically determined. Assertive style carries a vague message, and is
subject to fashion swings that lead people to borrow, ignore, or differentiate their styles from those of others. Emblemic style, on the other
hand, transmits a clear message of conscious affiliation and identity to a
specific receiving audience. Emblemic styles may change slowly due to
errors of reproduction, or rapidly when the referent changes. Neither
assertive nor emblemic styles are mutually exclusive. Iconographic style
is a special form of symbolic style in which components correspond
specifically to spoken ones, often containing conscious messages that are
clear, purposeful, and aimed at a particular audience, as with religious
symbolism (Plog 1990; Sackett 1990; Wiessner 1990).

Technologic style manifests itself as variation in manufacturing attributes. Potters in one society may coil their vessels from the right to the
left, while others may coil from the left to the right. Some potters may

refine their clay by kneading, while another group may favor foot tread-
ing. One people may employ a particular variety of clay or temper that
constitutes a conscious or inadvertent statement about raw material preferences and availability.

Although there can be more than one way to make and use something,
enculturation, the process by which individuals learn the potter's trade
according to socially accepted norms, dictates that artisans will express
a limited range of techniques. Due to this specificity, technologic stylistic
elements may correlate closely with group affiliation. The concept of
technologic style changes the way archaeologists view the interplay of
style, form, and function. Style resides in both decorative and technologic
attributes. Stylistic analysis must include the way something is made, its
composition, and its intended function. It dictates that group affiliation
can be inferred from ceramic construction techniques and raw material
choices. Underhill (1944:86) illustrated how technological distinctions
can be made for modern Pueblo groups. For example, the Rio Grande
Pueblos favor volcanic sand temper, while Santa Ana and Zia Pueblos
prefer crushed volcanic rock, and the potters of Taos and Picuris prefer
a micaceous clay that requires no additional temper (Underhill 1944:86).

Although Sackett (1985) argues that technologic style is passive,
Wiessner (1990) correctly states that it may switch from passive to active
if conditions require. Technologic stylistic attributes change slowly while
symbolic stylistic characteristics are dynamic and rapidly changing. In
summary, style as symbolic behavior resides in both decorative and technologic attributes, and group affiliation can be inferred from ceramic
construction techniques, raw material choices, and decorative motifs. The
concept of technologic style serves as an aspect of middle-range theory
that researchers (Rice 1987; Van der Leeuw and Pritchard 1984) have
long sought to convert technical analysis of ceramics into explanations
of human behavior.

ASSUMPTIONS ABOUT STYLE AND CERAMIC PRODUCTION

The concept of technologic style, then, is a powerful tool to examine
southern New England "Iroquoian" ceramics. It is an excellent means to
test hypotheses about interaction formulated in terms of ceramic composition. Technologic style is learned behavior that is slow changing,
and represented as variation in manufacturing attributes. Because of the
enculturative nature of technologic style, it is possible to distinguish
social phenomena, especially group affiliation, using ceramic petrogra-

phy and macroscopic examination of technologic traits. The following assumptions about style and ceramic production guide this study.

Assumption One

Technologic style is a product of enculturation and thus is less likely to change than other forms of style in a given culture. Technologic style suggests that enculturation directs the manner of construction and choice of raw materials. The concept of technologic style means that method of construction, sources and composition of plastic and aplastic components, and execution of decorative designs and design combinations are significant clues to group affiliation (Sackett 1985, 1990).

Assumption Two

A group's ceramic traits are a mix of symbolic and technologic styles. Since both symbolic and technologic style can convey meaning, we must be aware of an interaction of the two (Plog 1990; Sackett 1990; Wiessner 1990). The way that stylistic traits are located, combined, and executed may suggest group affiliation. For example, linear plat designs (i.e., discrete layouts of incised vertical, horizontal, and oblique lines) on a Mohawk River valley vessel may be executed with a broad stylus, while southern New England renderings may be done with a small, sharp stylus, or even a fine cord. Even the size and thickness of the vessels related to their intended function can suggest group affiliation.

Assumption Three

Ceramic stylistic attributes can be changed, mixed, and matched. Many archaeologists reject the existence of a direct relationship between stylistic variation and social boundaries, but accept the idea that similarity between two groups' ceramics can be an expression of interaction or a shared ideology (Arnold 1985; Chilton 1996; Dincauze 1975; Hodder 1986; Lizee 1994b; Luedtke 1986b; Petersen 1990; Plog 1990; Sackett 1990; Wiessner 1990). Potters always have choices that are subject to revision from changing social environments and interaction with other groups. The similarity between two groups' ceramics can be an expression of identity, but at other times, we might expect to find great dissimilarities as potters strive to differentiate themselves from others.

Assumption Four

Raw materials for plastic and aplastic ceramic components are presumed to have been obtained locally. Ceramic raw materials are rarely imported from great distances. Most preindustrial potters obtain clay from within a radius of one to seven km of their settlement (Arnold 1985). The same rule holds true for temper materials—one-to-nine-km radius (Arnold 1985).

HYPOTHESES

From the above assumptions, treated like axioms, this study of "Iroquoian" pottery, phrased in terms of ceramic composition and manufacturing technology, derives four testable hypotheses to clarify the cultural historical relationships among Mohawk River valley, Hudson River valley, and southwestern New England potters by examining groupings of both stylistic and technologic attributes:

Hypothesis One

If southern New England groups share Mohawk River valley stylistic traits, one will see identical decorative motifs combined with differing local technologic elements. Here, New England Algonquian traits represented by design combinations, execution, and placement on vessels will be identical to those in the Mohawk River valley. In contrast, the manner of construction, firing techniques, and the use of local raw materials will remain typically southern New England in form. Paste may consist of specific types of crushed aplastic temper, and local southern New England illite clays will be used instead of central New York calcareous clays, for example.

Hypothesis Two

Mohawk River valley trade pots will contain Mohawk River valley symbolic and technologic traits. These pots should look endemic to the Mohawk River valley as to both symbolic and technologic style. Design elements should be executed in typical Mohawk River valley fashion, at typical locations on the vessel, and using Mohawk River valley tools. I base this distinction on the fact that Mohawk River valley ceramics tend to have larger collars and castellations and tend to be more globular in form than southern New England pots. By contrast, southern New England pottery tends to have smaller collars and castellations accompanied by conoidal (cone-shaped) bases. These contrasts are indicative of differing construction technologies and stylistic expressions. In addition, Mohawk River valley decorative motifs are generally larger and executed with a broad stylus. Mohawk River valley collar notches are usually wider and deeper than those on southern New England styles (Chilton 1996:114–122). Construction techniques for transported pots should be Iroquoian and, most important, the ceramic paste should contain typical Mohawk River valley tempering materials.

There is good ethnohistoric evidence for the Iroquois using drawing as the primary pottery construction technique (Kapches 1994). Drawing involves opening a large lump of paste by thrusting fingers or a fist into the center, then squeezing and pinching in an upward pulling movement to raise and thin the vessel walls (Rice 1987:125). Archaeological work has shown that many Iroquois vessels were fired during the summer months in hearths adjacent to temporary agricultural cabins (Kapches 1994). Iroquoian archaeologists infer that coiling came first in the archaeological record, but by terminal Woodland times (ca. 500 B.P.) most pottery was drawn. According to Kapches (1994:96), if there was not enough clay to shape the rim, the Iroquois added a flattened coil or fillet of clay to shape the rim and lip. The surface of the vessel was smoothed to receive this fillet, and because of this treatment, the prepared area was different in appearance from the remainder of the vessel. As with all add-ons, this union was a potential weak spot (Kapches 1994:96).

Hypothesis Three

If Mohawk River valley immigrants are making pots in southern New England, their ceramics will show a mixture of Mohawk River valley symbolic and technologic traits combined with local raw materials. Designs, temper, firing, and manner of construction should exhibit Mohawk River valley style, but the ceramic paste will be southern New England illite clay, and local tempering materials. Mohawk River valley potters adopting Connecticut River valley materials will manipulate those materials in traditional Mohawk River valley ways, for example, using sand for temper, or making drawn pots rather than coiled vessels. They will also continue to execute decorative styles in accustomed ways that differ from those of their Connecticut River valley neighbors.

Hypothesis Four

If Mohawk River valley symbolic traits were incorporated into the southern New England repertoire, one should see clear stylistic differ-

ences between the two regions. If, for the sake of this argument, we assume trait dispersal from a core area and assume that an "Iroquoian" motif is assimilated into southern New England, one would expect to see borrowed symbolic motifs applied with a typically southern New England technological style. This means that southern New England vessels should show contrasts in the fine details of motif size, manner of execution, placement of design, and design combinations. The ways the designs are applied, the tools used to make them, and the locations of the designs on the pot, might be more in keeping with a southern New England approach. That approach might include smaller motifs consisting of fine lines, possibly appearing "cramped," and shallower thumbnail or punctate impressions on narrower collars. Design elements might also be combined in ways not seen in the Mohawk River valley. This might include shoulder decorations and different motifs placed on collars beneath castellations. Other technologic traits such as the use of the coiling technique and the reliance upon local tempers will also indicate place of manufacture. Vessel size should be, on average, smaller. Vessel shapes will include more conoidal bases. In fact, there is no reason to assume that the designs in this discussion originated in the Mohawk River valley. Radiocarbon dates do not support such an assumption; rather, these may represent a series of pan-Northeastern decorative traits.

METHODOLOGICAL DISCUSSION

A problem with this approach is the lack of good archaeological context for much of the southern New England sample. Age differences between the samples can have important effects on symbolic stylistic combinations. What may appear as regional differences may be due to no more than lags in trait adoption, or small sample size (Lavin 1997). To maintain better chronological control on the samples, this study uses only Late Woodland and Contact period collared ceramics. In the Mohawk River valley this period includes from approximately the mid-fifteenth to the eighteenth centuries A.D., including Chance, Garoga, and Mohawk phases (Kuhn and Bamann 1987). In southern New England and eastern New York, this period includes castellated pots from assemblages in the Connecticut, Housatonic, and Hudson River valleys. While we cannot deny that a great deal of stylistic change must have taken place during more than 300 years, the lack of chronological data makes it impossible to detail where and when traits originated and circulated.

Others have called for a similar strategy using technological distinctions to study regional questions (MacEachern 1998; Welsch and Terrell 1998). In doing so, they have drawn inspiration from the French ap-

proach of *techniques et culture* or *technologie* that explores links between cognition and technical choice as reflected in material culture
patterning (Stark 1998a:2–3). French archaeologists have developed
methods for studying technologic style by examining the manufacturing
sequence or *chaîne opératoire* (Lemmonier 1986, 1992).

In an ethnoarchaeological survey of pottery production among 21 Af-
rican groups (speaking seven different languages), Gosselain (1998)
found that ceramic technological behaviors were so deeply embedded in
the social and economic aspects of daily life that they were often inex-
tricably woven into cultural practices. This is the difference between a
ceramic ecology approach, which attempts to explain ceramic production
in terms of material science, and the *chaîne opératoire* approach, which
takes into consideration the driving social and economic forces behind
production. Because technologic style, expressed as ceramic production
techniques, is completely embedded in social and economic systems,
analysis of production steps should provide clues for understanding cultural identities. The relationship between society and technology is complex, however, and archaeologists should beware of making simplistic
associations between group identity and the patterning of ceramic traits
(Gosselain 1998).

Close at home, Goodby (1998) has examined the lack of correlation
between ethnohistorically determined social boundaries and the uniform
Shantok-style ceramic industry of coastal southern New England (Shantok pottery is collared, round-based, thin, shell- or mineral-tempered pottery first identified in southeastern Connecticut). His study of 43 Shantok
vessel lots (a vessel lot comprises all sherds assignable to a single vessel)
from Wampanoag and Narragansett tribal areas shows they were tech-
nologically indistinguishable from one another and from those of the
Mohegan Pequot. Goodby thinks there must have been a single technological style throughout southern New England. The group unity expressed in Shantok pottery, according to Goodby (1998:176), is not
between political and social entities, but rather a gender-based affiliation
in which ceramic style was used by women potters in a debate over the
importance of unity among native peoples during the Contact period.
Goodby is to be commended for taking a "modern" approach to stylistic
variation in ceramics. He does not make pots equal people, but instead
demonstrates that Shantok-like traits are widely distributed in southeastern New England and not restricted solely to the Mohegan Pequots as
Rouse (1947) had argued. The role of the individual in stylistic expression is a cornerstone of Goodby's (1998) analysis. As I have stated
above, recognition of style as personal expression is the key to any sym-

bolic stylistic analysis. In this case, women potters, who may have been related and shared a technological tradition, may have used a combination of assertive and emblemic styles (the two are not mutually exclusive) to communicate shared values. Finally, Goodby's (1998) analysis views groups as open and fluid systems. He echoes Gosselain (1998) and MacEachern (1998) by not attempting to make simplistic associations between historically defined group identities and ceramic traits. Because of the interrelatedness among women potters in these groups, technologic stylistic analysis may not yield information about group boundaries on this level. As Gosselain (1998) discovered, technological analysis works best on a level where distinct groups are separated by strongly contrasting linguistic, social, ideological, and technological systems. This is the key to my approach in which I compare two strongly contrasting, but interacting groups.

COMPOSITIONAL ANALYSIS USING OPTICAL MINERALOGICAL TECHNIQUES

The four hypotheses formulated to clarify relationships between groups address issues of trait borrowing, trade in ceramic containers, and immigration by posing questions formulated in terms of the mineralogical characteristics of ceramic pastes. An important aspect of technologic style is the selection and combination of raw materials. As presented above, each geologic terrain gave potters distinct mineral choices that they combined as temper containing distinctive mineral suites. Ceramic petrography supports the study of these physical traits by means of optical mineralogical analysis with polarized light (Hodges 1963; Shepard 1936; Williams 1983).

Ceramic petrographers identify and describe aplastic constituents of ceramic pastes by optical analysis with the polarized light petrographic microscope. This approach relies upon application of the physics of light and crystal optic principles. Optic principles rest on the tenet that the internal structure, or crystal lattice, of each mineral type is distinct, and affects light transmission through the crystal in a unique way. Incoming light is polarized (vibrating in only one plane), and the crystal breaks that light into two polarized rays. The petrographic microscope makes it possible to eliminate one of the two polarized rays, leaving a single ray with vibrations confined to a single plane. Optical mineralogists call this plane polarized light. Using this principle, it is possible to identify transparent minerals precisely and diagnostically (Blatt 1992; MacKenzie and

Adams 1994; Philpotts 1989; Philpotts and Wilson 1994; Stoiber and Morse 1993).

Ceramic petrographers use these techniques to compare and contrast technological traits among diverse archaeological assemblages (Williams 1983). Shepard (1936) pioneered the use of optical techniques, showing that ceramics from Pecos Pueblo in New Mexico contained exotic and distinctive tempering materials. Previously, this had been unsuspected and all ceramics found at the site had been thought to be locally made. This approach is adaptable to the study of Northeastern ceramics because the region's geologic diversity dictates that ceramics from differing geographic subregions will contain distinctive suites of minerals. For example, some Hudson River valley ceramics contain a distinctive Adirondack metagabbro as temper (Chilton 1994a).

The ceramic data sets compiled to test the four hypotheses are drawn from watersheds draining various geologic regions in southwestern New England and eastern New York State. These watersheds contain terrains underlain by Lower Paleozoic marine sedimentary rocks, Precambrian and Paleozoic metamorphic rocks, and Early Mesozoic sedimentary formations. Each zone includes volcanic materials and is overlain by glacial drift containing rocks from zones farther to the north (Hunt 1967:Fig. 2.1). Volcanism and glaciation have produced an interesting mix of raw tempering materials throughout the study area, and the data sets display ceramic populations from a cross-section of this geographically diverse area.

Sample selection involved macroscopic sorting and grouping of sherds into vessel lots on the basis of surface treatment and paste. Vessel lot analysis emphasizes identification of attributes and does not generalize the sherds into types (Chilton 1994a). Vessel lots quantify the minimum number of vessels that could be present in an assemblage from which petrographic samples will be drawn. By sorting sherds into vessel lots before analysis, ceramic analysts ensure that individual samples represent separate vessels. Once sorting has been accomplished, analysis continues with a representative body or neck/collar sherd from each vessel lot sliced perpendicular to the vessel's rim. This study uses standard thin section preparation techniques (Humphries 1992). I studied the ceramic thin sections by optical microscopic means in polarized light. Observations for each sample were summarized on a worksheet and tabulated (Pretola 2000).

Organizing the data set by river drainage is at once convenient and also grounded in prehistoric reality. Using geographic approaches, many archaeologists have relied upon drainage systems to bound their data

(Kenyon 1983; Kroeber 1939:8–9; Luedtke 1986b). They also identify cultural subdivisions within drainages corresponding to coastal, transitional, and headwater groupings. Similar approaches appear to work for the Connecticut, Housatonic, and Hudson River valleys (Bender and Curtin 1990; Handsman and Richmond 1992; Massachusetts Historical Commission [MHC] 1984; Paynter 1979; Snow 1980:2–4).

The Connecticut River valley appears to reflect this cultural pattern in the Contact period. The lower reaches were homelands for diverse groups such as the Niantics, Mashantucket Pequots, and Mohegan Pequots. Other groups such as the Tunxis, Podunk, Agawam, Norwottuck, Woronoak, and Pocumtuck occupied an ecologically transitional zone between coastal environments and the northern reaches of the Connecticut River claimed by the Western Abenaki (Day 1979). Similarly, the Housatonic River had the Wappingers in its coastal reaches, and a branch of the Mahicans, who later became the Stockbridge, in the river's upper reaches (Frazier 1992). The Hudson River watershed was also occupied by the Wappingers in its coastal zone, and the Mahicans the transitional zone beyond West Point (Dunn 1994). The Mohawk River, a tributary of the Hudson, was the territory of the Mohawk, the easternmost unit of the Iroquois Confederacy. However, at the time of European contact, the Mahicans controlled the Mohawk River's mouth and a short distance upstream. Just how far back into prehistory these boundaries reflect reality is the subject of much speculation (Bender and Curtin 1990). It is clear from post-contact history that these geographic and social boundaries were extremely fluid. Aboriginal history in the Hudson River valley is marked by a series of wars culminating with the Mohawks' gaining access to the Hudson and the Dutch trade at Fort Orange (present-day Albany). Nor were there strict social boundaries; Chief Hendrick of the Mohawks had a Mahican mother (Frazier 1992:9).

The Connecticut River ceramic assemblage consists of 25 selected terminal Woodland sherds from as many distinct vessel lots, including two from the Springfield, Massachusetts, Fort Hill site dating between A.D. 1650 and 1675 (Johnson et al. 1989; Pretola and Johnson 1996; Young 1969); and five from the terminal Woodland component of the Guida Farm site, Westfield, Massachusetts (Byers and Rouse 1960; Chilton 1996; Fowler 1966; Howes 1943; Maloney 1989; MHC 1984; Young 1969); and seven from the early seventeenth-century Bark Wigwams site in Northampton, Massachusetts (Johnson and Bradley 1987). Additionally, there are two terminal Woodland samples from Deerfield, Massachusetts (Stillwater Bridge and Acorn Squash sites); one from Riverside, Gill, Massachusetts; one from the Falls River, Turners Falls, Massachusetts; three from Bennett Brook, Northfield, Massachusetts; and four from the Hockanum section of Hadley and South Hadley, Massachusetts (Figure 11.1).

The Housatonic assemblage consists of 24 sherds, four of which are from the Late Woodland component of the Chassell 2 site (19-BK-141), Stockbridge, Massachusetts (Chilton 1994b; Johnson 1994). Another sherd is from the Hop Brook #1 site (19-BK-147) in Tyringham, Massachusetts (Macomber 1992). These five Late Woodland and Early Contact sherds are from the upper reaches of the Housatonic River in what was historically the Mahican (Stockbridge) homeland. This study also uses 11 sherds from the Whitlock, Lover's Leap (6-LF-70), and Boulder Home (6-LF-113) sites in New Milford, Connecticut. These include Late Woodland and Early Contact assemblages from the transitional oak-hickory forests on the middle reaches of the river (Handsman and Richmond 1992). The remaining eight sherds in the Housatonic sample are from the Late Woodland component of site 294A-AF2-1 (CT# 55) on the east side of the Housatonic River in Milford, Connecticut (Mills et al. 1997). This site (Figure 11.1, #11) represents a major encampment of people ancestral to the Wappingers, a southeastern Connecticut coastal group. In this sample, shell-tempered pottery was avoided because only a study of mineral temper will answer the questions posed in this study. Both shell- and mineral-tempered vessel lots were prevalent in the ceramic assemblage from this drainage.

The Hudson River drainage sample (Figure 11.1) includes 10 sherds from the later components of the Goldkrest site (Lavin et al. 1996), and seven Late Woodland samples drawn from the Follett Collection of the Winney's Rift site (Brumbach and Bender 1986). Two absolute dates place the later components of the Winney's Rift site in the late sixteenth century.

The Mohawk Iroquois sample consists of 25 sherds from three sixteenth-century village sites: Garoga (nine samples), Klock (eight samples), and Smith (eight samples). These sites were occupied in sequence by the same community beginning with the Garoga site and ending with the Smith site (Kuhn and Bamann 1987). Several museums house artifact assemblages from the sites, but the largest and most important collections from which I have drawn my samples are curated at the New York State Museum.

PETROGRAPHIC ANALYSIS AND RESULTS

Mineral identification using optical techniques in polarized light shows Mohawk River valley potters used minerals and mineral complexes derived from Adirondack high-temperature, metamorphosed granulite and amphibolite facies rocks. These include olivine metagabbro corona textures, clinopyroxene/orthopyroxene intergrowths, welded feldspar crystals, and feldspar made dusty by intergrowths of spinel (Bohlen et al. 1985; Isachsen et al. 1991:23–44; Whitney and McLelland 1973, 1983). The mineral assemblage is dominated by feldspars such as plagioclase (oligoclase), some microcline, and microantiperthite. Pyroxenes include the orthopyroxene hypersthene, and clinopyroxenes pigeonite and augite. Other minerals include zircon, olivine, apatite, hornblende, and opaque minerals including ilmenite. These minerals are all derived from such Adirondack region rocks as metagabbro, metanorthosite, and granitic gneisses (Figure 11.2A).

Olivine is present as individual grains, sometimes with plagioclase and other feldspar crystals that indicate it is from a metanorthosite source. Other olivine examples are from crushed corona textures derived from the olivine metagabbro source. These distinctive textures originated when, during moderate temperature and pressure, associated crystals of olivine and plagioclase were slowly inverted to pyroxenes, garnet, and spinel-laced feldspar (Figure 11.2A). Because of the slow rate of metamorphism, however, the center of the crystals did not invert, producing features displaying rings of minerals with unaltered olivine and plagioclase at the center (Isachsen et al. 1991:Fig 4.10, Fig. 5.4; Whitney and McLelland 1973:Fig. 2).

All Hudson River valley ceramic samples also show distinctive Adirondack minerals characteristic of high temperature granulite and amphibolite facies metamorphism (Bohlen et al. 1985). These include plagioclase, the orthopyroxene hypersthene, clinopyroxenes augite and pigeonite, garnet, and amphiboles such as hornblende. The Adirondack source is confirmed by the presence of olivine metagabbro corona textures. This very distinctive texture is present in most Hudson River valley samples. These observations confirm reports by Chilton (1994a) and William M. Kelley (personal communication, 1995), who also identified Adirondack-derived tempering materials in Late Woodland sherds from the Goat Island Rockshelter in the Hudson River valley. Olivine crystals lacking evidence of corona textures are rare in the samples, suggesting that Hudson River valley potters did not use the metanorthosite sources and this may distinguish Hudson River valley tempers from those in the Mohawk River valley (Figure 11.2B).

It is somewhat speculative to infer how Hudson River valley potters acquired Adirondack tempering materials. There are three ways by which aboriginal potters could have procured them. One is going to the Adirondacks and collecting them during seasonal trips that might have been

Figure 11.2
Optical Micrographs of Ceramic Thin Sections Under Cross Polarized Light

A.

B.

C.

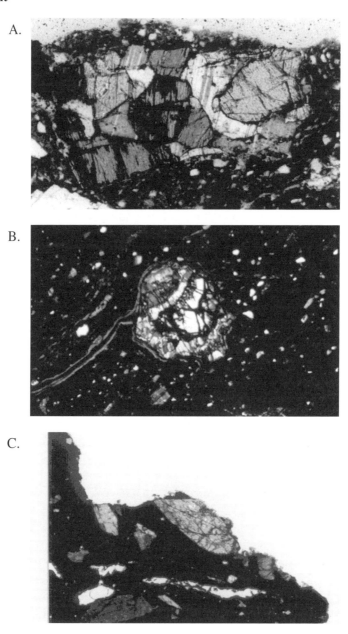

Figure 11.2 Continued

A. Mohawk River valley crushed olivine corona aplastic; crystals at center and lower
   left are olivine surrounded by clinopyroxene (second and third order interference
   colors) and plagioclase (first order grey and brown interference colors) (6.5×); B.
   Hudson River valley rounded aplastic grain, showing structure of Adirondack metagabbro corona (6.3×); C. New Milford, Connecticut sherd edge, showing a euhedral
   amphibole crystal probably hornblende; crushed mineral grain to the left is also an
   amphibole (2.5×); D. Connecticut River valley crushed aplastic grain of metamorphosed plagioclase that has been annealed with individual crystals sintered together at 120° angles (2.5×).

made for ritual purposes, among others (Bender and Curtin 1990). A
second could have been through trade with residents of the region, and
a third is collecting Adirondack materials from the drift and alluvial
deposits of the Hudson River valley. Each is plausible, but collecting
the material from local glacial and alluvial deposits is the most likely.
As mentioned previously, potters characteristically obtain tempering
materials within one to nine kilometers of home (Arnold 1985). Even
so, geologists estimate that Adirondack materials comprise only 10% of
the locally available rock and mineral resources of the Hudson River
valley (William M. Kelley, personal communication, 1996). These materials were carried south by Pleistocene ice lobes and then washed out
by stream action. Clearly, Hudson River valley potters were very selective.

   Optical mineralogic identification of the Housatonic River valley sample reveals four different tempering mixtures resulting from available
local geologic sources and movement of pots. Chassell site ceramics
contain feldspar, plagioclase, muscovite, biotite, microperthite, and pyroxenes reflecting a granite or granitic gneiss source. One sample, with

crushed shell as the primary temper, contains clay "impurities" pointing to a granitic source.

The Chassell and Hop Brook #1 sites are within a section of the Proto-North American (Continental) Terrane, where gneiss, including granitic gneiss and schist of the Grenville basement rock, can be obtained. Schists are also available from the region's marble and Taconic Allochthon deposits (Rogers 1985; Zen et al. 1983). The pottery sample from Hop Brook, however, tells a different story. Its temper contains olivine metagabbro coronas and other minerals consistent with an Adirondack source. Because it is coiled (see below) and lacks olivine from metanorthosite, it is most likely of Hudson River valley manufacture. This points to contact between inhabitants of the Hudson and Housatonic River valleys.

The New Milford, Connecticut, sample also indicates a relationship between the peoples of the Hudson and Housatonic River valleys. Four samples from the Whitlock site contain Adirondack tempering materials. Two other temper mixes are also represented in the New Milford sample. Four separate vessel lots, two from Whitlock and two from the Lover's Leap site, contain minerals consistent with crushed granitic igneous and metamorphic rock possibly combined with sand temper and clay "impurities" of the same source. The third paste type, restricted to the Boulder Home site, consists of inclusions (some possibly added sand temper) of quartz, feldspar, and clinopyroxenes combined with crushed amphiboles including hornblende. These minerals indicate granitic material has been combined with amphibole-rich igneous or metamorphic rock (Figure 11.2C). Although the sample is small, the fact that this temper class is restricted to one site may indicate a localized source. New Milford is in the *Iapetos* (Oceanic) Terrane, rich in schist and gneiss (including granitic gneiss) of the Hartland and Gneiss Dome belts, Connecticut Valley Synclinorium (Rogers 1985). Local rocks could account for all the minerals present in these two temper classes (Jackson and Hall 1982; Mose and Nagel 1982).

The Milford, Connecticut, sample also shows a variety of tempering materials. One Milford sample contains Adirondack tempering materials that also indicates contact between the Hudson and Housatonic populations even as far south as the Connecticut shore. Five samples have tempering minerals consistent with granitic sources. Two samples, however, combine greenschist facies minerals such as staurolite and sillimanite with granitic temper. This combination of granitic and greenschist minerals constitutes a fourth paste class for the Housatonic River valley. The Milford sample's temper is consistent with its location in the *Iapetos* (Oceanic) Terrane's Orange-Milford belt of the Connecticut Valley Synclinorium. Rocks here include schist, gneiss, and phyllite, including greenstone and greenschist (Rogers 1985). In summary, Housatonic River valley tempering diversity reflects the complex geology of the valley, while at the same time points to connections with Hudson River valley peoples.

Most Connecticut River valley samples show a combination of granitic igneous sources combined with greenschist facies metamorphic amphibolites, and suggest use of upland metamorphic rocks (Figure 11.2D). Phyllosilicates muscovite and biotite are common aplastics, as are hornblende and undulose metamorphic quartz. Examples of mylonite from the Bronson Hill anticlinorium, on the eastern edge of the Connecticut River valley, confirm that aplastic sources are from the crystalline metamorphic rocks east of the Connecticut Valley Newark Terrane. Small olivine crystals in the Bark Wigwams samples occur as individual aplastic grains and also as part of crushed granitic rock particles. These are dissimilar to the larger Adirondack examples used in the Mohawk and Hudson River valleys; and the Bark Wigwams olivines are presumed of local origin. Additionally, there are examples of well-rounded Connecticut River valley redstone clasts in the "impurities." These are often highly spherical and never crushed, indicating accidental inclusions in the plastic component of the paste. The presence of redstone "impurities" may prove to be diagnostic for Connecticut River valley ceramics when present.

The uniqueness of each river valley's aplastic mineral inclusions is most telling. Ceramic inclusions from the Housatonic watershed are more variable. This reinforces historic accounts of the strong cultural connections between native groups in the Hudson and Housatonic watersheds (Dunn 1994; Frazier 1992). Late Woodland ceramic samples from the Connecticut River drainage corroborate Dincauze's (1995) observations that central and northern Connecticut River valley pots were tempered with crushed granitic and metamorphic rocks similar to those from the Bronson Hill Anticlinorium.

These findings help to explain the diversity of inclusion types identified for the Northeast (Chilton 1996:86–88). The high diversity of inclusions noted for the Connecticut River valley is probably a function of the variations in mineral composition represented in differing outcrops of granitic material in the uplands along the margin of the valley and unconsolidated sediments within the valley. The more mobile Algonquian settlement pattern may have allowed potters to use diverse sources of ceramic raw materials more than did sedentary people. The use of upland granitic and greenschist facies aplastics is distinct and shows that native potters were being very selective since valley lowland bedrock consists of Mesozoic redstones and basalts of the Newark Series (Hubert et al. 1982). There are no examples of purposely added Mesozoic aplastics, although sandstone clasts can be seen as paste "impurities" in some thin sections.

MACROSCOPIC OBSERVATIONS

Late Woodland collared ceramic vessels from the Hudson River valley and southern New England were constructed by techniques that contrast with those used on Mohawk River valley ceramics. On the basis of orientations of inclusions, pores, and sherd breakage patterns, it is clear that the bodies of Mohawk River valley ceramics were drawn. Collars were either drawn, or attached as fillets to the neck or lower part of the collar. Often Mohawk River valley potters used a half-lap technology to apply collar fillets. For final shaping, potters appear to have pressed the collar into a form held against the vessel's inside. In contrast, Hudson River valley and southern New England collars were added, or shaped from two or more coils attached to the neck/collar base section of the vessel. Consistently a coil was shaped to form the top of the neck and the base of the collar, then additional coils might be added to bolster the neck/collar join and build the middle of the collar. Many times an additional coil was added to form the collar top and lip. In all cases, from the Hudson to the Connecticut River valleys, collars were coil-built. This reinforces and amplifies Chilton's (1996:97–100) findings, based upon macroscopic observations, that Mohawk River valley vessels were drawn or tier built, and southern New England vessels were coiled.

As discussed above, the way surface treatment and designs are applied can provide information for inferring group affiliation or, at least, learning and potting social environments. In this regard, there are distinct differences in the way collar designs were applied in the Mohawk River valley compared to the Hudson River valley and southern New England sites. In the Mohawk River drainage, designs were mainly applied with a broad stylus in bold strokes. Basal collar notching was primarily deep impression with the thumbnail, or other means. Eastern New York and southwestern New England potters applied their designs with a fine stylus, often with delicate strokes. By contrast, basal collar notching was narrow and shallow using the thumbnail or a sharp-edged tool.

The sequence of application was more variable among Mohawk River valley pots than it was for eastern New York and southwestern New England. The majority of Mohawk watershed collars were smoothed, then two to four horizontal lines were incised into the upper third of the collar. Following this, vertical lines were incised between the horizontal lines and the lip. Notches were then cut into the lip by thumbnail impression or the edge of a wedge-shaped tool. On some examples, the decorating technique diverged in that medium-to-broad diagonal lines were incised below the horizontal lines.

Alternatively, some Mohawk River valley potters wiped the central portion of the collar and basal notches after the horizontal lines had been incised. Then, diagonal lines were cut into the collar. This sequence may suggest that potters had been dissatisfied with the appearance of diagonal lines incised prior to collar notching and "erased" the surface in such a way as to avoid much damage to the notches. This may represent a conscious effort to conform to stylistic rules endorsed by the group (emblemic style) rather than individual taste (assertive style). On the other hand, Hudson River valley and southwestern New England collars were often smoothed or wiped, then the horizontal, vertical, and diagonal lines were applied. Basal notching was the last step. Generally, the basal notches were not wiped after execution.

As a rule, Hudson River drainage and southern New England ceramics tend to be smaller and have smaller and more finely executed decorations applied to their collars. Mohawk River valley ceramics, by contrast, tend to be larger, with medium-to-broad incised line decoration, and large basal notches. Despite this variability, Mohawk watershed, eastern New York, and southern New England ceramics all used similar design motifs. Although their combinations may have varied, these similarities, discussed above, point to shared motifs and shared meanings. There are no true solely "Iroquoian" motifs; they are just as common in eastern New York and southern New England, and even extend south into Pennsylvania.

Although archaeologists are becoming more aware of slips (Cotkin et al. 1999), Northeastern archaeologists rarely report them. However, my analysis found that a majority (76%) of the Mohawk River valley sample had a dark gray interior slip. The Hudson watershed Winney's Rift assemblage contained many Algonquian vessels with dark grey interior slips, while the sample from the Housatonic River valley had one possible example (Hop Brook #1). That vessel was manufactured in the Hudson River valley. In the Connecticut River drainage, three samples were slipped.

Food residues and sooting can cause encrustations on cooking vessels that mimic slips. In most cases however, the residues rarely penetrate the vessel's surface and appear discontinuous. Careful observation of the

Table 11.1
Hypotheses Test

Traits Needed for Hypothesis to be True

Hypothesis	Stylistic Motif Execution	Construction	Aplastic Raw Materials
#1 Borrowed Iroquoian	I	A	A
#2 Iroquoian Trade	I	I	I
#3 Iroquoian Residence	I	I	A
#4 Local Algonquians	A	A	A

Eastern New York and Southwestern New England Traits

River Drainage	Motif Execution	Construction	Aplastic Raw Materials	Hypothesis Supported
Hudson	A	A	A	4
Housatonic	A	A	A	4
Connecticut	A	A	A	4

A = Algonquian eastern New York and southwestern New England
I = Iroquoian Mohawk River valley

sherd before thin section preparation also helps to separate residues from slip applications. Ultimately, food residues often have a dull luster different from reduced ceramic in crossed polarized light and can often be readily distinguished during the optical microscope study.

HYPOTHESES TESTING AND CONCLUSIONS

As related above, four primary assumptions guide the interpretation of stylistic data in this ceramic study. Grounded in ceramic ecology, these assumptions show that very strong evidence must be presented before one can assert, on the basis of raw materials, that trade in raw materials or movement of pots, has taken place. On the basis of the optical mineralogy study, combined with the macroscopic technological study, it is possible to define what is an Iroquoian trait versus an Algonquian trait. I summarize these expectations, then compare my findings and summarize the results in Table 11.1.

Table 11.1 illustrates trait profiles necessary to demonstrate each hypothesis. Because I am testing for "Iroquoian" traits in Algonquian pottery, Table 11.1 presents, in tabular form, a summary of observations for the three eastern New York and southwestern New England drainages, while holding Mohawk River valley traits constant. Table 11.1 shows an A-A-A pattern for all three river drainages, and so presents a profile one would expect if hypothesis four were true. On the basis of this study, it is clear that incised geometric collar designs with basal collar notching and other pan-Northeastern decorative traits were incorporated and combined into a distinctly southwestern New England stylistic repertoire.

These conclusions make it clear that "Iroquoian" traits in southern New England ceramics are not the result of slavish copying, trade, or production by Iroquoian immigrants resident in southern New England. All eastern New York and southern New England samples used in this study are clearly of local Algonquian manufacture. There is evidence of trade or movement of people between the Hudson River valley Algonquians and central Housatonic River valley Algonquians, and this reinforces historical accounts of political and social affiliation. The absence of Hudson River valley aplastic inclusions in the Connecticut River drainage weakens arguments for social interaction of the same magnitude across the Berkshire Uplands. The nearly universal uses of granitic and greenschist facies aplastics in southwestern New England may render interaction between New England groups invisible. Only if distinctive inclusions are identified will it be possible to see other examples of intra-Algonquian trade or interaction.

These methods may be helpful in identifying Mohawk Iroquoian fishing stations in the Hudson River valley. Although ethnohistoric literature alludes to temporary fishing sites visited by Mohawk families in the seventeenth century, no archaeological manifestation has been clearly identified (Bender and Curtin 1990). The results of my study show that Mohawk fishing stations should yield distinctly Iroquoian pottery—that is, if Mohawk fishing parties brought pottery with them.

The great diversity in ceramic materials, decoration, and morphology in southern New England is probably a function of degree of social integration, production context, and scale (Chilton 1996:120; 1999:110). Ceramics from the middle central Connecticut River valley, although showing surface decoration and morphology typically identified with the Iroquois (but not uniquely so), are made of local materials, using local construction techniques. In contrast, ceramics from Mohawk Iroquois sites in the central Mohawk River valley show much more uniformity. This is undoubtedly a reflection of the higher degree of social integration known to have existed among sixteenth- and seventeenth-century Iroquois. Related aspects of production context and scale, although not clearly defined at this time, must also play a part in these phenomena.

One point this study has clearly made is that traditional arguments relying upon unilateral diffusion and trade from central New York sources cannot be invoked to explain southern New England terminal Woodland ceramic trait distributions. The dynamics producing the diversity seen in southern New England ceramics are much more complicated than existing models of Northeastern prehistory allow. What is needed is a more sophisticated model based upon a multidirectional flow of traits integrated with a more realistic, unified, theory of style and stylistic change than many archaeologists have used up to this time. One approach to this issue would be to inventory various stylistic traits and work to date precisely when they appear in time and space. Unfortunately, problems with the accuracy of radiocarbon dates for the last millennium make it a difficult proposition at the present time. For an initial attempt toward a new model, see Lavin (this volume).

The fact that early researchers saw similarities in stylistic motifs throughout the Northeast argues that Northeastern terminal Woodland populations interacted and followed a path of incorporation and recombination throughout the region. In contrast to earlier researchers, modern archaeologists should not assume that ceramic traits diffused eastward from central New York without chronometric evidence to demonstrate it. Nor should they ignore, or give up, the attempt to understand an extremely interesting chapter in Northeastern prehistory.

The concept of technologic style supports studies of group affiliation on a coarse, regional scale. This works in the Northeast where regional resource diversity allows the kinds of distinctions that my study has drawn. In similar ethnoarchaeological circumstances, for example, among South Cameroonian populations (Gosselain 1998) and Northern Mandara peoples (MacEachern 1998) of Africa, it is possible to make regional distinctions. In South Cameroons there is strong evidence that ceramic traits correlate with linguistic affiliation. The results of my study show clear distinctions between the ceramics of two culturally and linguistically distinct Northeastern peoples. Despite these cultural and linguistic differences, however, Algonquians and Iroquoians interacted in an open and fluid system that allowed association and mixture of people and ideas. Archaeologists will find that motifs were being adopted from different directions and being combined in differing ways just as Dincauze (1975) suggested more than 20 years ago. One point is very clear: use of the term "Iroquoian" to describe any eastern New York and southern New England ceramic trait is a misnomer, and should be abandoned.

ACKNOWLEDGMENTS

I wish to acknowledge, with thanks, the following people who helped me with sample acquisition: Robert Funk, Russell Handsman, Alberto Meloni, Ryan Kimberly, Susan Bender, Lucianne Lavin, Andrea Anderson, Nick Bellantoni, Eric Johnson, Brona Simon, Ricardo Elia, Mitch Mulholland, Claire Carlson, Dena Dincauze, and two amateur archaeologists who wish not to be named.

For intellectual inspiration, I wish to acknowledge Ellen-Rose Savulis, Elizabeth Chilton, Neal Salisbury, Eric Johnson, and Lucianne Lavin. For inspiration and superhuman patience, I acknowledge my dissertation committee: Dena Dincauze, Stephen Haggerty, and Donald Proulx, my committee chair. I also acknowledge the support of the Springfield Library and Museums Association, my employer who generously allowed me the time to conduct research. I also thank Jordan Kerber for several constructive comments, and for including my work in this volume. I must thank Barbara Luedtke who was always supportive and keenly interested in my petrographic work. I despair that my thanks are too little and too late.

I am responsible for preparing the figures, micrographs, and table. They have been redrawn from my dissertation (Pretola 2000). I alone am responsible for any errors or omissions.

12

Analysis and Interpretation of Early Ceramics from Sewalls and Amoskeag Falls, Merrimack River Valley, New Hampshire

Victoria Bunker

INTRODUCTION

We now know that it was nearly 3500 years ago that the earliest pottery was made and used by people in New England. This pottery was made by individuals who participated not only within their own cultural context, but also experimented with a new material—clay—thus creating a new type of implement—the ceramic pot. These potters, working by hand, eye, and touch, made substantial utilitarian wares. We believe that the first potters must have shared information and ideas—by emulation and conversation—resulting in the distribution across hundreds of miles of an innovative product that today is recognized and classified by archaeologists as the Vinette I type of cord-impressed pottery.

These first potters employed a series of decisions, which are encoded in the final product and visible in the sherds we find as archaeological remains. Because pottery-making is an additive technology, various stages of the manufacture process are retained in the final piece, evident as diagnostic traits or attributes. We can come close to understanding some of the decisions and techniques of these potters by investigating those attributes that reveal the way the vessels were made. Consequently, we can approach a better understanding of the very people who made the pottery.

The pottery I have examined for this study meets the criteria for classification within the Vinette I type of ceramics. Throughout New England, archaeologists consider Vinette I pottery as a hallmark for the Early Woodland or Early Ceramic period, dated to ca. 3000–2150 B.P. This pottery also marks the introduction of a new and different object into the material culture of the time. The Vinette type was first defined in New York State, and archaeologists have regarded the first Vinette ceramic associations as indicative of a separate cultural marker (Ritchie 1980:179 ff.). This pottery forms a "horizon style" that was "apparently the product of intensive social interaction" (Petersen and Sanger 1991: 126) over a wide geographic distance, spreading from interior New York throughout New England and into Canada.

Throughout the greater Northeast, this early pottery exhibits many shared attributes. Vessels have thick and straight walls with a conoidal base. These pots were manufactured by a coil technique and are usually gray, brown, or buff in color. They were heavily tempered with grit composed of coarse and poorly sorted, crushed rock and sands. Decorative motifs include some use of incision (Strauss and Goodby 1993; Petersen and Hamilton 1984), while both interior and exterior surfaces exhibit cord markings, created by impressing the surface with some type of a corded fiber. This fiber may have been in the form of cordage, fabric, basketry, or other weaving or textile, and was typically applied in a horizontal direction on vessel interiors and in multiple directions on the exterior of the pots. Individual pots are estimated to have had about a one-gallon capacity (Braun and Braun 1994:62–65; Petersen and Sanger 1991:126–131; Ritchie 1980:194; Ritchie and MacNeish 1949).

Recent analysis of the cordage used to finish the surfaces of these early vessels has provided new information about technology and tradition in northern New England. Through investigation of a large sample of casts taken from the surfaces of cord-impressed pottery, a better understanding of the perishable fiber industry of the time has been obtained. In particular, a distinction between artifacts from coastal and interior contexts has been noted with use of a "Z" twist (weft slant) at coastal sites and an "S" twist (weft slant) at non-coastal riverine sites. This is interpreted as a likely reflection of technological preferences and continuity, as well as degree of social interaction. The concept, as well as the actual method, of using cordage must have been communicated among individuals making this pottery (Petersen 1996; Petersen and Hamilton 1984; Petersen and Sanger 1991).

As with many other artifact classes, New England archaeologists have looked to New York State for definition of typology and chronology; types developed beyond our region have been eagerly applied here in an attempt to refine and to understand our own archaeological evidence. In

New England, many archaeologists have adopted the Vinette I classification as a marker of the Woodland period, even in the absence of independent chronological control or the full compliment of other
artifactual evidence for the tradition. However, by examining the relationship of early ceramics to other artifact types, we have learned that
pottery was made much earlier than we were aware, even appearing in
association with Terminal Late Archaic contexts and assemblages (Snow
1980:276). Regardless of chronological association, we have speculated
that the use and manufacture of pottery represents a "quantum leap" in
technology (Snow 1980:242).

Yet, New England archaeologists remain puzzled by the date and significance of this major technological innovation; answers to the questions
"when?" "how?" "why?" and "by whom?" was pottery introduced into
the material culture have eluded scholars for some time. This paper helps
us solve the puzzle by giving us the oldest known dates for the appearance of ceramics in New England's archaeological sequence. These ceramics consist of remains of two vessels that firmly anchor the
appearance of Vinette type pottery in the Merrimack River valley of New
Hampshire nearly 3500 years ago. They were excavated from
radiocarbon-dated contexts at the Beaver Meadow Brook site, at Sewall's
Falls, and the Eddy site, at Amoskeag Falls (Figure 12.1). Analysis of
the technological attributes of these remains provides insight into how
both early vessels were manufactured. This, in turn, opens the door for
a better understanding of decisions made by ancient potters—we may
consider the "sherds found at a site as the end result of a long series of
decisions about pottery manufacture, use, and disposal" (Luedtke 1985:
211).

RESEARCH APPROACH

I have chosen to explore and describe the technological attributes of
these two vessels partly because both are undecorated, and the earliest
ceramics of New England tend to have little to no decoration for analysis
of styles and motifs. Further, we "are hampered by the lack of a good
ceramic typology or chronology for New England" (Luedtke 1980a:49).
Yet I also believe that when we only apply classificatory typology, typically focusing on decorative motif, to local ceramics of any time period,
we are in danger of obscuring other kinds of information, especially
those data linked to manufacture technology. Indeed, physical criteria are
equally valid in developing cultural interpretations. Thus, my approach
has been to scrutinize individual attributes to develop a greater under-

Figure 12.1
Location of the Beaver Meadow Brook and Eddy Sites in the Merrimack River Valley, New Hampshire

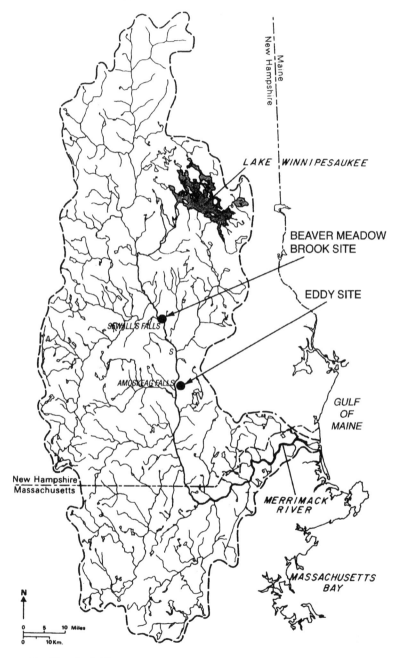

Prepared by Dennis E. Howe.

standing of the ceramic product and how it was actually made (Chilton 1999b; Dincauze 1975; Kenyon 1979, 1983).

Because each vessel is represented by sherds found as clusters in discrete archaeological contexts, there was no doubt in designating individual vessels. The Beaver Meadow Brook vessel was represented by over 500 sherds that were reconstructed to form over half the original pot. The Eddy site vessel was represented by over a dozen sherds that represent large portions of the original vessel walls.

Materials used to make the pots, including both the clay itself and aplastic tempering inclusions, were studied. While neither microscopic work nor clay or mineral sourcing were completed, visible attributes provide a sense of the materials selected by the potter. The texture and color of the sherds were compared to test tiles I made from clays found in deposits along the Merrimack River and to my collection of brick and earthenware from local manufactories for overall similarities and obvious matches. The kinds of aplastic temper used in each vessel was identified by examination through a hand lens. Only broad categories can be determined through this method; these include sands (of undifferentiated minerals), mica, quartz, feldspar, granite, fire-reddened rock, steatite, and shell. The temper quality and quantity were also described. Overall temper coarseness and overall particle size range were recorded. The relative proportion of temper-to-clay matrix was estimated by comparison to established density percentages (Rice 1987:349).

Vessel morphology was also recorded. Height and diameter of reconstructed pieces were measured and wall profiles characterized to estimate vessel size and shape. Other detail was evident in the configuration of the lip and rim elements. Wall thickness was measured to provide ranges and average wall thickness for each pot. The relatively thick walls created by these earliest potters may have been necessary to strengthen the heavy vessels, which tended to crack irregularly across their surfaces between coarse grit particles (Chilton 1999b:104).

Traits reflective of pot building and finishing were observed. Coil building was recognized by thickened bulges in wall surfaces, or distinctive hollow troughs and half-rounds along breaks. The surface treatment on the interior and exterior of the vessel was recorded. Attributes were selected to characterize the cordage applied by the potter on the pliable vessel surface in its "green" state. This is a time when basic vessel construction has been completed, and the potter holds and turns the vessel while deciding how to finish it off.

Cordage was applied to the interior and exterior surfaces of the Vinette type ceramics. The potters 3000 years ago must have been very familiar with various types of cordage, especially using baskets, lines, snares, and nets for hunting, fishing, and other daily activities. Yet, the exact type of tool used to impress the vessel walls has not yet been determined archaeologically. We speculate that a basket, a piece of basketry or netting, or a paddle wrapped with cordage or woven fabric could have been used. Conversely, the method may have been simpler and the potter's hand was the only tool used.

Surface treatment presumably finished and strengthened the actual construction by melding individual coils into the vessel wall. The rough surface could have served other functions as well, possibly providing a firmer grip or transferring heat more evenly (Chilton 1999b). Perhaps the impressions reflect a conservatism carried over from basketry in the making of containers with a certain appearance. Or the impressed surface may simply have been pleasing to the potter's eye.

Various attributes of the cordage itself were studied and recorded. Impressions were taken from several locations on the interior and exterior of each vessel. These impressions provided a "positive" cast that reveals the original cordage applied to the pot surface. The direction of the cordage twist was determined as either "S" or "Z" (Petersen 1996; Petersen and Hamilton 1984; Petersen and Sanger 1991), a trait believed to be a sensitive indicator of cultural geography between the coast and interior valleys of New England (Petersen 1996; Petersen and Hamilton 1984; Petersen and Sanger 1991). Another trait recorded was the gauge or number of twists per centimeter along a single strand of cordage, to obtain a sense of the tightness of the cord itself. The direction of cordage application, either horizontal, vertical, or cross-hatched, was also noted, to reflect the way the potter held the pot and reached the surfaces during finishing.

After a green (still wet) vessel dries, it is fired to create a hard and durable product. Hardness and color were examined as general indicators of firing. Hardness was measured on sherd surfaces using a scratch test with Moh's scale. Readings are suggestive of firing conditions; a moderate hardness (e.g., 4 or 5) may indicate that a nonkiln open fire was used (Rice 1987:355 ff.). Color may indicate other aspects of firing, including the atmosphere, duration, and temperature. For earthenwares containing natural iron impurities in the clays, firing in an open, oxygen-rich atmosphere can result in pottery with red and brown coloration (Rice 1987:333). Color was recorded using a Munsell color chart.

Further evaluation of the pottery suggested traits associated with use and subsequent discard. Among these were: the character of sherd breakage; and the presence of smudges, charred remains, cracks, and repair holes. Repeated heating and cooling during use in or near a fire can affect the appearance and the lifespan of a vessel. Smudges may form on surfaces smothered or placed in coals. Charred crusts may form as vessel contents burn and harden. Low-fired and coarsely tempered earthenware is brittle, porous, fragile, and easily broken. It is heavy and not easily transported. Water and steam can expand and contract among pores between clay and temper particles, causing fractures and propagating cracks. Repairs can be made by drilling holes into the walls to bind over cracks. Or a vessel may simply fracture beyond repair and be left to crumble in place.

BEAVER MEADOW BROOK SITE AND VESSEL

The Beaver Meadow Brook site is one of many archaeological locations that are known to cluster along the Merrimack River at Sewall's Falls, in Concord, New Hampshire (Figure 12.1). Excavations were conducted at various zones within the Sewall's Falls district, including river terraces and an island below the falls. Fieldwork was completed over the course of several field seasons, including a focused effort at the Beaver Meadow Brook site in 1985 and 1986 (Howe 1988; Starbuck 1982, 1984, 1985).

The Beaver Meadow Brook site is located on the south side of Beaver Meadow Brook, on a high terrace on the west bank of the Merrimack River. The site exhibited deep cultural stratigraphy with deposits extending to approximately one meter below present-day ground surface. A clear archaeological context was evident with dated features, artifacts, and clusters of materials separated both vertically and horizontally. The earliest site occupation occurred approximately 6000 years ago with final site occupation occurring some 2000 years ago (Howe 1988).

A concentration of distinctive interior-exterior Vinette I cord-impressed ceramics was discovered between 35 and 50 cm below surface in a clear stratigraphic layer at the site (Figure 12.2). Among these were approximately 500 sherds found together and reassembled to form a single vessel (Figure 12.3). Charcoal recovered from soils inside this collapsed pot was radiocarbon dated to 3150 ± 125 B.P. (GX-14011) (uncalibrated and uncorrected) (Howe 1988:82). The reconstruction provided nearly one-half of a total vessel, with rim and side-wall sections present, but the base missing. Attributes are summarized in Table 12.1.

The potter who constructed this vessel used clay mixed with shattered, angular pieces of quartz, as well as handfuls of sand containing mica and other small particles. The coarse temper was uniformly distributed

Figure 12.2
Beaver Meadow Brook Site Pottery

throughout the clay before the pot was made. The pot was built by coiling and smoothing the clay, and building rather thick walls with only slight variation in thickness along the face of the pot.

The maker finished the vessel by impressing surfaces with twinned fiber. The cordage was fine and uniform, tightly twisted in an "S" orientation. The impressions run horizontally on the interior, but are aligned in a cross hatch on the exterior. At the rim, the potter smoothed over the cord markings, erasing the impressions from the exterior surface near the vessel mouth to leave a smooth zone just below the lip. The vessel was fired in an open, oxygen-rich fire, producing a strong and durable pot of a pale brown color.

The potter created a moderately large-sized vessel, about three hands high and two hands across, with a capacity of about four to six quarts (a generous gallon) (Figure 12.3). This pot was substantial enough to have cooked acorns or extract nut oils (acorn shell and nut-meat remains were found nearby) or game foods (represented at the site by shell and

Figure 12.3
Beaver Meadow Brook Site Pottery Reconstruction

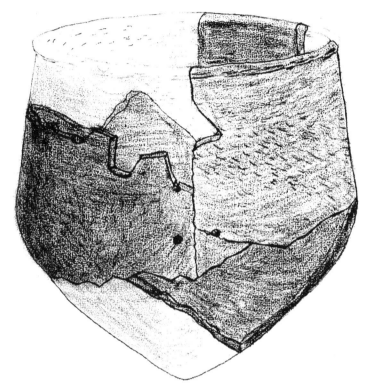

The vessel is estimated to have been 27 cm from base to rim. Based on Howe 1988:83. Prepared by Dennis E. Howe.

bone fragments of snake, turtle, fish, and beaver) (see Howe 1988:92, 95). Smudges indicate that the pot was used in or near a fire. Perhaps the pot was balanced among rocks or in coals and used for cooking. We may also surmise that the owner valued and cared for this pot. In an attempt to stall a break, three holes were drilled into one wall for binding over a crack with a lacing or a cord (see Howe 1988:82–83). However, the pot probably broke while being used and was left behind at the Beaver Meadow Brook site, where it continued to disintegrate and fracture into 500 or more angular and irregular sherds.

EDDY SITE AND VESSEL

The Eddy site, along with the Neville, Smyth, and other sites, forms a distinctive archaeological district at Amoskeag Falls, along the Mer-

Table 12.1
Attributes of the Beaver Meadow Brook Site Vessel

Reconstructed Height	30 cm
Reconstructed Diameter	26 cm
Vessel Shape	straight walls on upper body, lower body tapered
Rim and Lip Morphology	rim slightly everted an lip, lip smoothed to flat profile
Construction	coiled and smoothed
Wall Thickness	range = 0.8 to 1.1 cm; average = 0.99 cm
Aplastic Inclusions	sand, mica, coarse quartz
	temper 5%-10% of matrix
	inclusion size 0.1 to 0.5 cm diameter
Color	interior = brown to dark brown (7.5 YR 5/3 to 7.5 YR 3/3)
	exterior = yellowish to light-yellowish brown (10 YR 6/4 to 10 YR 5/4)
	core = very dark gray (7.5 YR 3/1)
Hardness	5 on Mohs scale
Surface Treatment	exterior = cordage applied horizontally and cross-hatched, smoothed over at rim
	interior = cordage applied horizontally
Cordage	twist = "S"
	cord width = 0.18 to 0.23 cm
	cord gauge = two twists per cm
Other Characteristics	vessel includes three repair holes on one face, areas of black smudging visible r surface; sherd breakage irregular and angular

rimack River in Manchester, New Hampshire (Figure 12.1). Amoskeag Falls is well-known to archaeologists for its vast and rich cultural deposits found on islands below the falls and multiple terrace tiers above the river on both the east and west sides of the Merrimack. Excavations and collections reveal an array of artifacts and features indicative of a long and continuous occupation history at Amoskeag, beginning some 8000 or more years ago (Dincauze 1976; Foster et al. 1981; Bunker 1992).

The Eddy site is located on the west bank of the Merrimack River, on an alluvial terrace below Amoskeag Falls (Figure 12.1). The site was excavated in 1985 and 1986 and exhibited deep cultural stratigraphy with deposits extending nearly two meters below present-day ground surface.

Figure 12.4
Eddy Site Pottery

CENTIMETERS

Vertical stratigraphy was easily recognized at the site through changes in artifact types and distribution, variation in sediment quality, and radiocarbon dates obtained from charcoal in features. A range of radiocarbon dates, from as early as approximately 7800 to 3300 B.P., reflects the occupation sequence at the site (Bunker 1992).

One of the features (Feature 5) excavated at the Eddy site contained 14 large (3 to 8 cm in size) and numerous small (under 3 cm in size) sherds of interior-exterior cord-impressed ceramics, which were recognized as Vinette I ceramics (Figure 12.4). This occurrence was discovered at a depth of 63 to 69 cm below ground surface in a discrete stratigraphic context (Bunker n.d.) (Figure 12.5). Feature 5 was a small

Figure 12.5
**Eddy Site Feature 5 with Pottery In Situ at 63–66 cm Below Ground
Surface**

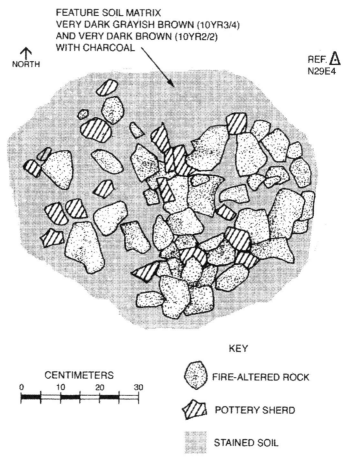

FEATURE SOIL MATRIX
VERY DARK GRAYISH BROWN (10YR3/4)
AND VERY DARK BROWN (10YR2/2)
WITH CHARCOAL

NORTH

REF. A
N29E4

KEY

FIRE-ALTERED ROCK

POTTERY SHERD

STAINED SOIL

CENTIMETERS
0   10   20   30

EDDY SITE FIELD DRAWING: FEATURE 5 WITH POTTERY *IN SITU*
EXCAVATION PLAN AT 63-66 CM BELOW SURFACE

Prepared by Dennis E. Howe.

circular hearth, measuring approximately 60 cm in diameter and characterized by the presence of stones, reddened and cracked by heat of the fire. Charcoal from the feature provided a radiocarbon date of 3315 ± 90 B.P. (G-12385) (uncalibrated and uncorrected). In addition to the early ceramics, this hearth also contained flakes and cores of quartz, flakes of volcanic stone, calcined turtle shell fragments, and other unidentifiable calcined bone (Bunker n.d.).

Table 12.2
Attributes of the Eddy Site Vessel

Reconstructed Height	unknown
Reconstructed Diameter	unknown
Vessel Shape	straight walls on body
Rim and Lip Morphology	unknown
Construction	coiled and smoothed
Wall Thickness	range = 0.8 to 1.3 cm; average = 1.09 cm
Aplastic Inclusions	sand, mica, coarse quartz, granite or fire-altered rock
	temper 5%-10% of matrix
	inclusion size 0.1 to 0.6 cm diameter
Color	interior = brown to dark gray (7.5 YR 5/2, 5 YR 4/2, 5 YR 4/3, 7.5 YR 4/1)
	exterior = red, yellowish red, reddish brown and strong brown (2.5 YR 5/6, 5 YR 5/6, 5 YR 4/4, 5 YR 5/4, 7.5 YR 5/4)
	core = very dark gray (7.5 YR 3/1)
Hardness	5 on Mohs scale
Surface Treatment	exterior = cordage applied obliquely, horizontally, and cross-hatched
	interior = cordage applied horizontally
Cordage	twist = "S"
	cord width = 0.12 to 0.15 cm
	cord gauge = three twists per cm
Other Characteristics	sherd breakage uneven and irregular

The cord-impressed sherds found in Feature 5 originated from a single vessel, which fell on its side and broke into sherds within the feature. The sherds were interspersed among the stones of the hearth, and those found near the top of the feature had their exterior surface facing up, while those at greater depths within the feature had their interior surfaces topside. A total of 14 larger and many smaller sherds from a single vessel were found in Feature 5. While these could not be completely reassembled, a large portion of the side walls of the original vessel is represented (Figure 12.4). Attributes are summarized in Table 12.2.

This vessel was constructed of clay mixed with sands, tiny flecks of mica, quartz, and irregular chunks of pinkish granite or fire-altered rock. Some of these bits were quite large, measuring over 0.5 cm in diameter, and protruded through both walls of the pot. The temper was evenly distributed, but large pieces are prominent among the cracks and breaks across the vessel. The potter built this vessel by coiling and smoothing the sides. Wall thickness varies across the vessel, with the basal area slightly thicker than upper sections of the pot.

The potter applied cordage when finishing the vessel. The fiber used to create the cordage was uniformly and tightly twinned, twisted in an "S" orientation. The cordage was applied horizontally on the interior of the vessel. On the exterior walls, cordage runs in horizontal and oblique directions, with areas aligned in a cross hatch. The potter fired this vessel in an open atmosphere, resulting in a bright reddish final pot with hard surfaces.

The pot was robust and heavy, used within the fire, probably balanced among the stones found in the hearth. Likely, it served as a container for cooking, perhaps used to cook the turtle and other game represented archaeologically by faunal remains found in association. The pot probably tipped over and broke within the fire and was left in place to crack and break further into sherds of uneven and irregular shapes over time.

DISCUSSION

The potters who made the vessels found at the Beaver Meadow Brook and Eddy sites used very similar techniques to build very similar pots. These two vessels exhibit traits that are echoed in other Vinette I ceramics found throughout the wider Northeast, as well as in the Merrimack watershed (Braun and Braun 1994; Dincauze 1976; Foster et al. 1981; Fowler 1966; Luedtke 1985; Sidney 1996). These traits include: use of heavy grit for tempering; construction of thick-walled straight-sided pots by a hand-built coiled technique; surface impression with cordage exhibiting an "S"-weft slant; firing in an open atmosphere; and use for cooking in or near a fire. The observed uniformities suggest that these potters participated in a single cultural tradition, geographically linked to the interior watersheds of what is recognized today as central and northern New England.

Some archaeologists have presumed that the first potters "knew very little" about clay and pottery making (Fowler 1966:53). These opinions developed partially through comparison of the thick walls and coarse temper seen in the early ceramics to the wafer-thin walls and nearly invisible temper observed among the latest pots in the New England sequence. Indeed, experiments with new technology result in a variety of products—some showing innovations, some showing imperfections. There is evidence of transition from use of steatite bowls in the use of crushed steatite as a tempering agent in some early ceramics (Weeks 1971). The shape and surfaces of Vinette I pots also echo baskets, possibly reflecting a transition in container making. But, the first ceramics were a highly successful innovation, and indicate that the first potters were conscious of requirements for making utilitarian wares that needed to withstand heating, cooking, and general use when they made their pottery. The Vinette type persisted in use for some 850 years and paved the way for potters to continue their experimentation and adaptation.

By studying the technical attributes of these two vessels in great detail, I believe we have improved our understanding of actual production steps and some of the variables contributing to decision-making for these prehistoric potters. The manufacture of these ceramics was not casual and the sherds we find at archaeological sites are not the products of novices.

The procedure followed to build these pots involved selection of clay and coarse, gritty tempering agents, which were readily available along the river and stream bankings where people lived and traveled. The clay was probably removed from exposed embankments and collected in blocks or chunks. It was likely to be firm and platy, with impurities. Temper was probably also gathered close at hand, including sands, gravels, or stone fragments crushed from rock in nearby hearths. The amount used was guided by the feel of the clay in the potter's hand and mixed into the moist clay to make a malleable material that could be rolled into coils.

The vessels were constructed by building and smoothing the coils into pots having thick walls, slightly everted lips, and simple shapes. The potters finished the vessel surfaces with cord impressions while the clay was still damp by pushing fiber deep into the pliable clay walls. When the pots were dry, they were fired, probably in or near a camp fire; a kiln was not used nor was the pot smothered beneath coals, slabs, or other materials, resulting in robust pots, ready for use. Each of these steps involved making a choice. Each step may have been accompanied by ritual, by teaching, or by gossip. When making decisions, each potter must "balance desirable and undesirable properties against one another" (Luedtke 1985:212), while working within the vocabulary of society and tradition. Making pottery also reflects an investment of time and resources. Each potter needed to decide on the type and function of the intended vessel, where to gather clay and temper, when to build the pot, when to fire it, how to use it, and when to repair or discard it. Pottery making required planning and knowledge.

Clay gathering is best accomplished in warm weather when clay deposits are accessible and free of ice and snow. Pot making is best done during warm, dry days so the vessel can dry evenly without cracking. How many days were needed? Were several pots made at one time? Did the potter support the vessel in the crook of the elbow and reach into it to finish the interior surface? Were the finger tips of one hand wrapped with a piece of a basket and angled down toward the base to make a series of horizontal impressions on the vessel interior? Was the pot turned and pressed along its natural curvature to finish the exterior with a series of overlapping impressions?

Vessel shape and size is governed by need and is specific to use. These early pots with thick walls would have been suitable for slow simmering next to a fire, in coals, or on the edge of a hearth. Perhaps it was nuts that were being reduced for oils in these early pots (Braun and Braun 1994:62). Their shapes were well-suited for cooking, with an open mouth large enough for adding ingredients or pouring out the contents.

What was the lifespan of one pot? Were pots made, used, and left as individual sites were occupied and departed? Heavy, brittle pottery was probably not easy to transport, but a valued piece could have been safely carried in a sling or basket. If a pot cracked or weakened, it could be reinforced and repaired by drilling holes through the walls to lace over cracks.

While many questions remain, this study has informed us that potters had acquired expertise in the arena of ceramic manufacture in New England by approximately 3500 years ago. Analysis of attributes reflecting technological aspects of pottery-making has defined some of the variables associated with ceramic manufacture and confirms that a set of practices was consistently followed by these early potters.

ACKNOWLEDGMENTS

I wrote this chapter as a tribute to Barbara Luedtke, and I honor her as a friend, dissertation advisor, mentor, and colleague. I thank Barbara for teaching me about scientific inquiry, archaeological investigation, and humanism. I also wish to thank the following individuals: Richard Boisvert; Bob Buchanan; Jane Carolan; Bob Goodby; Dennis Howe; Toni Howe; Jordan Kerber; David Starbuck; and all the volunteers who excavated with me at the Eddy site. Figures 12.1 and 12.5 were completed by the author, who also took the photographs in Figures 12.2 and 12.4. Dennis Howe prepared Figure 12.3.

References

Armour-Chelu, Marie, and Paul Andrews. 1994. Some Effects of Bioturbation by Earthworms (Oligochaeta) on Archaeological Sites. *Journal of Archaeological Science* 21(4):433–444.

Arnold, Dean E. 1985. *Ceramic Theory and Cultural Process*. New York: Cambridge University Press.

Aubrey, David. 1994. Geomorphological Investigation of Spectacle Island (Appendix A). In *The Spectacle Island Site: Middle to Late Woodland Adaptations in Boston Harbor, Suffolk County, Massachusetts*. Littleton, MA: Timelines, Inc. Report.

Barber, Russell J. 1982. *The Wheeler's Site: A Specialized Shellfish Processing Station on the Merrimac River*. Cambridge, MA: Harvard University, Peabody Museum Monograph 7.

———. 1983. Diversity in Shell Middens: The View from Morrill Point. *Man in the Northeast* 25:109–125.

Beauchamp, William M. 1901. *Wampum and Shell Articles Used by the New York Indians*. Albany, NY: University of the State of NY, New York State Museum Bulletin 8(41).

Bellantoni, Nicholas. 1987. *Faunal Resource Availability and Prehistoric Cultural Selection on Block Island, Rhode Island*. Storrs, CT: Ph.D. dissertation, Department of Anthropology, University of Connecticut.

Bender, Susan J., and Edward V. Curtin. 1990. *A Prehistoric Context for the Upper Hudson Valley: Report of the Survey and Planning Project*. On file at the New York State Office of Parks, Recreation, and Historic Preservation, Albany.

Bendremer, Jeffrey C. 1993. *Late Woodland Settlement and Subsistence in Eastern Connecticut*. Storrs, CT: Ph.D. dissertation, Department of Anthropology, University of Connecticut.

Bernstein, David J. 1987. *Prehistoric Subsistence at Greenwich Cove, Rhode Island*. Binghamton, NY: Ph.D. dissertation, Department of Anthropology, Binghamton University.

————. 1990. Prehistoric Seasonality Studies in Coastal Southern New England. *American Anthropologist* 92(1):96–115.

————. 1991. *A Stage IB Archaeological Survey of the van der Kolk Land Division Project, Mount Sinai, New York*. On file at the Institute for Long Island Archaeology, State University of New York, Stony Brook.

————. 1993a. *Prehistoric Subsistence on the Southern New England Coast: The Record from Narragansett Bay*. San Diego, CA: Academic Press.

————. 1993b. *Archaeological Data Recovery at the van der Kolk Site, Mount Sinai, Town of Brookhaven, Suffolk County, New York*. On file at the Institute for Long Island Archaeology, State University of New York, Stony Brook.

————. 1999. Prehistoric Use of Plant Foods on Long Island and Block Island Sounds. In *Current Northeast Paleoethnobotany*, edited by J.P. Hart, pp. 101–119. Albany, NY: New York State Museum Bulletin 494.

Bernstein, David J., Robert M. Cerrato, and Heather E. Wallace. 1994. *Late Woodland Use of Coastal Resources at Mount Sinai Harbor, Long Island, New York*. Paper presented at the 59th annual meeting of the Society for American Archaeology, Anaheim, CA.

Bernstein, David J., Michael J. Lenardi, and Daria Merwin. 1993. *Archaeological Investigations at Eagles Nest, Mount Sinai, Town of Brookhaven, Suffolk County, New York*. On file at the Institute for Long Island Archaeology, State University of New York, Stony Brook.

Bernstein, David J., Michael J. Lenardi, Daria Merwin, and Stephen Zipp. 1997. *Archaeological Investigations on the Solomon Property, Mount Sinai, Town of Brookhaven, Suffolk County, New York*. On file at the Institute for Long Island Archaeology, State University of New York, Stony Brook.

Bigelow, Henry B., and William C. Schroeder. 1953. *Fishes of the Gulf of Maine*. Washington, DC: Fishery Bulletin of the Fish and Wildlife Service 53. U.S. Government Printing Office.

Binford, Lewis R. 1962. Archaeology as Anthropology. *American Antiquity* 28(2):217–225.

————. 1969. A New Method of Calculating Dates from Kaolin Pipe Stem Samples. *Southeastern Archaeological Conference Newsletter* 9(1):19–21.

Binzen, Timothy. 1997. *Mohican Lands and Colonial Corners: Weataug, Wechquadnach and the Connecticut Colony 1675–1750*. Storrs, CT: M.A. thesis, Department of Anthropology, University of Connecticut.

Blancke, Shirley. 1978. *Analysis of Variation in Point Morphology as a Strategy in the Reconstruction of the Culture History of an Archaeologically Disturbed Area*. Boston, MA: Ph.D. dissertation, Department of Anthropology, Boston University.

———. 1981. *Survey of Pre-Contact Sites and Collections in Concord, Final Report*. On file at the Massachusetts Historical Commission, Boston.

———. 1987. *Archaeological Site Examination of the Bedford Street Housing Asparagus Farm Area, Concord, Massachusetts*. On file at the Massachusetts Historical Commission, Boston.

———. 1988. *Bedford Street Survey, Concord, Massachusetts (Site 19-MD-100, Survey No. 2)*. On file at the Massachusetts Historical Commission, Boston.

———. 1998. *Volunteer Intensive Archaeological Survey of the Sleepy Hollow North Cemetery Expansion: Final Report, Concord, MA*. On file at the Massachusetts Historical Commission, Boston.

———. 1999. *Archaeological Data Recovery at Sleepy Hollow North Cemetery Expansion: Final Report, Phase 1. Concord, MA*. On file at the Massachusetts Historical Commission, Boston.

———. 2001. *Archaeological Data Recovery at Sleepy Hollow North Cemetery Expansion: Final Report, Phase 2. Concord, MA*. (in prep.)

Blatt, Harvey. 1992. *Sedimentary Petrology*. 2nd ed. New York: W.H. Freeman & Co.

Bohlen, Steven R., John W. Valley, and Eric J. Essene. 1985. Metamorphism in the Adirondacks. I. Petrology, Pressure and Temperature. *Journal of Petrology* 26:971–992.

Boissevain, Ethel. 1943. Observations on a Group of Shell Heaps on Cape Cod. *Bulletin of the Massachusetts Archaeological Society* 5(3):6–11.

Boisvert, Richard, Anthony R. Philpotts, and Barbara L.A. Calogero. 1993. *Seeking the Source of So Called "Argillite" in New Hampshire*. Paper presented at the 58th annual meeting of the Society for American Archaeology, Pittsburgh, PA.

Boisvert, Richard, Monisha Tasker, and Anthony R. Philpotts. 1996. *Lithic Source Analysis of New Hampshire Hornfels*. Paper presented at the 36th annual meeting of the Northeastern Anthropological Association, Plymouth, NH.

Bolton, Reginald P. 1909. The Indians of Washington Heights. In *The Indians of Greater New York and the Lower Hudson*, edited by C. Wissler, pp. 74–109. Hudson-Fulton, NY: Anthropological Papers of the American Museum of Natural History III.

Bouck, Jill, Richard L. Burt, and James B. Richardson III. 1983. *Prehistoric Cultural Resources and Site Locations, Martha's Vineyard*. On file at the Massachusetts Historical Commission, Boston.

Bowman, William, and Gerald Zeoli. 1978. Discovery of a New Major Aboriginal Lithic Source. *Bulletin of the Massachusetts Archaeological Society* 39:35–47.

Bradley, James W. 1987. *Evolution of the Onondaga Iroquois: Accommodating Change, 1500–1655*. New York: Syracuse University Press.

Bragdon, Kathleen J. 1996. *Native Peoples of Southern New England, 1500–1650*. Norman, OK: University of Oklahoma Press.

Braun, David P. 1974. Explanatory Models for the Evolution of Coastal Adaptation in Prehistoric Eastern New England. *American Antiquity* 39(4): 582–596.

Braun, Esther K., and David P. Braun. 1994. *The First Peoples of the Northeast*. Lincoln, MA: Lincoln Historical Society.

Brumbach, Hetty Jo. 1975. "Iroquoian" Ceramics in "Algonkian" Territory. *Man in the Northeast* 10:17–28.

———. 1979. Early Ceramics and Ceramic Technology in the Upper Hudson Valley. *The Bulletin*, Journal of the New York State Archaeological Association 76:21–22.

———. 1995. Algonquian and Iroquoian Ceramics in the Upper Hudson River Drainage. *Northeast Anthropology* 49:55–66.

Brumbach, Hetty Jo, and Susan J. Bender. 1986. Winney's Rift: A Late Woodland Village Site in the Upper Hudson River Valley. *The Bulletin*, Journal of the New York State Archaeological Association 92:1–7.

Bullen, Ripley P. 1948. Culture Dynamics in Eastern Massachusetts. *American Antiquity* 14(1):36–48.

———. 1949. *Excavations in Northeastern Massachusetts*. Andover, MA: Phillips Academy, Papers of the Robert S. Peabody Foundation for Archaeology 1(3).

Bullen, Ripley P., and Edward Brooks. 1948. Three Burials at the Hughes Site, Nantucket, Massachusetts. *Bulletin of the Massachusetts Archaeological Society* 10(1):14–15.

Bullock, P., N. Fedoroff, A. Jongerius, G. Stoops, T. Tursina, and U. Babel. 1985. *Handbook for Soil Thin Section Description*. Wolverhampton, England: International Society of Soil Science. Waine Research Publications.

Bunker, Victoria. 1992. Stratified Components of the Gulf of Maine Archaic Tradition at the Eddy Site, Amoskeag Falls. In *Early Holocene Occupation in Northern New England*, edited by B.S. Robinson, J.B. Petersen, and A.K. Robinson. Occasional Publications in Maine Archaeology 9: 135–148. Augusta.

———. 2001. *A Hornfels Workshop on the Ossipee River*. Paper presented at the joint spring meeting of the Massachusetts and New Hampshire Archaeological Societies, Franklin Pierce College, Rindge, NH.

———. n.d. *The Eddy Site*. On file at the New Hampshire Division of Historical Resources, Concord.

Bunker, Victoria, and Jane Potter. 1993. *Archaeological Research Study: Data Recovery at the Mason Site (27 MR 120), A Stone Tool Manufacture Site on the Merrimack River.* On file at the New Hampshire Division of Historical Resources, Concord.

————. 1994. *The Nashua Project: Archaeological Data Recovery at the Mine Falls Part I and II Site (27 HB 32 and 33) and the Dead Pine Tree Site (27 HB 34), Nashua, New Hampshire.* On file at New Hampshire Division of Historical Resources, Concord.

Butler, Eva, and Wendell S. Hadlock. 1949. Dogs of the Northeastern Woodland Indians. *Bulletin of the Massachusetts Archaeological Society* 10(2):17–35.

Byers, Douglas S. 1979. *The Nevin Shellheap: Burials and Observations.* Andover, MA: Phillips Academy. Papers of the Robert S. Peabody Foundation for Archaeology 9.

Byers, Douglas S., and Frederick Johnson. 1940. *Two Sites on Martha's Vineyard.* Andover, MA: Phillips Academy. Papers of the Robert S. Peabody Foundation for Archaeology 1.

Byers, Douglas S., and Irving Rouse. 1960. A Re-Examination of the Guida Farm. *Bulletin of the Archaeological Society of Connecticut* 30:3–43.

Byram, Scott. 1998. Fishing Weirs in Oregon Coast Estuaries. In *Hidden Dimensions: The Cultural Significance of Wetland Archaeology*, edited by K. Bernick, pp. 198–219. Vancouver, BC: University of British Columbia Press.

Calogero, Barbara L.A. 1991. *Macroscopic and Petrographic Identification of the Rock Types Used for Stone Tools in Central Connecticut.* Storrs, CT: Ph.D. dissertation, Department of Anthropology, University of Connecticut.

————. 1993. Lithic Misidentification. *Man in the Northeast* 43:87–90.

Calogero, Barbara L.A., and Anthony R. Philpotts. 1987. *Stone Selection in Prehistoric Central Connecticut.* Paper presented at the 52nd annual meeting of the Society for American Archaeology, Toronto, Canada.

————. 1995. Rocks and Minerals Used by Tool Knappers in New England. *Northeast Anthropology* 59:1–17.

————. 2001. *Report on Three Lithographic Thin Sections from the Sleepy Hollow Expansion Site, Concord, MA.* On file at the Massachusetts Historical Commission, Boston.

Calogero, Barbara L.A., Anthony R. Philpotts, and Marc Banks. 1995. *Petrographic Identification and Source of Tridymite-Bearing Hornfels Used Prehistorically in Central Connecticut.* Paper presented at the 1995 regional conference of the Geological Society of Connecticut, Cromwell.

Cannon, A., H.P. Schwarcz, and M. Knyf. 1999. Marine-Based Subsistence Trends and the Stable Isotope Analysis of Dog Bones from Namu, British Columbia. *Journal of Archaeological Science* 26(4):399–407.

Carlson, Catherine C. 1985. *Summary Statement of Methodology and Results on Aboriginal Fish Weir Library Research (including annotated bibliography)*. On file at Timelines, Inc., Littleton, MA.

———. 1988. *Analysis of Shell Samples from the 500 Boylston Street Archaeological Project*. On file at Timelines, Inc., Littleton, MA.

———. 1990. Letter report. On file at Timelines, Inc., Littleton, MA.

Carty, Frederick M., and Arthur E. Spiess. 1992. The Neponset Paleoindian Site in Massachusetts. *Archaeology of Eastern North America* 20:19–37.

Cassedy, Daniel F. 1998. *From the Erie Canal to Long Island Sound: Technical Synthesis of the Iroquois Pipeline Project, 1989–1993*. Atlanta, GA: Garrow and Associates Report.

Ceci, Lynn. 1984. Shell Midden Deposits as Coastal Resources. *World Archaeology* 16(1):62–74.

———. 1990a. Radiocarbon Dating "Village Sites" in Coastal New York: Settlement Pattern Change in the Middle to Late Woodland. *Man in the Northeast* 39:1–28.

———. 1990b. Wampum as a Peripheral Resource in the Seventeenth-Century World System. In *The Pequots of Southern New England*, edited by L. Hauptman and J. Wherry, pp. 48–63. Norman, OK: University of Oklahoma Press.

Cerrato, Robert M., Heather E. Wallace, and Kent G. Lightfoot. 1991. Tidal and Seasonal Patterns in the Chondrophore of the Soft-Shell Clam *Mya arenaria*. *Biological Bulletin* 181:307–311.

Chaffin, William L. 1886. *History of the Town of Easton, Massachusetts*. Cambridge, MA: John Wilson and Son.

Chamberlain, Barbara Glau. 1964. *These Fragile Outposts*. Yarmouth, MA: Parnassus Imprints.

Chapdelaine, Claude. 1990. The Mandeville Site and the Definition of a New Regional Group within the St. Lawrence Iroquoian World. *Man in the Northeast* 39:53–63.

Childs, S. Terry. 1984a. Prehistoric Ceramic Analysis, Technology and Style. In *Chapters in the Archeology of Cape Cod, I: Results of the Cape Cod National Seashore Archeological Survey 1979–1981*, vol. 2, edited by F.P. McManamon, pp. 157–194. Boston, MA: Division of Cultural Resources, North Atlantic Regional Office, National Park Service.

———. 1984b. Prehistoric Ceramic Remains. In *Chapters in the Archeology of Cape Cod, I: Results of the Cape Cod National Seashore Archeological Survey 1979–1981*, vol. 2, edited by F.P. McManamon, pp. 195–278. Boston, MA: Division of Cultural Resources, North Atlantic Regional Office, National Park Service.

Chilmark Planning Board, Chilmark Conservation Commission, and the Martha's Vineyard Commission. 1985. *Chilmark Master Plan, Including the Open Space Plan*. On file at the Chilmark Conservation Commission, Chilmark, MA.

Chilton, Elizabeth S. 1994a. *The Goat Island Rockshelter: New Light from Old Legacies*. Amherst, MA: Department of Anthropology Research Report 29. University of Massachusetts.

———. 1994b. Ceramic Attribute Analysis: Chassell 2 Site (Appendix B). In *Data Recovery of the Chassell 2 (19-BK-141) and Kamposa Bog (19-BK-143) Sites, Stockbridge, Massachusetts*, by E.S. Johnson. Amherst, MA: University of Massachusetts Archaeological Services Report.

———. 1996. *Embodiments of Choice: Native American Ceramic Diversity in the New England Interior*. Amherst, MA: Ph.D. dissertation, Department of Anthropology, University of Massachusetts.

———. 1998. The Cultural Origins of Technical Choice: Unraveling Algonquian and Iroquoian Ceramic Traditions in the Northeast. In *The Archaeology of Social Boundaries*, edited by M.T. Stark, pp. 132–160. Washington, DC: Smithsonian Institute Press.

———. 1999a. Mobile Farmers of Pre-Contact Southern New England: The Archaeological and Ethnohistorical Evidence. In *Current Northeast Paleoethnobotany*, edited by J.P. Hart, pp. 157–176. Albany, NY: New York State Museum Bulletin 494.

———. 1999b. Ceramic Research in New England: Breaking the Typological Mold. In *The Archaeological Northeast*, edited by M.A. Levine, K.E. Sassaman, and M.S. Nassaney, pp. 97–111. Westport, CT: Bergin & Garvey.

———. 2001. "Towns They Have None": Diverse Subsistence and Settlement Strategies in Native New England. In *Northeast Subsistence-Settlement Change:* A.D. *700–*A.D. *1300*, edited by J.P. Hart and C. Reith. New York State Museum Bulletin. Under review.

Chilton, Elizabeth S., and Dianna L. Doucette. 1998. *Summary Report on Archaeological Investigations and a Proposal for an Archaeological Field School, Lucy Vincent Beach Site (19-DK-148), Chilmark, Martha's Vineyard, Massachusetts*. On file at the Massachusetts Historical Commission, Boston.

———. 1999. *Summary Report on Burial #3 Lucy Vincent Beach Site (19-DK-148)*. On file at the Massachusetts Historical Commission, Boston.

Christenson, Andrew L. 1985. The Identification and Study of Indian Shell Middens in Eastern North America: 1643–1861. *North American Archaeologist* 6(3):227–243.

Chute, Newton E. 1966. Geology of the Norwood Quadrangle, Norfolk and Suffolk Counties, Massachusetts. *Geological Survey Bulletin* 1163-B. Reston, VA: U.S. Geological Survey.

Claassen, Cheryl P. 1991a. Normative Thought and Shell Midden Archaeology. In *Archaeological Method and Theory*, vol. 3, edited by M.B. Schiffer, pp. 249–298. Tucson, AZ: University of Arizona Press.

———. 1991b. Gender, Shellfishing, and the Shell Mound Archaic. In *Engen-*

dering Prehistory: Women and Production, edited by J. Gero and M. Conkey, pp. 276–300. London: Basil Blackwell.

Clapp, Ebenezer. 1859. *History of Dorchester, Massachusetts*. Boston, MA: Dorchester Antiquarium and Historical Society.

Coates, Laura, and Michael Haynie. 1999. *The Great Divide: Attribute Analysis of the Lucy Vincent Beach Site Prehistoric Ceramics*. Undergraduate research paper prepared for Anthropology 197, Harvard University, Spring 1999. Ms. in possession of the authors.

Conkey, Margaret W. 1990. Experimenting with Style in Archaeology: Some Historical and Theoretical Issues. In *The Uses of Style in Archaeology*, edited by M.W. Conkey and C.A. Hastorf, pp. 5–17. New York: Cambridge University Press.

Connecticut, State of. 1837. *Resolves and Private Laws, From the Year 1789 to the Year 1836*, Vols. 1 and 2.

Connor, Paul F. 1971. *The Mammals of Long Island, New York*. Albany, NY: Bulletin 416. New York State Museum and Science Service, University of the State of New York.

Cotkin, Spencer J., Christopher Carr, Mary Louise Cotkin, Alfred E. Dittert, and Daniel T. Kremser. 1999. Analysis of Slips and Other Inorganic Surface Materials on Woodland and Early Fort Ancient Ceramics, South-Central Ohio. *American Antiquity* 64(2):316–342.

Courty, Marie, Paul Goldberg, and Richard Macphail. 1989. *Soils and Micromorphology in Archaeology*. New York: Cambridge University Press.

———. 1994. Ancient People—Lifestyle and Cultural Patterns. *Transactions of the 15th World Congress of Soil Science* 6a:250–269. International Society of Soil Science, Mexico.

Crabtree, Donald E. 1972. *An Introduction to Flintworking*. Pocatello, ID: Occasional Papers of the Idaho State University Museum 28.

Currie, Douglas R. 1994. Micromorphology of a Native American Cornfield. *Archaeology of Eastern North America* 22:63–72.

Davidson, D.A., S.P. Carter, and T.A. Quine. 1992. An Evaluation of Micromorphology as an Aid to Archaeological Interpretation. *Geoarchaeology* 7:55–65.

Day, Gordon M. 1979. Western Abenacki. In *Northeast: Handbook of North American Indians*, vol. 15, edited by B.G. Trigger, pp. 148–159. Washington, DC: Smithsonian Institute Press.

Décima, Elena B., and Dena F. Dincauze. 1998. The Boston Back Bay Fish Weirs. In *Hidden Dimensions: The Cultural Significance of Wetland Archaeology*, edited by K. Bernick, pp. 157–172. Vancouver, BC: University of British Columbia Press.

Diamond, Joseph E. 1994. *Kingston Incised Pottery: An Update*. Paper presented at the Archaeology of the Hudson Valley Conference, New York State Museum, Albany.

Didier, Mary Ellen. 1974. X-Ray Diffraction Analysis of Some of the Savich

Farm Point Material. *Eastern States Archaeological Federation Bulletin* 33:12.

———. 1975. The Argillite Problem Revisited: An Archaeological and Geological Approach to a Classical Archaeological Problem. *Archaeology of Eastern North America* 3:90–100.

Dincauze, Dena F. 1968. *Cremation Cemeteries in Eastern Massachusetts.* Cambridge, MA: Harvard University. Papers of the Peabody Museum of Archaeology and Ethnology, vol. 59, no. 1.

———. 1969. Review of *The Connecticut Valley Indian*, by William R. Young. *American Antiquity* 34(1):129.

———. 1974. An Introduction to Archaeology in the Greater Boston Area. *Archaeology of Eastern North America* 2:39–67.

———. 1975. Ceramic Sherds from the Charles River Basin. *Bulletin of the Archaeological Society of Connecticut* 39:5–19.

———. 1976. *The Neville Site: 8,000 Years at Amoskeag, Manchester, New Hampshire*. Cambridge, MA: Harvard University, Peabody Museum Monographs 4.

———. 1985. Significance and Problems Statement; Research Design. Chapters in *Reconnaissance Archaeological Study for the 500 Boylston Street Project*, compiled by M. Roberts. Littleton, MA: Timelines, Inc. Report.

———. 1990. A Capsule Prehistory of Southern New England. In *The Pequots in Southern New England*, edited by L.M. Hauptman and J.D. Wherry, pp. 19–32. Norman, OK: University of Oklahoma Press.

———. 1995. Watching Our Tempers. *Conference on New England Archaeology Newsletter* 14:34.

———. 1996. Deconstructing Shell Middens in New England. *The Review of Archaeology* 17(1):45–49.

———. 1998. Boylston Street Fish Weirs. In *Archaeology of Prehistoric Native America: An Encyclopedia*, edited by G. Gibbons, pp. 88–91. New York: Garland.

Doucette, Dianna L. 2001. *Geoarchaeological Approach to Understanding Early and Middle Archaic Native American Features and Burial Practices in New England*. Dissertation prospectus submitted to the Department of Anthropology, Harvard University, Cambridge, MA. Ms. in possession of the author.

Dunford, Frederick J. 1998. *Late Woodland Period Shell Midden Diversity on Cape Cod, Massachusetts: Political, Ritual, and Daily Life*. Paper presented at the 63rd annual meeting of the Society for American Archaeology, Seattle.

Dunn, Shirley W. 1994. *The Mohicans and Their Land 1609–1730*. Fleischmanns, NY: Purple Mountain Press.

Emperaire, José. 1955. *Les Nomades de la Mer*. 2nd ed. Paris: Gallimard.

Feder, Kenneth L. 1981. The Farmington River Archaeological Project: Focus on a Small River Valley. *Man in the Northeast* 22:131–146.

Fenton, William N. 1948. The Present Status of Anthropology in Northeastern North America: A Review Article. *American Anthropologist* 50(1):494–515.

Filios, Elena L. 1989. The End of the Beginning or the Beginning of the End: The Third Millennium B.P. in Southern New England. *Man in the Northeast* 38:79–93.

Finch, James K. 1909. Aboriginal Remains on Manhattan Island. In *The Indians of Greater New York and the Lower Hudson*, edited by C. Wissler, pp. 64–73. Hudson-Fulton, NY: Anthropological Papers of the American Museum of Natural History III.

Flannery, Regina. 1939. *An Analysis of Coastal Algonquian Culture*. Washington, DC: The Catholic University Press, Anthropological Series 7.

Foster, Donald, Victoria Kenyon, and George P. Nicholas. 1981. Ancient Lifeways at the Smyth Site, NH 38–4. *New Hampshire Archeologist* 22(2):1–91.

Foster, M.K., J. Campisi, and M. Mithun, editors. 1984. *Extending the Rafters: Interdisciplinary Approaches to Iroquoian Studies*. Albany, NY: State University of New York Press.

Fowler, William S. 1948. Classification of Some Massachusetts Pottery. *Bulletin of the Massachusetts Archaeological Society* 10:4–6.

———. 1956. Sweet-Meadow Brook: A Pottery Site in Rhode Island. *Bulletin of the Massachusetts Archaeological Society* 18(1):1–23.

———. 1966. Ceremonial and Domestic Products of Aboriginal New England. *Bulletin of the Massachusetts Archaeological Society* 27(3–4).

———. 1974. Two Indian Burials in North Middleboro. *Bulletin of the Massachusetts Archaeological Society* 35(3–4):14–18.

Frazier, Patrick. 1992. *The Mohicans of Stockbridge*. Lincoln, NE: University of Nebraska Press.

Funk, Robert. 1976. *Recent Contributions to Hudson Valley Prehistory*. Albany, NY: New York State Museum Memoir 22.

Gardner, Russell H. 1996. Last Royal Dynasty of the Massachusetts. *Bulletin of the Massachusetts Archaeological Society* 57(1):18–26.

Ge', T., Marie Courty, W. Matthews, and J. Wattez. 1993. Sedimentary Formation Processes of Occupation Surfaces. In *Formation Processes in Archaeological Context*, edited by P. Goldberg, D.T. Nash and M.D. Petraglia, pp. 149–164. Madison, WI: Prehistory Press. Monographs in World Archaeology 17.

Goldberg, Paul. 1992. Micromorphology, Soils, and Archaeological Sites. In *Soils in Archaeology*, edited by V.T. Holiday, pp. 145–168. Washington, DC: Smithsonian Institute Press.

Goldberg, Paul, David Nash, and Michael Petraglia, editors. 1993. *Formation Processes in Archaeological Context*. Madison, WI: Prehistory Press. Monographs on World Archaeology 17.

Goldberg, Paul, and Ian Whitbread. 1993. Micromorphological Study of a Bedouin Tent Floor. In *Formation Processes in Archaeological Context*, edited by P. Goldberg, D.T. Nash, and M.D. Petraglia, pp. 165–188. Madison, WI: Prehistory Press. Monographs in World Archaeology 17.

Goodby, Robert G. 1992. *Diversity as a Typological Construct: Reconstructing Late Woodland Ceramics from Narragansett Bay*. Paper presented at the 32nd annual meeting of the Northeastern Anthropological Association, Bridgewater, MA.

———. 1994. *Style, Meaning and History: A Contextual Study of 17th Century Native American Ceramics from Southeastern New England*. Providence, RI: Ph.D. dissertation, Department of Anthropology, Brown University.

———. 1995. Native American Ceramics from the Rock's Road Site, Seabrook, New Hampshire. *New Hampshire Archeologist* 35(1):46–60.

———. 1998. Technological Patterning and Social Boundaries: Ceramic Variability in Southern New England, A.D. 1000–1675. In *The Archaeology of Social Boundaries*, edited by M.T. Stark, pp. 161–182. Washington, DC: Smithsonian Institute Press.

Gookin, Daniel. 1970. *Historical Collections of the Indians in New England*, edited by J.H. Fiske. Worcester, MA: Towtaid. (orig. 1792).

Gosselain, Olivier P. 1998. Social and Technical Identity in a Clay Crystal Ball. In *The Archaeology of Social Boundaries*, edited by M.T. Stark, pp. 78–106. Washington, DC: Smithsonian Institute Press.

Gramly, Richard M. 1980. Raw Materials Source Areas and "Curated" Tool Assemblages. *American Antiquity* 45(4):823–833.

———. 1982. The Vail Site: A Paleo-Indian Encampment in Maine. *Bulletin of the Buffalo Society of Natural Sciences* 30:44.

———. 1984. Mount Jasper: A Direct-Access Lithic Source Area in the White Mountains of New Hampshire. In *Prehistoric Quarries and Lithic Production*, edited by J.E. Ericson and B.A. Purdy, pp. 11–21. New York: Cambridge University Press.

Gramly, Richard M., and Gretchen A. Gwynne. 1979. Two Late Woodland Sites on Long Island Sound. *Bulletin of the Massachusetts Archaeological Society* 40(1):5–19.

Griffin, James B. 1944. *The Iroquois in American Prehistory*. Ann Arbor, MI: University of Michigan Press. Michigan Academy of Science, Arts, Letters, and Papers 29.

———. 1946. Cultural Change and Continuity in Eastern United States Archaeology. In *Man in Northeastern North America*, edited by F. Johnson, pp. 37–95. Andover, MA: Phillips Academy. Papers of the Robert S. Peabody Foundation for Archaeology 3.

Grimes, John, W. Eldridge, B.G. Grimes, A. Vaccaro, F. Vaccaro, J. Vaccaro, N. Vaccaro, and A. Orsini. 1984. Bull Brook II. New Experiments upon the Record of Eastern PaleoIndian Cultures. *Archaeology of Eastern North America* 12:159–183.

Grumet, Robert S. 1978. *"We Are Not So Great Fools": Changes in Upper*

Delawaran Socio-Political Life, 1630–1758. New Brunswick, NJ: Ph.D. dissertation, Department of Anthropology, Rutgers University.

———. 1995. *Historic Contact: Indian People and Colonists in Today's Northeastern United States in the Sixteenth through Eighteenth Centuries.* Norman, OK: University of Oklahoma Press.

Guernsey, Samuel J. 1916. Notes on Explorations of Martha's Vineyard. *American Anthropologist* 18(1):81–97.

Gwynne, Gretchen A. 1979. Prehistoric Archaeology at Mount Sinai Harbor, Suffolk County, New York. *The Bulletin*, Journal of the New York State Archaeological Association 77:14–25.

———. 1982. *The Late Archaic Archaeology of Mount Sinai Harbor, New York.* Stony Brook, NY: Ph.D. dissertation, Department of Anthropology, State University of New York.

———. 1984. A Late Archaic House Pattern on Long Island. *The Bulletin*, Journal of the New York State Archaeological Association 88:1–8.

———. 1985. The Rudge-Breyer Site: A Late Archaic Base Camp. *The Bulletin*, Journal of the New York State Archaeological Association 91:1–12.

Haley and Aldrich, Inc. 1985. *Report on Subsurface Investigations and Foundation Design Recommendations: Proposed Development, 500 Boylston Street, Boston, Massachusetts.* Boston, MA: Haley and Aldrich, Inc. Report.

Halligan, Jessi J. 2000. *Maushop's Legacy: Cultural Continuity on Martha's Vineyard, Massachusetts, 7000 Years Ago to the Present.* Senior honors thesis, Department of Anthropology, Harvard University, Cambridge, MA.

Hamell, George R. 1987. Mythical Realities and European Contact in the Northeast during the Sixteenth and Seventeenth Centuries. *Man in the Northeast* 33:63–87.

Handsman, Russell. 1988. Algonkian Women Resist Colonialism. *Artifacts* 16(3–4):29–31.

———. 1989. *The Fort Hill Project: Native Americans in Western Connecticut and an Archaeology of Living Traditions.* Washington, CT: American Indian Archaeological Institute.

———. 1990. *Corn and Culture, Pots and Politics: How to Listen to the Voices of Mohegan Women.* Paper presented at the 23rd annual meeting of the Society for Historical Archaeology, Tucson, AZ.

Handsman, Russell, and Trudy Lamb Richmond. 1992. *Confronting Colonialism: The Mahican and Schagticoke People and Us.* Paper prepared for an advanced seminar at the School for American Research, Santa Fe, NM.

Hansen, Wallace. 1956. *Geology and Mineral Resources of the Hudson and Maynard Quadrangles, Massachusetts.* Washington, DC: Geological Survey Bulletin 1038.

Hanson, Lindley S. 1995. Turbidites, Debris Flows, and Type-1 Melange of the

Carrabassett Formation, East Branch Pleasant River. In *Guidebook to the Field Trips in North-Central Maine*, edited by L.S. Hanson, pp. 229–238. Dubuque, IA: William C. Brown. New England Intercollegiate Geological Conference 85th annual meeting, Millinocket, ME.

Harrington, Jean C. 1954. Dating Stem Fragments of Seventeenth and Eighteenth Century Clay Tobacco Pipes. *Quarterly Bulletin of the Archaeological Society of Virginia* 9(1):9–13.

Harrington, Mark R. 1909. Ancient Shell Heaps near New York City. In *The Indians of Greater New York and the Lower Hudson*, edited by C. Wissler, pp. 169–179. Hudson-Fulton, NY: Anthropological Papers of the American Museum of Natural History III.

Harris, Edward. 1989. *Principles of Archaeological Stratigraphy*, 2nd ed. London: Academic Press.

Harrison, Burr, and Valerie McCormack. 1990. *Investigations at the Bassett Knoll Site*. Paper presented at the 30th annual meeting of the Northeastern Anthropological Association, Burlington, VT.

Hather, J. 1991. The Identification of Charred Archaeological Remains of Vegetative Parenchymous Tissue. *Journal of Archaeological Science* 18(6): 661–675.

Hayes, Charles F. III, editor. 1980. *Proceedings of the 1979 Iroquois Pottery Conference*. Research Records 13. Rochester Museum and Science Center, Rochester, NY.

Haynes, Henry. 1886. Localities of Quarries Worked by the Indians for Material for Their Stone Implements. *Proceedings of the Boston Society of Natural History* 23:333–336.

Heath, Dwight B., editor. 1969. *A Journal of the Pilgrims at Plymouth (Mourt's Relation-1622)*. New York: Corinth Books.

Herbster, Holly. 1996. *The Archaeology of Squibnocket Ridge*. Paper presented at the 36th annual meeting of the Northeastern Anthropological Association, Plymouth, NH.

Herbster, Holly, and Suzanne G. Cherau. 1998. *Data Recovery Program at the Lot 13 Site (19-DK-144), Squibnocket Ridge, Chilmark, Massachusetts*. Pawtucket, RI: Public Archaeology Laboratory, Inc. Report.

———. 1999. *Archaeological Data Recovery Program within the Herring Creek Archaeological District, Wampanoag Aquinnah Shellfish Hatchery Project (WASH), Aquinnah, Martha's Vineyard, Massachusetts*. Pawtucket, RI: Public Archaeology Laboratory, Inc. Report 938.

———. 2001. *Intensive (Locational) Archaeological Survey, Pioggia Property, Aquinnah, Massachusetts*. Pawtucket, RI: Public Archaeology Laboratory, Inc. Report 1195.

Herbster, Holly, and Suzanne Glover. 1993. *Archaeological Investigations at Squibnocket Ridge, Chilmark, Massachusetts*. Pawtucket, RI: Public Archaeology Laboratory, Inc. Report 458.

Hermes, O. Don, Barbara E. Luedtke, and Duncan Ritchie. 2001. Melrose Green

Rhyolite: Its Geologic Setting and Petrographic and Geochemical Characteristics. *Journal of Archaeological Science* 28(9):913–928.

Hermes, O. Don, and Duncan Ritchie. 1997. Application of Petrographic and Geochemical Methods to Sourcing Felsitic Archaeological Materials in Southeastern New England. *Geoarchaeology* 12(1):1–30.

Hodder, Ian. 1979. Economic and Social Stress and Material Culture Patterning. *American Antiquity* 44(3):446–454.

———. 1982. *Symbols in Action: Ethnoarchaeological Studies of Material Culture*. New York: Cambridge University Press.

———. 1986. *Reading the Past: Current Approaches to Interpretation in Archaeology*. New York: Cambridge University Press.

———. 1987. The Contextual Analysis of Symbolic Meanings. In *The Archaeology of Contextual Meanings*, edited by I. Hodder, pp. 1–10. New York: Cambridge University Press.

Hodge, Frederick Webb, editor. 1906. *Handbook of American Indians North of Mexico*. Washington, DC: Bureau of American Ethnology Bulletin 30. U.S. Government Printing Office.

Hodges, H.W.M. 1963. The Examination of Ceramic Materials in Thin Section. In *The Scientist and Archaeology*, edited by E. Pyddoke, pp. 101–110. New York: Roy Publishers.

Hoffman, Curtiss R. 1991. *A Handbook of Indian Artifacts from Southern New England*. Middleboro, MA: From the original text of William S. Fowler. Massachusetts Archaeological Society, Special Publication 4.

Howe, Dennis. 1988. The Beaver Meadow Brook Site: Prehistory on the West Bank at Sewall's Falls, Concord, New Hampshire. *New Hampshire Archeologist* 29(1):49–107.

Howes, William J. 1943. Aboriginal New England Pottery. *Bulletin of the Massachusetts Archaeological Society* 5:1–5.

Hubert, John F., James Michael Gilchrist, and Alan A. Reed. 1982. Jurassic Redbeds of the Connecticut Valley: (1) Brownstones of the Portland Formation; (2) Playa-Playa Lake–Oligomictic Lake Model for Parts of the East Berlin, Shuttle Meadow and Portland Formations. In *Guidebook for Fieldtrips in Connecticut and South Central Massachusetts*, edited by R. Joesten and S.S. Quarrier. Guidebook No. 5, pp. 103–141. Hartford, CT: State Geological and Natural History Survey of Connecticut, Natural Resources Center, Department of Environmental Protection.

Humphries, D.W. 1992. *The Preparation of Thin Sections of Rocks, Minerals, and Ceramics*. New York: Oxford University Press.

Hunt, Charles B. 1967. *Physiography of the United States*. San Francisco, CA: W.H. Freeman & Co.

Huntington, E. Gail. 1959. An Archaeological Study from Martha's Vineyard. *Dukes County Intelligencer* 1:2. Edgartown, MA: Dukes County Historical Society.

————. 1969. *An Introduction to Martha's Vineyard and a Guided Tour of the Island*. Edgartown, MA: Dukes County Historical Society.

Hurd, D. Hamilton, editor. 1884. *History of Plymouth County, Massachusetts*. Philadelphia, PA: J.W. Lewis.

Isachsen, Y.W., E. Landing, J.M. Lauber, L.V. Rickard, and W.B. Rogers, editors. 1991. *Geology of New York: A Simplified Account*. Educational Leaflet 28. Albany, NY: The University of the State of New York, State Education Department.

Jackson, Richard A., and Leo Hall. 1982. An Investigation into the Stratigraphy and Tectonics of the Kent Area, Western Connecticut. In *Guidebook for Fieldtrips in Connecticut and South Central Massachusetts*, edited by R. Joesten and S.S. Quarrier. Guidebook No. 5, pp. 213–246. Hartford, CT: State Geological and Natural History Survey of Connecticut, Natural Resources Center, Department of Environmental Protection.

Jercinovic, Michael. 1997a. Microprobe Results on Kaolinite Nodules. E-mail to Michael Volmar, March 26.

————. 1997b. Microprobe Results on Pottery Fragment. E-mail to Michael Volmar, April 4.

Johnson, Eric S. 1993. *"Some by Flatteries and Others by Threatenings": Political Strategies among Native Americans of Seventeenth-Century Southern New England*. Amherst, MA: Ph.D. dissertation, Department of Anthropology, University of Massachusetts.

————. 1994. *Data Recovery of the Chassell 2 (19-BK-141) and Kamposa Bog (19-BK-143) Sites, Stockbridge, Massachusetts*. Amherst, MA: University of Massachusetts Archaeological Services Report.

————. 2000a. The Politics of Pottery: Material Culture and Political Process among Algonquians of 17th-Century Southern New England. In *Interpretations of Native North American Life: Material Contributions to Ethnohistory*, edited by M.S. Nassaney and E.S. Johnson, pp. 118–145. Gainesville, FL: University of Florida Press.

————. 2000b. Community and Confederation: A Political Geography of Contact-Period Southern New England. In *The Archaeological Northeast*, edited by M.A. Levine, K.E. Sassaman, and M.S. Nassaney, pp. 139–154. Westport, CT: Bergin & Garvey.

Johnson, Eric S., and James W. Bradley. 1987. The Bark Wigwams Site: An Early Seventeenth Century Component in Central Massachusetts. *Man in the Northeast* 33:1–26.

Johnson, Eric S., Emily P. Gray, Daniel Hughes, Sioux McKinney, and Timothy Silva. 1989. *Report on the Fort Hill Site, Springfield, Massachusetts: Archaeological Site Examination by the University of Massachusetts Summer Field School, 1989*. On file at the Department of Anthropology, University of Massachusetts, Amherst.

Johnson, Eric S., and Thomas F. Mahlstedt. 1985. The Charles Read Archaeological Collection, Seekonk, Massachusetts. *Bulletin of the Massachusetts Archaeological Society* 46(2):56–61.

Johnson, Frederick, editor. 1942. *The Boylston Street Fishweir: A Study on the Archaeology, Biology, and Geology of a Site on Boylston Street in the Back Bay District of Boston, Massachusetts.* Andover, MA: Phillips Academy. Papers of the Robert S. Peabody Foundation for Archaeology 2.

———. 1949. *The Boylston Street Fishweir II: A Study on the Archaeology, Biology, and Geology of a Site on Boylston Street in the Back Bay District of Boston, Massachusetts.* Andover, MA: Phillips Academy. Papers of the Robert S. Peabody Foundation for Archaeology 4(1).

Johnston, Richard B., and Kenneth A. Cassavoy. 1978. The Fishweirs at Atherley Narrows, Ontario. *American Antiquity* 43(4):697–709.

Judson, Sheldon. 1949. The Pleistocene Stratigraphy of Boston, Massachusetts, and its Relation to the Boylston Street Fishweir. In *The Boylston Street Fishweir II*, edited by F. Johnson, pp. 7–48. Andover, MA: Phillips Academy. Papers of the Robert S. Peabody Foundation for Archaeology 4(1).

Kalin, Robert J., and Kent G. Lightfoot. 1989. The Remsen Hill Site, Mount Sinai, Long Island, New York: A Preliminary Excavation. *The Bulletin*, Journal of the New York State Archaeological Association 99:14–24.

Kapches, Mima. 1994. The Hill Site: A Possible Late Early Iroquoian Ceramic Firing Site in South-Central Ontario. *Northeast Anthropology* 48:91–102.

Kaplan, Lawrence, Mary B. Smith, and Lesley Sneddon. 1990. The Boylston Street Fishweir: Revisited. *Economic Botany* 44(4):516–528.

Kaye, Clifford A. 1964. Outline of Pleistocene Geology of Martha's Vineyard, Massachusetts. Washington, DC: U.S. Geological Survey Professional Paper 501C. *Geological Survey Research*, pp. 134–139.

Kaye, Clifford A., and Elso S. Barghoorn. 1964. Late-Quaternary Sea-Level Change and Crustal Rise at Boston, Massachusetts, with Notes on the Autocompaction of Peat. *Geological Society of America Bulletin* 75(1): 63–80.

Kellogg, Douglas C. 1995. How Has Coastal Erosion Affected the Prehistoric Settlement Pattern of the Boothbay Region of Maine? *Geoarchaeology* 10:65–83.

Kenyon, Victoria B. 1977. *Rhyolite at the Sumner Falls Site, VT.* On file at Boston University, Boston, MA.

———. 1979. A New Approach to the Analysis of New England Prehistoric Pottery. *Man in the Northeast* 18:81–84.

———. 1983. *River Valleys and Human Interaction: A Critical Evaluation of Middle Woodland Ceramics in the Merrimack River Valley.* Boston, MA: Ph.D. dissertation, Department of Anthropology, Boston University.

Kerber, Jordan E. 1988. Where are the Late Woodland Villages in the Narragansett Bay Region? *Bulletin of the Massachusetts Archaeological Society* 49(2):66–71.

———. 1994. *Archaeological Investigations at the Lambert Farm Site, Warwick, Rhode Island: An Integrated Program of Research and Education by the Public Archaeology Laboratory, Inc.*, Vol. I. Pawtucket, RI: Public Archaeology Laboratory, Inc. Report.

———. 1997a. *Lambert Farm: Public Archaeology and Canine Burials along Narragansett Bay.* Fort Worth, TX: Harcourt Brace College Publishers.

———. 1997b. Native American Treatment of Dogs in Northeastern North America. *Archaeology of Eastern North America* 25:81–96.

———. 1999. Coastal and Maritime Archaeology in New England: Current Research Issues and Future Directions. *Conference on New England Archaeology Newsletter* 18:1–7.

Kerber, Jordan E., editor. 1984. *Prehistoric Human Occupation of Potowomut Neck: Brown University Field Methods Project.* On file at the Rhode Island Historical Preservation Commission, Providence, RI.

Kerber, Jordan E., Alan D. Leveillee, and Ruth L. Greenspan. 1989. An Unusual Dog Burial Feature at the Lambert Farm Site, Warwick, Rhode Island: Preliminary Observations. *Archaeology of Eastern North America* 17: 165–174.

Kraft, Herbert C. 1975a. The Late Woodland Pottery of the Upper Delaware Valley: A Survey and Reevaluation. *Archaeology of Eastern North America* 3:101–140.

———. 1975b. *The Archaeology of the Tocks Island Area.* South Orange, NJ: Archaeological Research Center, Seton Hall University Museum.

———. 1978. *The Minisink Site.* Elizabeth, NJ: Archaeo-Historic Research.

Kroeber, Alfred L. 1939. *Cultural and Natural Areas of North America.* Berkeley, CA: Publications in American Archaeology and Ethnology 38.

Kuhn, Robert D. 1986. Interaction Patterns in Eastern New York: A Trace Element Analysis of Iroquoian and Algonkian Ceramics. *The Bulletin*, Journal of the New York State Archaeological Association 92:9–21.

———. 1987. Trade and Exchange among the Mohawk-Iroquois: A Trace Element Analysis of Ceramic Smoking Pipes. *North American Archaeologist* 8(4):305–315.

———. 1996. A Comparison of Mohawk and Onondaga Projectile Point Assemblages. *Journal of Middle Atlantic Archaeology* 12:27–34.

Kuhn, Robert D., and Susan E. Bamann. 1987. A Preliminary Report on Attribute Analysis of Mohawk Ceramics. *The Bulletin*, Journal of the New York State Archaeological Association 94:40–46.

Kuhn, Robert D., Robert E. Funk, and James F. Pendergast. 1993. The Evidence for a St. Lawrence Iroquoian Presence on Sixteenth Century Mohawk Sites. *Man in the Northeast* 45:77–86.

Lalish, Beth G. 1979. *The Petrography of Archaeological Materials in New*

Hampshire. Durham, NH: Senior thesis, Department of Anthropology, University of New Hampshire.

Largy, Tonya Baroody. 1979. *A Consideration of Two Lithic Materials from the Castle Hill Site, Wayland, Massachusetts*. On file at the University of Massachusetts, Boston.

Largy, Tonya Baroody, and Peter Burns. 2001. *Summary Report on Fauna from Lucy Vincent Beach Features*. Ms. in possession of the authors.

Largy, Tonya Baroody, and Duncan Ritchie. 2002. Local Lithic Materials in Archaic Technologies: Mylonite and Amphibolite from the Castle Hill Site, Wayland, Massachusetts. *Bulletin of the Massachusetts Archaeological Society* 63(1,2):51–65.

Larson, Edwin E., and Peter W. Birkeland. 1982. *Putnam's Geology*. New York: Oxford University Press.

Lavin, Lucianne. 1980. Analysis of Ceramic Vessels from the Ben Hollister Site, Glastonbury, Connecticut. *Bulletin of the Archaeological Society of Connecticut* 43:3–46.

———. 1984. Connecticut Prehistory: A Synthesis of Current Archaeological Investigations. *Bulletin of the Archaeological Society of Connecticut* 47: 5–40.

———. 1986. Pottery Classification and Cultural Models in Southern New England Prehistory. *North American Archaeologist* 7(1):1–14.

———. 1987. The Windsor Ceramic Tradition in Southern New England. *North American Archaeologist* 8(1):23–40.

———. 1988a. Coastal Adaptations in Southern New England and Southern New York. *Archaeology of Eastern North America* 16:101–120.

———. 1988b. The Morgan Site, Rocky Hill, Connecticut: A Late Woodland Farming Community in the Connecticut River Valley. *Bulletin of the Archaeological Society of Connecticut* 51:7–22.

———. 1988c. Analysis of Prehistoric Pottery. In *Archaeological Excavation of the Wicker's Creek Site, Dobbs Ferry, Westchester County, New York*, Volumes 1 and 2, pp. 61–65. New York: Greenhouse Consultants Report.

———. 1997. Diversity in Southern New England Ceramics: Three Case Studies. *Bulletin of the Archaeological Society of Connecticut* 60:83–96.

———. 1998. The Windsor Tradition: Pottery Production and Popular Identity in Southern New England. *Northeast Anthropology* 56:1–17.

———. 2001. The Schaghticoke Nation and the Moravian Movement: Tribal Revitalization without Assimilation in Highland Connecticut. In *Archaeology of the Appalachian Highlands*, edited by L.P. Sullivan and S.C. Prezzano, pp. 252–263. Knoxville, TN: University of Tennessee Press.

Lavin, Lucianne, Fred W. Gudrian, and Laurie Miroff. 1993. Pottery Production and Cultural Process: Prehistoric Ceramics from the Morgan Site. In *From Prehistory to the Present: Studies in Northeastern Archaeology in*

Honor of Bert Salwen, edited by N.A. Rothschild and D. Wall. *Northeast Historical Archaeology* 21–22:44–63.

Lavin, Lucianne, and Renee Kra. 1994. Prehistoric Pottery Assemblages from Southern Connecticut: A Fresh Look at Ceramic Classification in Southern New England. *Bulletin of the Archaeological Society of Connecticut* 57:35–51.

Lavin, Lucianne, and Laurie Miroff. 1992. Aboriginal Pottery from the Indian Ridge Site, New Milford, Connecticut. *Bulletin of the Archaeological Society of Connecticut* 55:39–51.

Lavin, Lucianne, Marina E. Mozzi, J. William Bouchard, and Karen Hartgen. 1996. The Goldkrest Site: An Undisturbed, Multicomponent Site in the Heart of Mahikan Territory. *Journal of Middle Atlantic Archaeology* 12: 113–129.

Leavenworth, Peter S. 1999. "The Best Title that Indians Can Claime": Native Agency and Consent in the Transferral of Penacook-Pawtucket Land in the Seventeenth Century. *New England Quarterly* 72(2):275–300.

Lemmonier, P. 1986. The Study of Material Culture Today: Towards an Anthropology of Technical Systems. *Journal of Anthropological Archaeology* 5:147–186.

———. 1992. *Elements for an Anthropology of Technology.* Ann Arbor, MI: Anthropology Papers 88. Museum of Anthropology, University of Michigan.

Lenardi, Michael J. 1998. *Lithic Analysis of the Eagles Nest Site, Long Island, New York: A Proposed Reduction Sequence of Quartz Artifacts Based upon Archaeological and Experimental Studies.* Stony Brook, NY: Ph.D. dissertation, Department of Anthropology, State University of New York.

Lenig, Donald. 1965. *The Oak Hill Horizon and its Relation to the Development of Five Nations Iroquois Culture.* Buffalo, NY: Researches and Transactions of the New York State Archaeological Association 15(1).

Lightfoot, Kent G. 1985. Shell Midden Diversity: A Case Example from Coastal New York. *North American Archaeologist* 6(4):289–324.

Lightfoot, Kent G., and Robert M. Cerrato. 1989. Regional Patterns of Clam Harvesting along the Atlantic Coast of North America. *Archaeology of Eastern North America* 17:31–46

Lightfoot, Kent G., Robert M. Cerrato, and Heather E. Wallace. 1993. Prehistoric Shellfish Gathering Strategies: Implications from the Growth Patterns of Soft-Shell Clams (*Mya arenaria*). *Antiquity* 67(255):358–369.

Lightfoot, Kent G., Robert Kalin, and James Moore. 1987. *Prehistoric Hunter-Gatherers of Shelter Island, New York: An Archaeological Study of the Mashomack Preserve.* Berkeley, CA: Contributions of the University of California Archaeological Research Facility 46. Department of Anthropology, University of California.

Little, Elizabeth A. 1986. Observations on the Methods of Collection, Use, and Seasonality of Shellfish on the Coasts of Massachusetts. *Bulletin of the Massachusetts Archaeological Society* 47(2):46–59.

Lizee, Jonathan M. 1989. *Niantic, Hackney Pond, and Shantok: An Examination of the Late Woodland and Contact Period Ceramic Typology in Southern New England.* Paper presented at the 29th annual meeting of the Northeastern Anthropological Association, Montreal.

———. 1994a. *Prehistoric Ceramic Sequences and Patterning in Southern New England: The Windsor Tradition.* Storrs, CT: Ph.D. dissertation, Department of Anthropology, University of Connecticut.

———. 1994b. *Cross-Mending Northeastern Ceramic Typologies.* Paper presented at the 34th annual meeting of the Northeastern Anthropological Association, Genesee, NY.

Lizee, Jonathan M., Hector Neff, and Michael D. Glascock. 1995. Clay Acquisition and Vessel Distribution Patterns: Neutron Activation Analysis of Late Windsor and Shantok Tradition Ceramics from Southern New England. *American Antiquity* 60(3):515–530.

Lopez, Julius. 1957. Some Notes on Interior Cord-Marked Pottery from Coastal New York. *Pennsylvania Archaeologist* 27(1):23–32.

Lopez, Julius, and Stanley Wisniewski. 1958. Discovery of a Possible Ceremonial Dog Burial in the City of Greater New York. *Bulletin of the Archaeological Society of Connecticut* 29:14–19.

Luedtke, Barbara E. 1975. *Survey of Twelve Islands in Boston Harbor.* On file at the Massachusetts Historical Commission, Boston.

———. 1976. *Lithic Material Distributions and Interaction Patterns during the Late Woodland Period in Michigan.* Ann Arbor, MI: Ph.D. dissertation, Department of Anthropology, University of Michigan.

———. 1978a. Survey in the Coastal Zone. In *Conservation Archaeology in the Northeast: Toward a Research Orientation*, edited by A.E. Spiess, pp. 95–101. Peabody Museum Bulletin 3. Peabody Museum of Archaeology and Ethnology. Cambridge, MA: Harvard University.

———. 1978b. Chert Sources and Trace-Element Analysis. *American Antiquity* 43(3):413–423.

———. 1979. Identification of Sources of Chert Artifacts. *American Antiquity* 44(4):744–756.

———. 1980a. The Calf Island Site and the Late Prehistoric Period in Boston Harbor. *Man in the Northeast* 20:25–76.

———. 1980b. Coastal Zone Archaeology in Boston Harbor. In *Proceedings of the Coastal-Archaeology Session, International Geographical Union Commission on the Coastal Environment*, edited by M.L. Schwartz and G.P. Moran, pp. 13–18. Bellingham, WA: Bureau for Faculty Research, Western Washington University.

———. 1980c. Survey of the University of Massachusetts Nantucket Field Station. In *Widening Horizons*, edited by C. Hoffman, pp. 95–129.

Attleboro, MA: Trustees of the Massachusetts Archaeological Society.

———. 1980d. *Neutron Activation Analysis of New England Volcanics*. Paper presented at the 45th annual meeting of the Society for American Archaeology, Philadelphia, PA.

———. 1984a. *Preliminary Report on an Archaeological Survey of the Southern Half of Long Island, MA*. On file at the Massachusetts Historical Commission, Boston.

———. 1984b. Lithic Material Demand and Quarry Production. In *Prehistoric Quarries and Lithic Production*, edited by J.E. Ericson and B.A. Purdy, pp. 65–76. New York: Cambridge University Press.

———. 1985. *The Camp at the Bend in the River: Prehistory at the Shattuck Farm Site*. Boston, MA: Massachusetts Historical Commission Occasional Publications in Archaeology and History 4.

———. 1986a. Flexible Tools for Constructing the Past. *Man in the Northeast* 31:89–98.

———. 1986b. Regional Variation in Massachusetts Ceramics. *North American Archaeologist* 7(2):113–135.

———. 1987a. The Pennsylvania Connection: Jasper at Massachusetts Sites. *Bulletin of the Massachusetts Archaeological Society* 48(2):37–47.

———. 1987b. *Results of Geophysical Testing at the Hill Site, 19-SU-56*. On file at the Massachusetts Historical Commission, Boston.

———. 1988. Where are the Late Woodland Villages in Eastern Massachusetts? *Bulletin of the Massachusetts Archaeological Society* 49(2):58–65.

———. 1990. *Report on an Archaeological Survey of World's End, Massachusetts*. On file at the Massachusetts Historical Commission, Boston.

———. 1992. *An Archaeologist's Guide to Chert and Flint*. Los Angeles, CA: Archaeological Research Tools 7. Institute of Archaeology, University of California. (Reprinted 1994).

———. 1993. Lithic Source Analysis in New England. *Bulletin of the Massachusetts Archaeological Society* 54(2):56–60.

———. 1996a. *The Archaeology of Thompson Island*. On file at the Massachusetts Historical Commission, Boston.

———. 1996b. Creating and Interpreting Cultural Identity. *Conference on New England Archaeology Newsletter* 15:1–6.

———. 1997. *Lithic Procurement and Use on the Boston Harbor Islands*. Paper presented at the 62nd annual meeting of the Society for American Archaeology, Nashville, TN.

———. 1998a. A Possible Late Middle Woodland Tool Kit from Thompson Island, Massachusetts. *Northeast Anthropology* 55:15–30.

———. 1998b. Analysis of the Copper Bead from Calf Island, Massachusetts. *North American Archaeologist* 19(2):163–171.

———. 1998c. Worked Ballast Flint at Aptucxet. *Northeast Historical Archaeology* 27:33–50.

————. 1999a. What Makes a Good Gunflint? *Archaeology of Eastern North America* 27:71–79.

————. 1999b. Gunflints in the Northeast. *Northeast Anthropology* 57:27–43.

————. 2000. Archaeology on the Boston Harbor Islands after 25 Years. *Bulletin of the Massachusetts Archaeological Society* 61(1):2–11.

————. n.d. Lithic Procurement and Use on the Boston Harbor Islands. In *Complexity, Agency and Stone Tools*, edited by A.S. Dowd. New York: Cambridge University Press. In press.

Luedtke, Barbara E., O. Don Hermes, and Duncan Ritchie. 1998. Rediscovery of the Wyoming Quarry Site, Melrose, Massachusetts. *Bulletin of the Massachusetts Archaeological Society* 59(1):25–30.

Luedtke, Barbara E., and J. Thomas Meyers. 1984. Trace Element Variation in Burlington Chert: A Case Study. In *Prehistoric Chert Exploitation: Studies from the Midcontinent*, edited by B.M. Butler and E.E. May, pp. 287–298. Carbondale, IL: Center for Archaeological Investigations Occasional Paper No. 2, Southern Illinois University.

Luedtke, Barbara E., and Peter S. Rosen. 1993. Archaeological Geology on Long Island, Boston Harbor. In *Field Trip Guidebook for the Northeastern United States: 1993 Boston GSA*, edited by J.T. Cheney and J.C. Hepburn, pp. T-1–T-15. Amherst, MA: Contribution No. 67. Department of Geology and Geography, University of Massachusetts.

MacEachern, Scott. 1998. Scale, Style, and Cultural Variation: Technological Traditions in the Northern Mandara Mountains. In *The Archaeology of Social Boundaries*, edited by M.T. Stark, pp. 107–131. Washington, DC: Smithsonian Institute Press.

MacKenzie, W.S., and A.E. Adams. 1994. *A Color Atlas of Rocks and Minerals in Thin Section*. New York: John Wiley and Sons.

MacNeish, Richard S. 1952. *Iroquois Pottery Types: A Technique for the Study of Iroquois Pottery*. Ottawa: National Museum of Canada Bulletin 124. Canada Department of Resources and Development.

Macomber, Gerald M. 1992. *Archaeological Site Examinations of Seven Prehistoric Sites in Proposed Segment 2x of Tennessee Gas Pipeline Company's Northeast Settlement Project-Phase 2 in Lee and Tyringham, Massachusetts*. Office of Public Archaeology Report 106, Boston University. (draft)

Macphail, Richard, Marie Courty, and Arthur Gebhardt. 1990. Soil Micromorphological Evidence of Early Agriculture in North-West Europe. *World Archaeology* 22(1):53–69.

Macphail, Richard, and Paul Goldberg. 1990. The Micromorphology of Tree Subsoil Hollows: Their Significance to Soil Science and Archaeology. In *Soil Micromorphology: A Basic and Applied Science*, edited by L. Douglas, pp. 431–440. Amsterdam: Elsevier.

Macpherson, Jennifer, Holly Herbster, and Suzanne Cherau. 1999. *Intensive Lo-*

cational Archaeological Survey, Bluffs Golf Club, Oak Bluffs, Massachusetts. Pawtucket, RI: Public Archaeology Laboratory, Inc. Report.

Maloney, Robin. 1989. Ceramics of the Guida Site and Walter S. Rodimon Collections: Another Piece of the Puzzle. *Bulletin of the Massachusetts Archaeological Society* 50(1):30–36.

Mandell, Daniel R. 1996. *Behind the Frontier: Indians in Eighteenth-Century Eastern Massachusetts.* Lincoln, NE: University of Nebraska Press.

Mason, Roger D., Mark L. Peterson, and Joseph A. Tiffany. 1998. Weighing vs. Counting: Measurement Reliability and the California School of Midden Analysis. *American Antiquity* 63(2):303–324.

Massachusetts Historical Commission (MHC). 1982. *Historic and Archaeological Resources of the Boston Area: A Framework for Preservation Decisions.* Boston, MA: Office of the Secretary of State.

———. 1984. *Historic and Archaeological Resources of the Connecticut Valley.* Boston, MA: Office of the Secretary of State.

———. 1987. *Historic and Archaeological Resources of Cape Cod and the Islands.* Boston, MA: Office of the Secretary of State.

Masthay, Carl, and Frank T. Siebert. 1997. *Map of New England Showing Distribution of Native American Algonquian Languages or Dialects.* In possession of the authors.

Mayer, Sandy. n.d. *Ceramics at Fort Ninigret, Charlestown, Rhode Island.* On file at the Rhode Island Historical Preservation Commission, Providence.

McBride, Kevin A. 1984. *Prehistory of the Lower Connecticut River Valley.* Storrs, CT: Ph.D. dissertation, Department of Anthropology, University of Connecticut.

———. 1986. *National Register Nomination of the Great Salt Pond Archaeological District, Block Island, Rhode Island.* On file at the Rhode Island Historical Preservation Commission, Providence.

———. 1990. The Historical Archaeology of the Mashantucket Pequots, 1637–1900. In *The Pequots of Southern New England*, edited by L.M. Hauptman and J.D. Wherry, pp. 96–116. Norman, OK: University of Oklahoma Press.

———. 1995. Source and Mother of the Fur Trade: Native-Dutch Relations in Eastern New Netherland. In *Enduring Traditions: The Native Peoples of Southern New England*, edited by L. Weinstein, pp. 31–52. Westport, CT: Bergin & Garvey.

McBride, Kevin A., and Robert E. Dewar. 1981. Prehistoric Settlement in the Lower Connecticut River Valley. *Man in the Northeast* 22:37–66.

McBride, Kevin A., Robert E. Dewar, and William M. Wadleigh. 1979. *North-Central Lowlands Archaeological Survey, South Windsor, Connecticut.* Storrs, CT: Archaeology Research Monographs 1. Department of Anthropology, University of Connecticut.

McBride, Kevin A., William M. Wadleigh, Robert E. Dewar, and Mary G.

Soulsby. 1980. *Prehistoric Settlement in Eastern Connecticut: The North-Central Lowlands and Northeastern Highlands Surveys: 1979.* Storrs, CT: Archaeology Research Monographs 1. Department of Anthropology, University of Connecticut.

McManamon, Francis P., editor. 1986. *Chapters in the Archeology of Cape Cod, V: The Indian Neck Ossuary.* Boston, MA: Division of Cultural Resources, North Atlantic Regional Office, National Park Service.

McWeeney, Lucinda. 1999. *Analysis of Charred Botanical Remains for the Lucy Vincent Site, Martha's Vineyard, Massachusetts.* Ms. in possession of the author.

———. 2000. *Additional Charcoal Identification for the Lucy Vincent Site, Martha's Vineyard, Massachusetts.* Ms. in possession of the author.

Mills, Tracey, Daniel Cassedy, and Nancy Asch Sidell. 1997. *Iroquois Gas Transmission System Phase III, Archaeological Data Recovery Report. Vol. III, The Connecticut Sites, Part IV.* Atlanta, GA: Garrow and Associates Report.

Mires, Ann Marie. 1998. *Burial Summary: Lucy Vincent Beach Site (19-DK-148).* On file at the Massachusetts Historical Commission, Boston.

Moeller, Roger W. 1992. *Analyzing and Interpreting Late Woodland Features.* Bethlehem, CT: Archaeological Services.

Moravian Church. 1743–1760. Transcripts of Moravian Contact with the Schaghticoke. *Moravian Archives* Box 111. Bethlehem, PA.

———. 1751–1758. Catalog of Indians at Pachgatgoch. *Moravian Archives* Box 115. Bethlehem, PA.

Morenon, E. Pierre. 1981. *Archaeological Resources in an Urban Setting: The Warwick, Rhode Island Case Study, Volume 2: Technical Data.* Providence, RI: Papers in Archaeology 5. Public Archaeology Program, Rhode Island College.

Mose, Douglas G., and Susan Nagel. 1982. Chronology of Metamorphism in Western Connecticut: Rb-Sr Ages. In *Guidebook for Fieldtrips in Connecticut and South Central Massachusetts*, edited by R. Joesten and S.S. Quarrier. Guidebook No. 5, pp. 247–262. Hartford, CT: State Geological and Natural History Survey of Connecticut, Natural Resources Center, Department of Environmental Protection.

Moss, Madonna L., and Jon M. Erlandson. 1998. A Comparative Chronology of Northwest Coast Fishing Features. In *Hidden Dimensions: The Cultural Significance of Wetland Archaeology*, edited by K. Bernick, pp. 180–198. Vancouver, BC: University of British Columbia Press.

Mrozowski, Stephen A. 1980. Aboriginal Ceramics. In *Burr's Hill: A 17th Century Wampanoag Burial Ground in Warren, Rhode Island*, edited by S.G. Gibson, pp. 84–87. Providence, RI: Haffenreffer Museum of Anthropology, Brown University.

———. 1994. The Discovery of a Native American Cornfield on Cape Cod. *Archaeology of Eastern North America* 22:47–62.

Mulholland, Mitchell T. 1988. Territoriality and Horticulture: A Perspective for Prehistoric Southern New England. In *Holocene Human Ecology in Northeastern North America*, edited by G.P. Nicholas, pp. 137–164. New York: Plenum.

Mulholland, Mitchell T., Christopher Donta, and Thomas L. Arcuti. 1998. *Community-Wide Archaeological Reconnaissance Survey of Chilmark, Massachusetts*. Amherst, MA: University of Massachusetts Archaeological Services Report.

Naylor, Richard S., and Suzanne Sayer. 1976. The Blue Hills Igneous Complex, Boston Area, Massachusetts. In *Geology of Southeastern New England*, edited by B. Cameron, pp. 135–146. Princeton, NJ: Science Press.

Nelson, Charles M. 1989. Radiocarbon Age of the Dog Burial from Squantum, Massachusetts. *Bulletin of the Massachusetts Archaeological Society* 50(1):29.

Newby, Paige, and Thompson Webb III. 1994. Radiocarbon-Dated Pollen and Sediment Records from near the Boylston Street Fishweir Site in Boston, Massachusetts. *Quaternary Research* 41(2):214–224.

Niemczycki, Mary Ann. 1984. *The Origin and Development of the Seneca and Cayuga Tribes of New York State*. Rochester, NY: Research Records 17. Rochester Museum and Science Center.

———. 1986. The Genesee Connection: The Origins of Iroquois Culture in West-Central New York. *North American Archaeologist* 7(1):15–44.

———. 1991. Cayuga Archaeology: Where Do We Go from Here? *The Bulletin*, Journal of the New York State Archaeological Association 102:27–33.

Oldale, Robert N. 1992. *Cape Cod and the Islands: The Geologic Story*. East Orleans, MA: Parnassus Imprints.

Parker, Arthur C. 1916. The Origin of the Iroquois as Suggested by Their Archaeology. *American Anthropologist* 18:479–507.

———. 1923. *Outline of the Algonkian Occupancy in New York*. Rochester, NY: New York State Archaeological Association. Lewis H. Morgan Chapter, Researches and Transactions 4.

Paynter, Robert. 1979. Processual Cultural Ecology of the Middle Connecticut River Valley. In *Ecological Anthropology of the Middle Connecticut River Valley*, edited by R. Paynter, pp 1–15. Amherst, MA: Department of Anthropology Research Report 18. University of Massachusetts.

Pendergast, James P. 1996. Problem Orientation for St. Lawrence Iroquoian Archaeological Research. *Journal of Middle Atlantic Archaeology* 12: 53–60.

Petersen, James B. 1980. *The Middle Woodland Ceramics of the Winooski Site A.D. 1–1000*. Vermont Archaeological Society, New Series, Monograph 1.

———. 1985. Ceramic Analysis in the Northeast: Resume and Prospect. In *Ceramic Analysis in the Northeast: Contributions to Methodology and*

Culture History, edited by J.B. Petersen. Rindge, NH: Occasional Publications in Northeastern Anthropology 9(4):5–25.

———. 1990. Evidence of the Saint Lawrence Iroquoians in Northern New England: Population Movement, Trade, or Stylistic Borrowing. *Man in the Northeast* 40:31–39.

———. 1996. Fiber Industries from Northern New England: Ethnicity and Technological Traditions during the Woodland Period. In *A Most Indispensable Art: Native Fiber Industries from Eastern North America*, edited by J.B. Petersen, pp. 100–119. Knoxville, TN: University of Tennessee Press.

Petersen, James B., and Nathan D. Hamilton. 1984. Early Woodland Ceramic and Perishable Fiber Industries from the Northeast: A Summary and Interpretation. *Annals of Carnegie Museum* 53(14):413–445.

Petersen, James B., and Marjory W. Power. 1985. Three Middle Woodland Ceramic Assemblages from the Winooski Site. In *Ceramic Analysis in the Northeast: Contributions to Methodology and Culture History*. Rindge, NH: Occasional Publications in Northeastern Anthropology 9(2): 109–159.

Petersen, James B., Brian S. Robinson, Daniel F. Belknap, James Stark, and Lawrence K. Kaplan. 1994. An Archaic and Woodland Period Fish Weir Complex in Central Maine. *Archaeology of Eastern North America* 22: 197–222.

Petersen, James B., and David Sanger. 1991. An Aboriginal Ceramic Sequence for Maine and the Maritime Provinces. In *Prehistoric Archaeology in the Maritime Provinces: Past and Present Research*, edited by M. Deal and S. Blair, pp. 121–178. New Brunswick, Canada: Reports in Archaeology 8. The Council of Maritime Premiers, Maritime Committee on Archaeological Cooperation.

Philpotts, Anthony R. 1989. *Petrography of Igneous and Metamorphic Rocks*. Englewood Cliffs, NJ: Prentice Hall.

———. 1990. *Principles of Igneous and Metamorphic Petrology*. Englewood Cliffs, NJ: Prentice Hall.

Philpotts, Anthony R., and Angel Martello. 1986. Diabase Feeder Dikes for the Mesozoic Basalts in Southern New England. *American Journal of Science* 286(2):105–126.

Philpotts, Anthony R., and Nancy Wilson. 1994. Application of Petrofabric and Phase Equilibria Analysis to the Study of a Potsherd. *Journal of Archaeological Science* 21:607–618.

Plog, Stephen. 1990. Sociopolitical Implications of Stylistic Variation in the American Southwest. In *The Uses of Style in Archaeology*, edited by M.W. Conkey and C.A. Hastorf, pp. 61–72. New York: Cambridge University Press.

Pollock, Stephen G. 1987. Chert Formation in an Ordovician Volcanic Arc. *Journal of Sedimentary Petrology* 57(1):75–87.

Pollock, Stephen G., Nathan D. Hamilton, and Richard Boisvert. 1996. The Mount Jasper Lithic Source, Berlin, New Hampshire. In *Guidebook to the Field Trips in Northern New Hampshire and Adjacent Regions of Maine and Vermont*, edited by M.R. Van Baalen, pp. 245–253. Mount Washington, NH: New England Intercollegiate Geological Conference 88th annual meeting.

Pollock, Stephen G., Nathan D. Hamilton, and Richard A. Doyle. 1995. Geology and Archaeology of Chert in the Munsungun Lake Formation. In *Guidebook to the Field Trips in North-Central Maine*, edited by L.S. Hanson, pp. 159–181. Dubuque, IA: William C. Brown. New England Intercollegiate Geological Conference 85th annual meeting, Millinocket, ME.

Pratt, Peter P. 1976. *Archaeology of the Oneida Iroquois, Vol. 1.* Rindge, NH: Occasional Publications in Northeastern Anthropology 1.

Pretola, John P. 1994. *Western Massachusetts Lithic Resources: A Tale of Two Chalcedonies.* Paper presented at the annual meeting of the Eastern States Archaeological Federation, Albany, NY.

———. 1995. *Optical Mineralogical Techniques for Sourcing Fine-Grained Quartz: A Feasibility Study Using Quartz Polymorph Ratios.* Paper presented at the annual meeting of the Geological Society of America, Northeast Section, Cromwell, CT.

———. 2000. *Northeastern Ceramic Diversity: An Optical Mineralogy Approach.* Amherst, MA: Ph.D. dissertation, Department of Anthropology, University of Massachusetts.

———. 2001. A Feasibility Study Using Silica Polymorph Ratios for Sourcing Chert and Chalcedony Lithic Materials. *Journal of Archaeological Science* 28(7):721–739.

Pretola, John P., and Eric S. Johnson. 1996. *The Springfield Fort Hill Site and the Agawam Indian Community in the Late Seventeenth Century.* Paper presented at the 95th annual meeting of the American Anthropological Association, San Francisco, CA.

Prezzano, Susan C. 1996. Household and Community: The Development of Iroquois Agricultural Village Life. *Journal of Middle Atlantic Archaeology* 12:7–16.

Prothers, Donald, and Lucianne Lavin. 1990. Chert Petrography and Its Potential as an Analytical Tool in Archaeology. *Geological Society of America Centennial Special Volume* 4:561–584.

Public Archaeology Laboratory, Inc. (PAL). 1998. *Native American Cultural Contexts for Archaeological Research, Martha's Vineyard, Massachusetts.* Pawtucket, RI: Public Archaeology Laboratory, Inc. Report.

Puniello, Anthony J. 1980. Iroquois Series Ceramics in the Upper Delaware Valley, New Jersey and Pennsylvania. In *Proceedings of the 1979 Iroquois Pottery Conference*, edited by C.F. Hayes III, pp. 147–155. Rochester, NY: Research Records 13. Rochester Museum and Science Center.

———. 1993. Evidence of the Niantic Indians in the Archaeological Record.

In *From Prehistory to the Present: Studies in Northeastern Archaeology in Honor of Bert Salwen*, edited by N.A. Rothschild and D. Wall. *Northeast Historical Archaeology* 21–22:79–95.

Rainey, Mary Lynne. 1991. *Phase I Intensive Archaeological Surveys for the Algonquin Gas Transmission Company Proposed 1.9 Mile 36-Inch Pipeline Loop and Temporary Materials Storage Site in Medway, Massachusetts, FERC Docket No. CP 90-643-000 and 1.8 Mile 10-Inch Pipeline Replacement in Milford and Medway, Massachusetts, FERC Docket No. CP 88-187-001.* Pawtucket, RI: Public Archaeology Laboratory, Inc. Report 400–4.

Rankin, Douglas W. 1995. Early Devonian Explosive Silicic Volcanism and Associated Early and Middle Devonian Clastic Sedimentation that Brackets the Acadian Orogeny, Traveler Mountain. In *Guidebook to Field Trips in North-Central Maine*, edited by L.S. Hanson, pp. 135–146. Dubuque, IA: William C. Brown. New England Intercollegiate Geological Conference 85th annual meeting, Millinocket, ME.

Ricard, Lori. 1999. *Historical Artifacts at the Lucy Vincent Beach Site, Chilmark, Martha's Vineyard, Massachusetts.* Undergraduate research paper prepared for Anthropology 197, Harvard University, Spring 1999. Ms. in possession of the author.

Rice, Prudence M. 1987. *Pottery Analysis: A Sourcebook.* Chicago, IL: University of Chicago Press.

Rice, Robin L. 1988. *Diatom Data from the Boylston Street Fishweir Project Core 8.* On file at Timelines, Inc., Littleton, MA.

Richardson, James B. III. 1985. Prehistoric Man on Martha's Vineyard. *Oceanus* 28(1):35–42.

Richardson, James B., and James L. Swauger. 1996. The Petroglyphs Speak: Rock Art and Iroquois Origins. *Journal of Middle Atlantic Archaeology* 12:43–51.

Ritchie, Duncan. 1979. *Middle Archaic Lithic Technology in Eastern and Southeastern Massachusetts.* Paper presented at the Conference on Northeastern Archaeology, University of Massachusetts, Amherst.

———. 1980. Prehistoric Cultural Resources in the Suburban Fringe: A Preliminary Assessment of the Sudbury/Assabet Drainage. In *Widening Horizons*, edited by C. Hoffman, pp. 80–94. Attleboro, MA: Trustees of the Massachusetts Archaeological Society.

———. 1981. *An Archaeological Survey of the Arrowhead Realty Trust Property near the Massachusetts Hill Hornfels/Braintree Slate Quarry, Milton, Massachusetts.* Providence, RI: Public Archaeology Laboratory Report, Department of Anthropology, Brown University.

———. 1982. Rozenas I & II Sites (7I/HP). In *Prehistoric Site Summaries, Final Report of the Interstate Highway 495 Archaeological Data Recovery Program, Volume II*, edited by P.F. Thorbahn, pp. 216–234. Providence, RI: Public Archaeology Laboratory, Department of Anthropology, Brown University.

————. 1985. *Archaeological Investigations at the Hartford Avenue Rockshelter, Uxbridge, Massachusetts: The Data Recovery Program*. Pawtucket, RI: Public Archaeology Laboratory, Inc. Report 40–2.

————. 1986. *Lithic Resource Use and Evidence for Woodland Period Trade or Exchange Networks in Southeastern New England: The Braintree Hornfels*. Paper presented at the Conference on New England Archaeology, University of Massachusetts, Boston.

————. 1987. *A Preliminary Analysis of Prehistoric Cultural Material from the Signal Hill (Neponset/Wamsutta) Site (19-NF-70)*. Pawtucket, RI: Public Archaeology Laboratory, Inc. Report 110.

————. 1998. *Petrographic and Geochemical Characterization of the Braintree Hornfels: An Approach to Prehistoric Quarrying in the Massachusett Hill Quarry Complex*. Paper presented at the annual meeting of the Geological Society of America, Northeast Section, Portland, ME.

Ritchie, Duncan, and Richard A. Gould. 1985. Back to the Source: A Preliminary Account of the Massachusett Hill Quarry Complex. In *Stone Tool Analysis: Essays in Honor of Don E. Crabtree*, edited by M.G. Plew, J.C. Woods, and M.G. Pavesic, pp. 35–53. Albuquerque, NM: University of New Mexico Press.

Ritchie, William A. 1932. The Algonkin Sequence in New York. *American Anthropologist* 34:406–415.

————. 1946. Archaeological Manifestations and Relative Chronology in the Northeast. In *Man in Northeastern North America*, edited by F. Johnson, pp. 96–105. Andover, MA: Phillips Academy. Papers of the Robert S. Peabody Foundation for Archaeology 3.

————. 1959. *The Stony Brook Site and its Relation to Archaic and Transitional Cultures on Long Island*. Albany, NY: Bulletin 372. New York State Museum and Science Service, University of the State of New York, State Education Department.

————. 1969. *The Archaeology of Martha's Vineyard*. New York: Natural History Press.

————. 1980. *The Archaeology of New York State*, Rev. ed. Harrison, NY: Harbor Hill.

Ritchie, William A., and Richard S. MacNeish. 1949. The Pre-Iroquoian Pottery of New York State. *American Antiquity* 15(2):97–124.

Robbins, Maurice. 1959. Some Indian Burials from Southeastern Massachusetts, Part 2: The Wapanucket Burials. *Bulletin of the Massachusetts Archaeological Society* 20(4):61–67.

————. 1980. *Wapanucket: An Archaeological Report*. Attleboro, MA: Massachusetts Archaeological Society.

Roberts, Michael, compiler. 1985. *Reconnaissance Archaeological Study for the 500 Boylston Street Project*. Littleton, MA: Timelines, Inc. Report.

Robinson, Paul A. 1990. *The Struggle Within: The Indian Debate in Seventeenth-Century Narragansett Country*. Binghamton, NY: Ph.D. dissertation, Department of Anthropology, State University of New York.

Rogers, Edward H. 1943. The Indian River Village Site, Milford, Connecticut. *Bulletin of the Archaeological Society of Connecticut* 15:17–78.

Rogers, John. 1985. *Bedrock Geological Map of Connecticut*. Hartford, CT: Connecticut Geological and Natural History Survey, in cooperation with the U.S. Geological Survey.

Rollins, Harold B., Daniel H. Sandweiss, and Judith C. Rollins. 1990. Mollusks and Coastal Archaeology: A Review. In *Archaeological Geology of North America*, edited by N.P. Lasca and J. Donahue, pp. 467–478. Boulder, CO: Geological Society of America, Centennial Special Volume 4.

Rosen, Peter S., Benno M. Brenninkmeyer, and Lynn Maybury. 1993. Holocene Evolution of Boston Inner Harbor, Massachusetts. *Journal of Coastal Research* 9(2):363–377.

Ross, Michael R. 1991. *Recreational Fisheries of Coastal New England*. Amherst, MA: University of Massachusetts Press.

Rouse, Irving. 1945. Styles of Pottery in Connecticut. *Bulletin of the Massachusetts Archaeological Society* 7:1–18.

———. 1947. Ceramic Traditions and Sequences in Connecticut. *Bulletin of the Archaeological Society of Connecticut* 21:10–25.

———. 1960. The Classification of Artifacts in Archaeology. *American Antiquity* 25(3):313–323.

———. 1972. *Introduction to Prehistory*. New York: McGraw-Hill.

Rubertone, Patricia E. 1989. Archaeology, Colonialism, and 17th-Century Native America: Towards an Alternative Interpretation. In *Conflict in the Archaeology of Living Traditions*, edited by R. Layton pp. 32–45. London: Unwin Hyman.

Sackett, James R. 1985. Style and Ethnicity in the Kalahari: A Reply to Wiessner. *American Antiquity* 50(1):154–159.

———. 1990. Style and Ethnicity in Archaeology: The Case For Isochrestism. In *The Uses of Style in Archaeology*, edited by M.W. Conkey and C.A. Hastorf, pp. 32–43. New York: Cambridge University Press.

Salisbury, Neal. 1982. *Manitou and Providence: Indians, Europeans, and the Making of New England 1500–1643*. New York: Oxford University Press.

Salwen, Bert. 1978. Indians of Southern New England and Long Island: Early Period. In *Northeast: Handbook of North American Indians*, vol. 15, edited by B.G. Trigger, pp. 160–176. Washington, DC: Smithsonian Institute Press.

Sandor, Jonathan A., and N.S. Nash. 1995. Ancient Agricultural Soils in the Andes of Southern Peru. *Soil Science Society of America* 59(1):170–178.

Sanger, David, and Mary Jo (Elson) Sanger. 1986. Boom and Bust on the River: The Story of the Damariscotta Oyster Shell Heaps. *Archaeology of Eastern North America* 14:65–78.

Schaper, Hans F. 1989. Shell Middens in the Lower Hudson Valley. *The Bul-*

letin, Journal of the New York State Archaeological Association 98:13–24.

Shattuck, Lemuel. 1835. *History of the Town of Concord*. Boston, MA: Russell, Odiorne, and Co.

Shaw, Leslie C. 1994. Improved Documentation in Shell Midden Excavations: An Example from the South Shore of Cape Cod. In *Cultural Resource Management: Archaeological Research, Preservation Planning, and Public Education in the Northeastern United States*, edited by J.E. Kerber, pp. 115–138. Westport, CT: Bergin & Garvey.

———. 2001. *Shell Analysis for the Lucy Vincent Site, Martha's Vineyard, Massachusetts*. Ms. in possession of the author.

Shelford, Victor E. 1963. *The Ecology of North America*. Urbana, IL: University of Illinois Press.

Shepard, Anna O. 1936. The Technology of Pecos Pottery. In *The Pottery of Pecos, Part 2*, edited by A.V. Kidder and A.O. Shepard, pp. 389–587. Andover, MA: Papers of the Phillips Academy Southwestern Expedition 7.

Shimer, Hervey W. 1918. Post-Glacial History of Boston. *Proceedings of the American Academy of Arts and Sciences* 53(6):441–463.

Sidney, Earl J. 1996. *Parsons Point, 27-CA-4*. On file at the State Conservation and Rescue Archaeology Program, Concord, NH.

Silver, Annette L. 1991. *The Abbott Interaction Sphere: A Consideration of the Middle Woodland Period in Coastal New York and a Proposal for a Middle Woodland Exchange System*. New York: Ph.D. dissertation, Department of Anthropology, New York University.

Simmons, William S. 1970. *Cautantowwit's House: An Indian Burial Ground on the Island of Conanicut in Narragansett Bay*. Providence, RI: Brown University Press.

———. 1989. *The Narragansett*. New York: Chelsea House Publishers.

Simon, Brona G. 1991. Prehistoric Land Use and Changing Conditions at Titicut Swamp in Southeastern Massachusetts. *Man in the Northeast* 42:63–74.

Sirkin, Les. 1982. Wisconsin Glaciation of Long Island, New York to Block Island, Rhode Island. In *Late Wisconsin Glaciation of New England*, edited by G.J. Larson and B.D. Stone, pp. 35–59. Dubuque, IA: Kendall/Hunt Publishing Co.

Skehan, James W., Nicholas Rast, Edward Kohut, J. Christopher Hepburn, and Stephen W. Grimes. 1998. Precambrian and Paleozoic Mylonites of the Boston Avalon. In *Guidebook to Field Trips in Rhode Island and Adjacent Regions of Connecticut and Massachusetts*, edited by D.P. Murray, pp. A3-1–A3-24. Kingston, RI: New England Intercollegiate Geological Conference 90th annual meeting, University of Rhode Island.

Skinner, Alanson B. 1909. The Lenapé Indians of Staten Island. In *The Indians of Greater New York and the Lower Hudson*, edited by C. Wissler, pp. 3–

62. Hudson-Fulton, NY: Anthropological Papers of the American Museum of Natural History III.

——. 1919a. *Explorations of Aboriginal Sites at Throgs Neck and Clasons Point, New York City.* New York: Contributions, Museum of the American Indian, Heye Foundation 4(4).

——. 1919b. *The Pre-Iroquoian Algonkian Indians of Central and Western New York.* Indian Notes and Monographs 7.

——. 1921. *Notes on Iroquois Archaeology.* Indian Notes and Monographs, Miscellaneous Series, 18.

——. 1923. *General Archaeological Criteria of Early Algonkian Culture.* Rochester, NY: New York State Archaeological Association. Lewis H. Morgan Chapter, Researches and Transactions 4.

——. 1961. *The Indians of Manhattan Island and Vicinity.* Port Washington, NY: Ira J. Friedman (orig. 1909).

Smith, Carlyle S. 1947. An Outline of the Archaeology of Coastal New York. *Bulletin of the Archaeological Society of Connecticut* 21:3–9.

——. 1950. *The Archaeology of Coastal New York.* New York: Anthropological Papers of the American Museum of Natural History, vol. 43(2).

Smith, O.G. 1987. *Archaeological Systematics and the Analysis of Iroquoian Ceramics: A Case Study from the Crawford Lake Area, Ontario.* Montreal: Ph.D. dissertation, Department of Anthropology, McGill University.

Snow, Dean R. 1980. *The Archaeology of New England.* New York: Academic Press.

——. 1991. Mohawk. *The Bulletin*, Journal of the New York State Archaeological Association 102:34–39.

——. 1995. Migration in Prehistory: The Northern Iroquois Case. *American Antiquity* 60(1):59–79.

Solecki, Ralph. 1947. An Indian Burial at Aqueduct, Long Island. *Bulletin of the Archaeological Society of Connecticut* 21:44–49.

——. 1950. The Archaeological Position of Historic Fort Corchaug, Long Island, and its Relation to Contemporary Forts. *Bulletin of the Archaeological Society of Connecticut* 24:3–40.

——. 1957. Shantok Influence on Eastern Long Island. *American Antiquity* 23(2):171–173.

Starbuck, David R. 1982. Excavations of Sewall's Falls in Concord, New Hampshire (NH 31–30). *New Hampshire Archeologist* 23:1–36.

——. 1984. Further Excavations at Sewall's Falls (NH 31–30). *New Hampshire Archeologist* 25(1):1–11.

——. 1985. Three Seasons of Site Survey and Excavation at Sewall's Falls (NH 31–30). *New Hampshire Archeologist* 26(1):87–102.

Stark, Miriam T. 1998a. Technical Choices and Social Boundaries in Material Culture Patterning: An Introduction. In *The Archaeology of Social*

Boundaries, edited by M.T. Stark, pp. 1–11. Washington, DC: Smithsonian Institute Press.

Stark, Miriam T., editor. 1998b. *The Archaeology of Social Boundaries*. Washington, DC: Smithsonian Institute Press.

Starna, William A., and Robert E. Funk. 1994. The Place of the In Situ Hypothesis in Iroquoian Archaeology. *Northeast Anthropology* 47:45–54.

Stein, Julie K. 1992. The Analysis of Shell Middens. In *Deciphering a Shell Midden*, edited by J.K. Stein, pp. 1–24. San Diego, CA: Academic Press.

Stoiber, Richard E., and Stearns A. Morse. 1993. *Crystal Identification with the Polarizing Microscope*. Melbourne, FL: Robert E. Krieger Publishing Co.

Strauss, Alan E. 1992. Jack's Reef Corner Notched Points in New England: Site Distribution, Raw Material Preference, and Implications for Trade. *North American Archaeologist* 13(4):333–350.

Strauss, Alan E., and Robert Goodby. 1993. The Slough Pond Site, Brewster, Mass. *Bulletin of the Massachusetts Archaeological Society* 54(1):25–37.

Strauss, Alan E., and O. Don Hermes. 1996. Anatomy of a Rhyolite Quarry. *Archaeology of Eastern North America* 24:159–171.

Strauss, Alan E., and Daniel P. Murray. 1988. A Model for the Prehistoric Distribution of Poor to Moderate Grade Raw Materials from Their Source in Southeastern New England: The Attleboro Red Felsite Example. *Archaeology of Eastern North America* 16:43–54.

Stuiver, Minze, and Thomas F. Braziunas. 1993. Sun, Ocean, Climate and Atmospheric $^{14}CO_2$: An Evaluation of Causal and Spectral Relationships. *The Holocene* 3(4):289–305.

Stuiver, M., G.S. Burr, K.A. Hughen, B. Kromer, G. McCormac, J.V.D. Plicht, M. Spurk, P.J. Reimer, E. Bard, and J.W. Beck. 1998a. INTCAL 98 Radiocarbon Age Calibration, 24,000–0 Cal BP. *Radiocarbon* 40(3): 1041–1083.

Stuiver, Minze, Paula J. Reimer, and Thomas F. Braziunas. 1998b. High-Precision Radiocarbon Age Calibration for Terrestrial and Marine Samples. *Radiocarbon* 40(3):1127–1151.

Stuiver, Minze, and Paula J. Reimer. 1993a. Extended ^{14}C Data Base and Revised Calib 3.0 ^{14}C Age Calibration Program. *Radiocarbon* 35:215–230.

———. 1993b. *CALIB User's Guide Rev 3.0.3*. Seattle, WA: Quaternary Isotope Laboratory, University of Washington.

Temple, Josiah H. 1988. *History of Framingham, Massachusetts: 1640–1885*. Somersworth, NH: New England History Press, in collaboration with the Framingham Historical and Natural History Society, Framingham, MA (orig. 1887).

Thompson, Margaret. 1985. Evidence for a Late Precambrian Caldera in Boston, Massachusetts. *Geology* 13:641–643.

Thompson, Margaret, and O. Don Hermes. 1990. Ash-Flow Stratigraphy in the

Mattapan Volcanic Complex, Greater Boston, Massachusetts. In *Geology of the Composite Avalon Terrane of Southern New England*, edited by A.D. Socci, J.W. Skehan, and G.W. Smith. *Geological Society of America Special Paper* 245:85–96.

Thorbahn, Peter F., and Deborah C. Cox. 1983. *Extended Phase II Testing and Analysis of Six Prehistoric Sites in the Northern Section of the Route 146 Project, Sutton and Uxbridge, Massachusetts*. Providence, RI: Public Archaeology Laboratory Report, Department of Anthropology, Brown University.

Thwaites, Reuben Gold, editor. 1896. *The Jesuit Relations and Allied Documents*. 73 vols. Cleveland, OH: Burrows Brothers.

Tilden, William S. 1887. *History of the Town of Medfield, 1650–1886*. Boston, MA: George H. Ellis.

Tipping, R., S. Carter, and D. Johnston. 1994. Soil Pollen and Soil Micromorphological Analyses of Old Ground Surfaces on Biggar Common, Borders Region, Scotland. *Journal of Archaeological Science* 21(3):387–402.

Tooker, Elisabeth, editor. 1970. *Iroquois Culture, History, and Prehistory*. Albany, NY: Proceedings of the 1965 Conference on Iroquois Research. University of the State of New York.

Trigger, Bruce G. 1981. Prehistoric Social and Political Organization: An Iroquoian Case Study. In *Foundations of Northeastern Archaeology*, edited by D.R. Snow, pp. 1–50. New York: Academic Press.

———. 1985. *Natives And Newcomers*. Montreal: McGill-Queens University Press.

Trumbull, J. Hammond, and Charles J. Hoadley, editors. 1850–1890. *Public Records of the Colony of Connecticut, 1633–1725*. (16 vols.) Hartford, CT: Case, Lockwood, and Brainard. Reprint.

Tryon, Christian A., and Anthony R. Philpotts. 1997. Possible Sources of Mylonite and Hornfels Debitage from the Cooper Site, Lyme, Connecticut. *Bulletin of the Archaeology Society of Connecticut* 60:3–12.

Tuck, James A. 1978. Northern Iroquoian Prehistory. In *Northeast: Handbook of North American Indians*, vol. 15, edited by B.G. Trigger, pp. 322–333. Washington, DC: Smithsonian Institute Press.

Ulan, Linda. 1988. *Tree Ring Analysis: 500 Boylston Street Archaeological Project*. On file at Timelines, Inc., Littleton, MA.

Ulery, April L., and R.C. Graham. 1993. Forest Fire Effects on Soil Color and Texture. *Soil Science Society of America* 57(1):135–140.

Underhill, Ruth M. 1944. Pueblo Crafts. In *Indian Handcrafts*, vol. 7., edited by W.W. Beatty. Washington, DC: Education Division, United States Indian Service.

U.S. Coastal Survey. 1846. *Outer Shore of Martha's Vineyard, from Nashaquitsa Cliff, East*. U.S. Coastal Survey Map, Register No. 202. Original map sheets housed in the U.S. National Archives, College Park, Maryland.

U.S. Department of Agriculture. 1986. *Soil Survey of Dukes County, Massachusetts.* Soil Conservation Service, United States Department of Agriculture, Washington, DC.

U.S. Geological Survey (USGS). 1949. *Squibnocket Quadrangle, Dukes County, Massachusetts, 15-Minute Series.* Department of the Interior, U.S. Geological Survey, Washington, DC.

———. 1972. *Squibnocket Quadrangle, Dukes County, Massachusetts, 7.5-Minute Series.* Department of the Interior, U.S. Geological Survey, Washington, DC.

Van der Leeuw, Sander E., and Alison C. Pritchard, editors. 1984. *The Many Dimensions of Pottery: Ceramics in Archaeology and Anthropology.* Amsterdam: Universiteit van Amsterdam.

Vargas, Tiziana. 1999. *The Lucy Vincent Beach Site Lithic Analysis: An Analysis of the Lithic Assemblage in Correlation to Primary Features.* Undergraduate research paper prepared for Anthropology 196, Harvard University, Fall 1999. Ms. in possession of the author.

Veneman, Peter. 1994. *Soil Descriptions for Massachusetts.* Amherst, MA: U.S. Department of Agriculture, Soil Conservation Service.

Volmar, Michael. 1998. *The Micromorphology of Landscapes: An Archaeological Approach in Southern New England.* Amherst, MA: Ph.D. dissertation, Department of Anthropology, University of Massachusetts.

———. 1999. *What is this Thing?: Micromorphology at RI-118.* Paper presented at the annual meeting of the Geological Society of America, Northeast Division, Providence, RI.

———. 2000. *Sleepy Hollow Expansion Archaeological Site Soil Micromorphology Report.* On file at the Massachusetts Historical Commission, Boston.

Walker, Iain C. 1977. *Clay Tobacco-Pipes, with Particular Reference to the Bristol Industry.* Ottawa: Parks Canada.

Waller, Joseph N., and Duncan Ritchie. 1997. *Intensive Archaeological Survey of the Sleepy Hollow North Cemetery Expansion, Concord, Massachusetts.* Pawtucket, RI: Public Archaeology Laboratory, Inc. Report 818.

———. 2001. *Archaeological Data Recovery Program: Pine Hawk Site (19-MD-793), Acton, MA.* Pawtucket, RI: Public Archaeology Laboratory, Inc. Report 1027-3.

Warrick, Gary. 1988. Estimating Ontario Iroquoian Village Duration. *Man in the Northeast* 36:21–60.

Weeks, Janice. 1971. Steatite Tempered Pottery in New England. *Man in the Northeast* 2:51–65.

Weinstein, Laurie. 1991. Land, Politics and Power: The Mohegan Indians in the 17th and 18th Centuries. *Man in the Northeast* 42:9–16.

Welsch, Robert L., and John Edward Terrell. 1998. Material Culture, Social Fields, and Social Boundaries on the Sepik Coast of New Guinea. In *The Archaeology of Social Boundaries*, edited by M.T. Stark, pp. 50–77. Washington, DC: Smithsonian Institute Press.

Werner, David J. 1972. The Zimmerman Site, 35-PI-14. In *Archaeology in the Upper Delaware Valley*, edited by W.F. Kinsey, pp. 55–130. Harrisburg, PA: The Pennsylvania Historical and Museum Commission.

White, Leslie A. 1959. *The Evolution of Culture*. New York: McGraw-Hill.

Whitney, Philip R., and James M. McLelland. 1973. Origin of Coronas in Meta-gabbros of the Adirondack Mountains, New York. *Contributions to Mineralogy and Petrology* 39:81–98.

———. 1983. Origin of Biotite-Hornblende-Garnet Coronas between Oxides and Plagioclase in Olivine Metagabbro, Adirondack Region, New York. *Contributions to Mineralogy and Petrology* 82:34–41.

Wiegand, Ernest A. 1987. The Prehistoric Ceramics of Southwestern Connect-icut: An Overview and Reevaluation. *Bulletin of the Archaeological Society of Connecticut* 50:23–42.

Wiessner, Polly. 1983. Style and Social Information in Kalahari San Projectile Points. *American Antiquity* 48(2):253–276.

———. 1985. Style or Isochrestic Variation? A Reply to Sackett. *American Antiquity* 50(1):160–166.

———. 1990. Is There a Unity to Style? In *The Uses of Style in Archaeology*, edited by M.W. Conkey and C.A. Hastorf, pp. 105–112. New York: Cambridge University Press.

Williams, D.F. 1983. Petrology of Ceramics. In *The Petrology of Archaeological Artifacts*, edited by D.R.C. Kemp and A.P. Harvey, pp. 301–329. New York: Clarendon Press.

Williams, Lorraine E. 1972. *Fort Shantok and Fort Corchaug: A Comparative Study of Seventeenth Century Culture Contact in the Long Island Sound Area*. New York: Ph.D. dissertation, Department of Anthropology, New York University.

Willoughby, Charles C. 1909. *Pottery of the New England Indians*. Cedar Rapids, IA: The Torch Press.

———. 1927. An Ancient Indian Fish-Weir. *American Anthropologist* 29(1):105–108.

Wintemburg, William J. 1931. *Distinguishing Characteristics of Algonkian and Iroquoian Cultures*. Ottawa: Canadian National Museum Annual Report for 1929.

Wobst, H. Martin. 1977. Stylistic Behavior and Information Exchange. In *Papers for the Director: Research Essays in Honor of James B. Griffin*, edited by C.E. Cleland, pp. 317–342. Ann Arbor, MI: Anthropology Papers 61. Museum of Anthropology, University of Michigan.

Wolf, Eric R. 1982. *Europe and the People without History*. Berkeley, CA: University of California Press.

Wood, William. 1977. *New England's Prospect*, edited by A.T. Vaughan. The Commonwealth Series, W.E.A. Bernhard, general editor. Amherst, MA: University of Massachusetts Press (orig. 1634).

Wyatt, Ronald J. 1977. The Archaic on Long Island. *Annals of the New York Academy of Sciences* 288:400–410.

Wyman, Jeffries. 1867. Examination of Shell-Heaps Found in Salisbury, Massachusetts. *Proceedings of the Boston Society of Natural History* 11:242–243.

Yesner, David R. 1983. On Explaining Changes in Prehistoric Coastal Economies: The View from Casco Bay. In *The Evolution of Maritime Cultures on the Northeast and Northwest Coasts of America*, edited by R.J. Nash, pp. 77–90. Publication 11. Burnaby, BC: Department of Archaeology, Simon Fraser University.

Young, William R. 1969. A Survey of the Available Knowledge on the Middle Connecticut Valley Indians—Prehistoric and Historic. In *An Introduction to the Archaeology and History of the Connecticut Valley Indian*, edited by W.R. Young, pp. 33–61. Springfield, MA: Springfield Museum of Science.

Zen, E-an. 1989. Tectonostratigraphic Terranes in the Northern Appalachians: Their Distribution, Origin, and Age; Evidence for Their Existence. In *Fieldtrip Guidebook T359*, edited by E. Zen, J.C. Hepburn, W.S.F. Kidd, P. Robinson, J.W. Skehan, and J.B. Thompson, Jr., pp. 1–26. Washington, DC: American Geophysical Union.

Zen, E-an, Richard Goldsmith, and Norman L. Hatch. 1983. *Bedrock Geologic Map of Massachusetts*. Washington, DC: USGS, in cooperation with the Commonwealth of Massachusetts Department of Public Works.

Zhang, Q.L., and Paul F. Hendrix. 1995. Earthworm (*Lumbricus rubellus* and *Aporrectodea caliginosa*) Effects on Carbon Flux in Soil. *Soil Science Society of America* 59(3):816–823.

Index

About the Contributors

DAVID J. BERNSTEIN is an Associate Professor of Anthropology, Department of Anthropology, State University of New York, Stony Brook.

SHIRLEY BLANCKE is an Associate Curator for Archaeology, Concord Museum, Concord, Massachusetts.

VICTORIA BUNKER is President, Victoria Bunker, Inc., Alton, New Hampshire.

BARBARA L.A. CALOGERO is an independent contract archaeologist in West Hartford, Connecticut.

ELIZABETH S. CHILTON is an Assistant Professor of Anthropology, Department of Anthropology, University of Massachusetts, Amherst.

ELENA DÉCIMA is formerly a contract archaeologist, Timelines, Inc., Littleton, Massachusetts.

DENA F. DINCAUZE is Emerita Professor of Anthropology, Department of Anthropology, University of Massachusetts, Amherst.

DIANNA L. DOUCETTE is a graduate student, Department of Anthropology, Harvard University, Cambridge, Massachusetts.

ROBERT G. GOODBY is an Assistant Professor of Anthropology, Department of Anthropology, Franklin Pierce College, Rindge, New Hampshire.

JORDAN E. KERBER is an Associate Professor of Anthropology and Curator of Collections, Longyear Museum of Anthropology, Department of Sociology and Anthropology, Colgate University, Hamilton, New York.

LUCIANNE LAVIN is Director and General Manager, American Cultural Specialists, LLC, Seymour, Connecticut.

BARBARA E. LUEDTKE was a Professor of Anthropology, Department of Anthropology, University of Massachusetts, Boston.

JOHN P. PRETOLA is Curator of Anthropology, Springfield Science Museum, Springfield, Massachusetts.

DUNCAN RITCHIE is a Senior Archaeologist, Public Archaeology Laboratory, Inc., Pawtucket, Rhode Island.

BRONA G. SIMON is State Archaeologist and Deputy State Historic Preservation Officer, Massachusetts Historical Commission, Boston.

MICHAEL A. VOLMAR is Curator, Fruitlands Museum, Harvard, Massachusetts.